QUOTABLE
SHAKESPEARE

QUOTABLE SHAKESPEARE:

A Thematic Selection of the Best of the Bard

Selected by

REYNER BARTON

BARNES
&NOBLE
BOOKS
NEW YORK

Originally published in 1946 as *Lend Me Your Ears*.

This edition published by Barnes & Noble, Inc.

1995 Barnes & Noble Books

ISBN 1-56619-880-1

Printed and bound in the United States of America

M 9 8 7 6 5 4 3 2 1

CONTENTS

FOREWORD

IN working at this selection of quotations from Shakespeare's plays and sonnets, I have used the three editions at my disposal: THE TEMPLE SHAKESPEARE, THE EVERYMAN and THE OXFORD SHAKESPEARE. They differ slightly; and I have not always given alternative references. This fact will explain what might appear to be some inaccuracies in the text; and I sincerely hope that it will explain them all! Then I have deliberately repeated certain speeches, the theme of which is embodied under more than one of the Subject Headings. To do so seemed to me to expedite reference. Where I have considered that the punctuation was misleading and confusing to a present-day reader, I have ventured to alter it, emphasising to the best of my ability the essential meaning of the lines.

Both in the original selection and subsequent revision of my work, I have received very valuable assistance from my wife; and I should like to thank her in this brief Foreword for her unfailing patience and perseverance in the help she has so willingly given me.

R. B.

Section I

TIME AND THE CALENDAR

Thy banks with pioned and twilled brims,
Which spongy April at thy hest betrims
To make cold nymphs chaste crowns.
(*The Tempest. Act 4. Scene 1. Iris speaking.*)
Pioned: overgrown with marsh-marigold, still called 'peony' in the
      neighbourhood of Stratford-on-Avon.
Twilled: covered with reeds or sedges.

Oh, how this spring of love resembleth
The uncertain glory of an April day,
Which now shows all the beauty of the sun
And by and by a cloud takes all away.
(*The Two Gentlemen of Verona. Act 1. Scene 3. Proteus speaking.*)

Oh, your desert speaks loud; and I should wrong it
To lock it in the wards of covert bosom,
When it deserves, with characters of brass,
A forted residence 'gainst the tooth of time
And razure of oblivion.
(*Measure For Measure. Act 5. Scene 1. The Duke speaking.*)

LEONATO   You will never run mad, niece.
BEATRICE   No, not till a hot January.
(*Much Ado About Nothing. Act 1. Scene 1.*)

I can see yet without spectacles, and I see no such matter. There's her
    cousin, an she were not possessed with a fury, exceeds her as much in
    beauty as the first of May doth the last of December.
(*Much Ado About Nothing. Act 1. Scene 1. Benedick speaking.*)

Why should proud Summer boast
Before the birds have any cause to sing?
Why should I joy in an abortive birth?
At Christmas I no more desire a rose
Than wish a snow in May's new-fangled mirth,
But like of each thing that in season grows.
(*Love's Labour's Lost. Act 1. Scene 1. Berowne speaking.*)

9

The seasons alter: hoary-headed frosts
Fall in the fresh lap of the crimson rose;
And on old Hiems' thin and icy crown,
An odorous chaplet of sweet Summer buds
Is, as in mockery, set.   The Spring, the Summer,
The chiding Autumn, angry Winter, change
Their wonted liveries, and the mazed world,
By their increase, now knows not which is which.
(*A Midsummer-Night's Dream.   Act 2.   Scene 1.   Titania speaking.*)

Yet I have not seen
So likely an ambassador of love.
A day in April never came so sweet,
To show how costly Summer was at hand,
As this fore-spurrer comes before his lord.
(*The Merchant of Venice.   Act 2.   Scene 9.   A servant speaking.*)

This night methinks is but the daylight sick:
It looks a little paler.   'Tis a day
Such as the day is when the sun is hid.
(*The Merchant of Venice.   Act 5.   Scene 1.   Portia speaking.*)

Why, this is like the mending of highways
In Summer, where the ways are fair enough!
(*The Merchant of Venice.   Act 5.   Scene 1.   Gratiano speaking.*)

Here feel we but the penalty of Adam,
The seasons' difference; as the icy fang,
And churlish chiding of the Winter's wind,
Which, when it bites and blows upon my body,
Even till I shrink with cold, I smile and say:
'This is no flattery.   These are counsellors
That feelingly persuade me what I am.'
(*As You Like It.   Act 2.   Scene 1.   The Banished Duke speaking.*)

Here shall he see
No enemy
But Winter and rough weather.
(*As You Like It.   Act 2.   Scene 5.   Amiens singing.*)

Blow, blow, thou Winter wind,
Thou art not so unkind
As man's ingratitude.
. . . .
Freeze, freeze, thou bitter sky,
That dost not bite so nigh
As benefits forgot.
(*As You Like It.   Act 2.   Scene 7.   Amiens singing.*)

And then he drew a dial from his poke,
And looking on it with lack-lustre eye
Says very wisely 'It is ten o'clock;
Thus may we see,' quoth he, 'how the world wags.
'Tis but an hour ago since it was nine
And after one hour more 'twill be eleven;
And so, from hour to hour, we ripe and ripe,
And then, from hour to hour, we rot and rot.
And thereby hangs a tale.'
(*As You Like It. Act 2. Scene 7. Jaques speaking.*)

               But whate'er you are
That in this desert inaccessible,
Under the shade of melancholy boughs,
Lose and neglect the creeping hours of time;
If ever you have looked on better days,
If ever been where bells have knolled to church,
If ever sat at any good man's feast,
If ever from your eyelids wiped a tear
And know what 'tis to pity and be pitied,
Let gentleness my strong enforcement be.
In the which hope I blush and hide my sword.
(*As You Like It. Act 2. Scene 7. Orlando speaking.*)

ROSALIND   I pray you, what is't o'clock?
ORLANDO   You should ask me, what time o' day; there's no clock in
    the forest.
(*As You Like It. Act 3. Scene 2.*)

No, no, Orlando! Men are April when they woo, December when they
    wed. Maids are May when they are maids, but the sky changes when
    they are wives.
(*As You Like It. Act 4. Scene 1. Rosalind speaking.*)

Let's take the instant by the forward top;
For we are old, and on our quick'st decrees
The inaudible and noiseless foot of time
Steals ere we can effect them.
(*All's Well That Ends Well. Act 5. Scene 3. The King of France speaking.*)

If you be not mad, be gone. If you have reason, be brief. 'Tis not that
    time of moon with me to make one in so skipping a dialogue.
(*Twelfth Night. Act 1. Scene 5. Olivia speaking.*)

As I am man,
My state is desperate for my master's love;
As I am woman . . . now alas the day! . . .
What thriftless sighs shall poor Olivia breathe!
Oh, time! Thou must untangle this, not I.
It is too hard a knot for me to untie.
(*Twelfth Night. Act 2. Scene 2. Viola speaking.*)

MALVOLIO 'If not, let me see thee a servant still.'
OLIVIA   Why, this is very Midsummer madness.
(*Twelfth Night. Act 3. Scene 4.*)

SIR TOBY   But see, but see! (*Enter Sir Andrew.*)
FABIAN   More matter for a May morning.
(*Twelfth Night. Act 3. Scene 4.*)

And thus the whirligig of time brings in his revenges.
(*Twelfth Night. Act 5. Scene 1. Feste speaking.*)

He makes a July's day short as December;
And with his varying childness cures in me
Thoughts that would thick my blood.
(*The Winter's Tale. Act 1. Scene 2. Polixenes speaking.*)

KING PHILIP   The yearly course that brings this day about
               Shall never see it but a holiday.
CONSTANCE   A wicked day, and not a holy day!
               What hath this day deserved? What hath it done
               That it in golden letters should be set
               Among the high tides in the calendar?
               Nay, rather turn this day out of the week;
               This day of shame, oppression, perjury.
(*King John. Act 3. Scene 1.*)

RICHARD   Why, uncle, thou hast many years to live.
JOHN OF GAUNT But not a minute, king, that thou canst give.
               Shorten my days thou canst with sullen sorrow
               And pluck nights from me, but not lend a morrow.
               Thou canst help time to furrow me with age,
               But stop no wrinkle in his pilgrimage.
(*Richard the Second. Act 1. Scene 3.*)

Oh, who can hold a fire in his hand
By thinking on the frosty Caucasus?
Or cloy the hungry edge of appetite
By bare imagination of a feast?
Or wallow naked in December snow
By thinking on fantastic Summer's heat?
(*Richard the Second. Act 1. Scene 3. Bolingbroke speaking.*)

Oh, call back yesterday! Bid time return!
And thou shalt have twelve thousand fighting men.
(*Richard the Second. Act 3. Scene 2. Salisbury speaking.*)

. . . it would be argument for a week, laughter for a month, and a good
jest for ever.
(*Henry the Fourth. Part One. Act 2. Scene 2. Prince Henry speaking.*)

So, when he had occasion to be seen,
He was but as the cuckoo is in June:
Heard, not regarded.
(*Henry the Fourth. Part One. Act 3. Scene 2. The King speaking.*)

No more, no more! Worse than the sun in March,
This praise doth nourish agues.
(*Henry the Fourth. Part One. Act 4. Scene 1. Hotspur speaking.*)

The time of life is short;
To spend that shortness basely were too long,
If life did ride upon a dial's point
Still ending at the arrival of an hour.
(*Henry the Fourth. Part One. Act 5. Scene 2. Hotspur speaking.*)

But thought's the slave of time, and life time's fool.
And time that takes survey of all the world
Must have a stop.
(*Henry the Fourth. Part One. Act 5. Scene 4. Hotspur speaking.*)

We see which way the stream of time doth run
And are enforced from our most quiet sphere
By the rough torrent of occasion.
(*Henry the Fourth. Part Two. Act 4. Scene 1. The Archbishop of York
speaking.*)

Oh, Westmoreland, thou art a Summer bird,
Which ever in the haunch of Winter sings
The lifting up of day!
(*Henry the Fourth. Part Two. Act 4. Scene 4. The King speaking.*)

Hung be the heavens with black, yield day to night!
Comets, importing change of times and states,
Brandish your crystal tresses in the sky;
And with them scourge the bad revolting stars
That have consented unto Henry's death!
King Henry the Fifth, too famous to live long!
(*Henry the Sixth. Part One. Act 1. Scene 1. Bedford speaking.*)

Thus sometimes hath the brightest day a cloud;
And after Summer evermore succeeds
Barren Winter, with his wrathful nipping cold:
So cares and joys abound as seasons fleet.
(*Henry the Sixth. Part Two. Act* 2. *Scene* 4. *Gloucester speaking.*)

Now, by the ground that I am banished from,
Well could I curse away a Winter's night,
Though standing naked on a mountain top
Where biting cold would never let grass grow,
And think it but a minute spent in sport.
(*Henry the Sixth. Part Two. Act* 3. *Scene* 2. *Suffolk speaking.*)

This battle fares like to the morning's war,
When dying clouds contend with growing light;
What time the shepherd, blowing of his nails,
Can neither call it perfect day nor night.
(*Henry the Sixth. Part Three. Act* 2. *Scene* 5. *The King speaking.*)

Now is the Winter of our discontent
Made glorious Summer by this sun of York.
(*Richard the Third. Act* 1. *Scene* 1. *Gloucester, afterwards Richard the Third, speaking.*)

This is the state of man: to-day he puts forth
The tender leaves of hopes; to-morrow blossoms,
And bears his blushing honours thick upon him;
The third day comes a frost, a killing frost,
And when he thinks, good easy man, full surely
His greatness is a-ripening, nips his root,
And then he falls, as I do.
(*Henry the Eighth. Act* 3. *Scene* 2. *Wolsey speaking.*)

PANDARUS   I'll be sworn 'tis true: he will weep you, an 'twere a man born in April.
CRESSIDA   And I'll spring up in his tears, an 'twere a nettle against May.
(*Troilus and Cressida. Act* 1. *Scene* 2.)

Time hath, my lord, a wallet at his back,
Wherein he puts alms for oblivion;
A great-sized monster of ingratitudes . . .
For Time is like a fashionable host
That slightly shakes his parting guest by the hand
And with his arms outstretched, as he would fly,
Grasps in the comer: welcome ever smiles,
And farewell goes out sighing.
(*Troilus and Cressida. Act* 3. *Scene* 3. *Ulysses speaking.*)

The end crowns all,
And that old common arbitrator, Time,
Will one day end it.
(*Troilus and Cressida. Act 4. Scene 5. Hector speaking.*)

Madam, an hour before the worshipped sun
Peered forth the golden window of the East,
A troubled mind drave me to walk abroad.
(*Romeo and Juliet. Act 1. Scene 1. Benvolio speaking.*)

At my poor house look to behold this night
Earth-treading stars that make dark heaven light.
Such comfort as do lusty young men feel
When well-apparelled April on the heel
Of limping Winter treads, even such delight
Among fresh female buds shall you this night
Inherit at my house.
(*Romeo and Juliet. Act 1. Scene 2. Capulet speaking.*)

JULIET   Wilt thou be gone? It is not yet near day.
It was the nightingale and not the lark
That pierced the fearful hollow of thine ear;
Nightly she sings on yond pomegranate-tree.
Believe me, love, it was the nightingale.

ROMEO   It was the lark, the herald of the morn,
No nightingale. Look, love, what envious streaks
Do lace the severing clouds in yonder East:
Night's candles are burnt out, and jocund day
Stands tip-toe on the misty mountain tops.
I must be gone and live, or stay and die.
(*Romeo and Juliet. Act 3. Scene 5.*)

Beware the Ides of March.
(*Julius Cæsar. Act 1. Scene 2. Soothsayer, speaking to Cæsar.*)
Ides of March: March 15th.

Come what come may,
Time and the hour runs through the roughest day.
(*Macbeth. Act 1. Scene 3. Macbeth speaking.*)

Ah, good father,
Thou seest, the heavens, as troubled with man's act,
Threaten his bloody stage: by the clock 'tis day,
And yet dark night strangles the travelling lamp.
Is't night's predominance, or the day's shame,
That darkness does the face of earth entomb
When living light should kiss it?
(*Macbeth. Act 2. Scene 4. Ross speaking.*)

                    Come, seeling night,
Scarf up the tender eye of pitiful day,
And with thy bloody and invisible hand
Cancel and tear to pieces that great bond
Which keeps me pale! Light thickens, and the crow
Makes wing to the rooky wood:
Good things of day begin to droop and drowse,
Whiles night's black agents to their preys do rouse.
(*Macbeth. Act 3. Scene 2. Macbeth speaking.*)

SEYTON   The queen, my lord, is dead.
MACBETH   She should have died hereafter;
          There would have been a time for such a word.
          To-morrow, and to-morrow, and to-morrow,
          Creeps in this petty pace from day to day
          To the last syllable of recorded time.
          And all our yesterdays have lighted fools
          The way to dusty death.
(*Macbeth. Act 5. Scene 5.*)

Time shall unfold what plaited cunning hides:
Who cover faults, at last shame them derides.
Well may you prosper!
(*King Lear. Act 1. Scene 1. Cordelia speaking.*)

CORNWALL   You know not why we came to visit you.
REGAN   Thus out of season, threading dark-eyed night.
(*King Lear. Act 2. Scene 1.*)

The April's in her eyes; it is love's Spring,
And these the showers to bring it on. Be cheerful.
(*Antony and Cleopatra. Act 3. Scene 2. Antony speaking.*)

CAPTAIN   The morn is fair. Good morrow, general.
ALL   Good morrow, general.
ANTONY   'Tis well blown, lads.
          This morning, like the spirit of a youth
          That means to be of note, begins betimes.
(*Antony and Cleopatra. Act 4. Scene 4.*)

                    For his bounty,
There was no Winter in't; an Autumn 'twas
That grew the more by reaping.
(*Antony and Cleopatra. Act 5. Scene 2. Cleopatra speaking.*)

Finish, good lady; the bright day is done,
And we are for the dark.
(*Antony and Cleopatra. Act 5. Scene 2. Iras speaking.*)

PHILARIO   What means do you make to him?
POSTHUMUS   Not any, but abide the change of time;
                Quake in the present Winter's state, and wish
                That warmer days would come.
(*Cymbeline. Act 2. Scene 4.*)

                            What should we speak of
When we are old as you?   When we shall hear
The rain and wind beat dark December, how,
In this our pinching cave, shall we discourse
The freezing hours away?
(*Cymbeline. Act 3. Scene 3. Arviragus speaking.*)

GUIDERIUS   Pray, draw near.
ARVIRAGUS   The night to the owl and morn to the lark less welcome.
IMOGEN   Thanks, sir.
(*Cymbeline. Act 3. Scene 6.*)

Thou art thy mother's glass, and she in thee
Calls back the lovely April of her prime;
So thou through windows of thine age shalt see,
Despite of wrinkles, this thy golden time.
(*Sonnet 3.*)

Those hours, that with gentle work did frame
The lovely gaze where every eye doth dwell,
Will play the tyrants to the very same
And that un-fair which fairly doth excel;
For never-resting time leads Summer on
To hideous Winter, and confounds him there.
(*Sonnet 5.*)

Shall I compare thee to a Summer's day?
Thou art more lovely and more temperate:
Rough winds do shake the darling buds of May,
And Summer's lease hath all too short a date.
(*Sonnet 18.*)

Devouring Time, blunt thou the lion's paws
And make the earth devour her own sweet brood;
Pluck the keen teeth from the fierce tiger's jaws
And burn the long-lived phœnix in her blood;
Make glad and sorry seasons as thou fleets
And do whate'er thou wilt, swift-footed Time,
To the wide world and all her fading sweets.
But I forbid thee one most heinous crime:
Oh, carve not with thy hours my love's fair brow,
Nor draw no lines there with thine antique pen.
(*Sonnet 19.*)

I tell the day, to please him thou art bright
And dost him grace when clouds do blot the heaven.
So flatter I the swart-complexioned night:
When sparkling stars twire not, *thou* gild'st the even.
But day doth daily draw my sorrows longer,
And night doth nightly make grief's strength seem stronger.
(*Sonnet* 28.)

Let this sad interim like the ocean be
Which parts the shore, where two contracted new
Come daily to the banks; that when they see
Return of love, more blessed may be the view.
Or call it Winter, which, being full of care,
Makes Summer's welcome thrice more wished, more rare.
(*Sonnet* 56.)

Like as the waves make towards the pebbled shore,
So do our minutes hasten to their end;
Each changing place with that which goes before,
In sequent toil all forwards do contend . . .
And Time that gave doth now his gift confound.
Time doth transfix the flourish set on youth
And delves the parallels in beauty's brow,
Feeds on the rarities of nature's truth,
And nothing stands but for his scythe to mow.
(*Sonnet* 60.)

How like a Winter hath my absence been
From thee, the pleasure of the fleeting year!
What freezings have I felt, what dark days seen!
What old December's bareness everywhere!
(*Sonnet* 97.)

From you have I been absent in the Spring;
When proud-pied April, dressed in all his trim,
Hath put a spirit of youth in everything
That heavy Saturn laughed and leaped with him.
Yet nor the lays of birds, nor the sweet smell
Of different flowers in odour and in hue,
Could make me any Summer's story tell,
Or from their proud lap pluck them where they grew.
(*Sonnet* 98.)

To me, fair friend, you never can be old;
For as you were when first your eye I eyed,
Such seems your beauty still.   Three Winters cold
Have from the forests shook three Summers' pride,

Three beauteous Springs to yellow Autumn turned
In process of the seasons have I seen,
Three April perfumes in three hot Junes burned,
Since first I saw you fresh, which yet are green.
(*Sonnet* 104.)

Love's not Time's fool, though rosy lips and cheeks
Within his bending sickle's compass come;
Love alters not with his brief hours and weeks,
But bears it out even to the edge of doom.
If this be error, and upon me proved,
I never writ . . . nor no man ever loved.
(*Sonnet* 116.)

SECTION II

HAPPINESS AND SORROW

Wish me partaker in thy happiness,
When thou dost meet good hap.
(*The Two Gentlemen of Verona. Act* 1. *Scene* 1. *Proteus speaking.*)

I do desire thee, even from a heart
As full of sorrows as the sea of sands,
To bear me company and go with me.
(*The Two Gentlemen of Verona. Act* 4. *Scene* 3. *Silvia speaking.*)

             Happy thou art not;
For what thou hast not, still thou striv'st to get,
And what thou hast, forget'st.
(*Measure For Measure. Act* 3. *Scene* 1. *The Duke speaking.*)

Oh, grief hath changed me since you saw me last,
And careful hours, with Time's deformèd hand,
Have written strange defeatures in my face.
(*The Comedy of Errors. Act* 5. *Scene* 1. *Ægeon speaking.*)

How much better is it to weep at joy then to joy at weeping!
(*Much Ado About Nothing. Act* 1. *Scene* 1. *Leonato speaking.*)

Never came trouble to my house in the likeness of your Grace; for trouble
    being gone, comfort should remain. But when you depart from me,
    sorrow abides and happiness takes his leave.
(*Much Ado About Nothing. Act* 1. *Scene* 1. *Leonato speaking.*)

Silence is the perfectest herald of joy: I were but little happy if I could say
   how much.
(*Much Ado About Nothing. Act 2. Scene 1. Claudio speaking.*)

She is never sad but when she sleeps; and not ever sad then. For I have
   heard my daughter say, she hath often dreamed of unhappiness and
   waked herself with laughing.
(*Much Ado About Nothing. Act 2. Scene 1. Leonato, speaking of Beatrice.*)

Happy are they that hear their detractions, and can put them to mending.
(*Much Ado About Nothing. Act 2. Scene 3. Benedick speaking.*)

No, no! 'Tis all men's office to speak patience
To those that wring under the load of sorrow,
But no man's virtue nor sufficiency
To be so moral when he shall endure
The like himself.
(*Much Ado About Nothing. Act 5. Scene 1. Leonato speaking.*)

Affliction may one day smile again; and till then, sit thee down, sorrow.
(*Love's Labour's Lost. Act 1. Scene 1. Costard speaking.*)

HOLOFERNES   I beseech your society.
NATHANIEL   And thank you too; for society, saith the text, is the happiness
   of life.
(*Love's Labour's Lost. Act 4. Scene 2.*)

And though the mourning brow of progeny
Forbid the smiling courtesy of love
The holy suit which fain it would convince,
Yet, since love's argument was first on foot,
Let not the cloud of sorrow justle it
From what it purposed; since, to wail friends lost
Is not by much so wholesome-profitable
As to rejoice at friends but newly found.
(*Love's Labour's Lost. Act 5. Scene 2. The King speaking.*)

In sooth, I know not why I am so sad.
It wearies me; you say it wearies you.
But how I caught it, found it, or came by it,
What stuff 'tis made of, whereof it is born,
I am to learn;
And such a want-wit sadness makes of me
That I have much ado to know myself.
(*The Merchant of Venice. Act 1. Scene 1. Antonio speaking.*)

Not in love neither? Then let's say you are sad
Because you are not merry; and 'twere as easy
For you to laugh and leap and say you are merry
Because you are not sad.
(*The Merchant of Venice. Act 1. Scene 1. Salarino speaking.*)

Happy in this, she is not yet so old
But she may learn; happier than this,
She is not bred so dull but she *can* learn;
Happiest of all is that her gentle spirit
Commits itself to yours to be directed,
As from her lord, her governor, her king.
(*The Merchant of Venice. Act 3. Scene 2. Portia speaking.*)

But, oh, how bitter a thing it is to look into happiness through another
    man's eyes!
(*As You Like It. Act 5. Scene 2. Orlando speaking.*)

My heart is heavy and mine age is weak;
Grief would have tears, and sorrow bids me speak.
(*All's Well That Ends Well. Act 3. Scene 4. The Countess of Rousillon
    speaking.*)

                            But I have
That honourable grief lodged here, which burns
Worse than tears drown.
(*The Winter's Tale. Act 2. Scene 1. Hermione speaking.*)

                    Adieu, my lord.
I never wished to see you sorry; now
I trust I shall.
(*The Winter's Tale. Act 2. Scene 1. Hermione speaking.*)

There might you have beheld one joy crown another; so and in such
    manner that it seemed sorrow wept to take leave of them, for their
    joy waded in tears.
(*The Winter's Tale. Act 5. Scene 2. Third Gentleman speaking.*)

Oh, if thou teach me to believe this sorrow,
Teach thou this sorrow how to make me die;
And let belief and life encounter so
As doth the fury of two desperate men
Which in the very meeting fall and die.
(*King John. Act 3. Scene 1. Constance speaking.*)

I will instruct my sorrows to be proud;
For grief is proud and makes his owner stoop.
To me and to the state of my great grief
Let kings assemble, for my grief's so great
That no supporter but the huge firm earth
Can hold it up.   Here I and sorrows sit.
Here is my throne; bid kings come bow to it.
(*King John.   Act 3.   Scene 1.   Constance speaking.*)

Look who comes here!   A grave unto a soul;
Holding the eternal spirit, against her will,
In the vile prison of afflicted breath.
(*King John.   Act 3.   Scene 4.   Philip of France, referring to Constance.*)

CARDINAL PANDULPH   You hold too heinous a respect of grief.
CONSTANCE   He talks to me that never had a son.
KING PHILIP   You are as fond of grief as of your child.
CONSTANCE   Grief fills the room up of my absent child,
                   Lies in his bed, walks up and down with me,
                   Puts on his pretty looks, repeats his words,
                   Remembers me of all his gracious parts,
                   Stuffs out his vacant garments with his form.
                   Then have I reason to be fond of grief.
(*King John.   Act 3.   Scene 4.*)

Methinks nobody should be sad but I.
Yet I remember, when I was in France,
Young gentlemen would be as sad as night
Only for wantonness.   By my Christendom,
So I were out of prison and kept sheep
I should be as merry as the day is long.
(*King John.   Act 4.   Scene 1.   Prince Arthur speaking.*)

Alack, why am I sent for to a king,
Before I have shook off the regal thoughts
Wherewith I reigned?   I hardly yet have learned
To insinuate, flatter, bow, and bend my limbs.
Give sorrow leave awhile to tutor me
To this submission.
(*Richard the Second.   Act 4.   Scene 1.   Richard speaking.*)

Might liquid tears or heart-offending groans
Or blood-consuming sighs recall his life,
I would be blind with weeping, sick with groans,
Look pale as primrose with blood-drinking sighs,
And all to have the noble duke alive.
(*Henry the Sixth.   Part Two.   Act 3.   Scene 2.   Queen Margaret speaking.*)

Why, Warwick, hath thy knee forgot to bow?
Old Salisbury, shame to thy silver hair,
Thou mad misleader of thy brain-sick son!
What! Wilt thou on thy death-bed play the ruffian,
And seek for sorrow with thy spectacles?
(*Henry the Sixth. Part Two. Act 5. Scene 1. The King speaking.*)

Oh, God! Methinks it were a happy life
To be no better than a homely swain;
To sit upon a hill as I do now,
To carve out dials quaintly, point by point,
Thereby to see the minutes how they run.
(*Henry the Sixth. Part Three. Act 2. Scene 5. The King speaking.*)

              Verily,
I swear 'tis better to be lowly born
And range with humble livers in content,
Than to be perked up in a glistering grief
And wear a golden sorrow.
(*Henry the Eighth. Act 2. Scene 3. Anne Bullen speaking.*)

My gracious silence, hail!
Would'st thou have laughed had I come coffined home,
That weep'st to see me triumph?
(*Coriolanus. Act 2. Scene 1. Coriolanus, to his wife, Virgilia.*)

FRIAR LAURENCE   So smile the heavens upon this holy act
                That after-hours with sorrow chide us not!
ROMEO   Amen! Amen! But come what sorrow can,
                It cannot countervail the exchange of joy
                That one short minute gives me in her sight.
(*Romeo and Juliet. Act 2. Scene 6.*)

Ah, Juliet, if the measure of thy joy
Be heaped like mine, and that thy skill be more
To blazon it, then sweeten with thy breath
This neighbour air. . . .
(*Romeo and Juliet. Act 2. Scene 6. Romeo speaking.*)

A pack of blessings lights upon thy back,
Happiness courts thee in her best array,
But, like a misbehaved and sullen wench,
Thou pout'st upon thy fortune and thy love.
Take heed, take heed, for such die miserable.
(*Romeo and Juliet. Act 3. Scene 3. Friar Laurence speaking.*)

How now, my lord!   Why do you keep alone,
Of sorriest fancies your companions making;
Using those thoughts which should indeed have died
With them they think on?   Things without all remedy
Should be without regard: what's done is done.
(*Macbeth.   Act 3.   Scene 2.   Lady Macbeth speaking.*)

What man!   Ne'er pull your hat upon your brows.
Give sorrow words: the grief that does not speak
Whispers the o'erfraught heart, and bids it break.
(*Macbeth.   Act 4.   Scene 3.   Malcolm speaking.*)

Canst thou not minister to a mind diseased,
Pluck from the memory a rooted sorrow,
Raze out the written troubles of the brain,
And with some sweet oblivious antidote
Cleanse the stuffed bosom of that perilous stuff
Which weighs upon the heart?
(*Macbeth.   Act 5.   Scene 3.   Macbeth speaking.*)

Though yet of Hamlet our dear brother's death
The memory be green, and that it us befitted
To bear our hearts in grief and our whole kingdom
To be contracted in one brow of woe,
Yet so far hath discretion fought with nature,
That we with wisest sorrow think on him
Together with remembrance of ourselves.
(*Hamlet.   Act 1.   Scene 2.   The King speaking.*)

Seems, madam!   Nay, it is; I know not 'seems'.
'Tis not alone my inky cloak, good mother,
Nor customary suits of solemn black,
Nor windy suspiration of forced breath,
No, nor the fruitful river in the eye,
Nor the dejected haviour of the visage,
Together with all forms, moods, shapes of grief
That can denote me truly.   These indeed seem,
For they are actions that a man might play.
But I have that within which passeth show;
These but the trappings and the suits of woe.
(*Hamlet.   Act 1.   Scene 2.   Hamlet speaking.*)

HAMLET   My excellent good friends!   How dost thou, Guildenstern?
              Ah, Rosencrantz!   Good lads, how do you both?
ROSENCRANTZ   As the indifferent children of the earth.

GUILDENSTERN Happy, in that we are not over-happy: on Fortune's cap
                  we are not the very button.
HAMLET   Nor the soles of her shoe?
ROSENCRANTZ Neither, my lord.
(*Hamlet. Act 2. Scene 2.*)

The violence of either grief or joy
Their own enactures with themselves destroy:
Where joy most revels, grief doth most lament;
Grief joys, joy grieves, on slender accident.
(*Hamlet. Act 3. Scene 2. Player King speaking.*)

Oh, how this mother swells up toward my heart!
Hysterica passio, down, thou climbing sorrow!
Thy element's below. Where is this daughter?
(*King Lear. Act 2. Scene 4. Lear speaking.*)

               Henceforth I'll bear
Affliction till it do cry out itself
'Enough! Enough!' and die.
(*King Lear. Act 4. Scene 6. Gloucester speaking.*)

Neither my place nor aught I heard of business
Hath raised me from my bed, nor doth the *general* care
Take hold on me; for my *particular* grief
Is of so flood-gate and o'erbearing nature
That it engluts and swallows other sorrows,
And it is still itself.
(*Othello. Act 1. Scene 3. Brabantio speaking.*)

CLEOPATRA What means this?
ENOBARBUS 'Tis one of those odd tricks which sorrow shoots
             Out of the mind.
(*Antony and Cleopatra. Act 4. Scene 2.*)

Nay, good my fellows, do not please sharp fate
To grace it with your sorrows: bid that welcome
Which comes to punish us; and *we* punish *it*,
Seeming to bear it lightly.
(*Antony and Cleopatra. Act 4. Scene 12. Antony speaking.*)

          But most miserable
Is the desire that's glorious: blessed be those,
How mean so'er, that have their honest wills
Which seasons comfort.
(*Cymbeline. Act 1. Scene 6. Imogen speaking.*)

Great griefs, I see, medicine the less; for Cloten
Is quite forgot.
(*Cymbeline. Act 4. Scene 2. Belarius speaking.*)

Why should this change of thoughts,
The sad companion, dull-eyed melancholy,
Be my so used a guest as not an hour
In the day's glorious walk or peaceful night . . .
The tomb where grief should sleep . . . can breed me quiet?
(*Pericles. Act 1. Scene 2. Pericles speaking.*)

CLEON   My Dionyza, shall we rest us here,
           And by relating tales of others' griefs
           See if 'twill teach us to forget our own?
DIONYZA   That were to blow at fire in hope to quench it.
(*Pericles. Act 1. Scene 4.*)

                    I thought as much.
One sorrow never comes but brings an heir
That may succeed as his inheritor.
(*Pericles. Act 1. Scene 4. Cleon speaking.*)

Oh, Helicanus! Strike me, honoured sir;
Give me a gash, put me to present pain,
Lest this great sea of joys rushing upon me
O'erbear the shores of my mortality
And drown me with their sweetness.
(*Pericles. Act 5. Scene 1. Pericles speaking.*)

When to the sessions of sweet silent thought
I summon up remembrance of things past,
I sigh the lack of many a thing I sought
And with old woes new-wail my dear times' waste.

Then can I drown an eye, unused to flow,
For precious friends hid in death's dateless night;
And weep afresh love's long since cancelled woe,
And moan the expense of many a vanished sight.
(*Sonnet 30.*)

Look what is best, that best I wish in thee:
This wish I have; then ten times happy me!
(*Sonnet 37.*)

The beast that bears me, tired with my woe,
Plods dully on, to bear that weight in me;
As if by some instinct the wretch did know
His rider loved not speed, being made from thee.
The bloody spur cannot provoke him on
That sometimes anger thrusts into his hide,
Which heavily he answers with a groan
More sharp to me than spurring to his side;
For that same groan doth put this in my mind:
My grief lies onward, and my joy behind.
(*Sonnet* 50.)

Ah, do not, when my heart hath 'scaped this sorrow,
Come in the rearward of a conquered woe;
Give not a windy night a rainy morrow,
To linger out a purposed overthrow.
(*Sonnet* 90.)

Section III

TREES, FLOWERS AND GARDENS

The king's son, Ferdinand,
With hair up-staring . . . then like reeds, not hair . . .
Was the first man that leap't; cried, 'Hell is empty
And all the devils are here.'
(*The Tempest. Act* 1. *Scene* 2. *Ariel speaking.*)
Reeds: Shakespeare uses the word to denote any grass-like, water-loving
plant.

Ceres, most bounteous lady, thy rich leas
Of wheat, rye, barley, vetches, oats and pease;
Thy turfy mountains, where live nibbling sheep,
And flat meads thatched with stover, them to keep. . . .
(*The Tempest. Act* 4. *Scene* 1. *Iris speaking.*)
Stover: used by Shakespeare to describe hay or straw.

You nymphs, called Naiads, of the windring brooks,
With your sedged crowns and ever-harmless looks,
Leave your crisp channels, and on this green land
Answer your summons; Juno does command.
(*The Tempest. Act* 4. *Scene* 1. *Iris speaking.*)
Sedge: any waterside plant in Shakespeare's plays.

Where the bee sucks, there suck I:
In a cowslip's bell I lie;
There I couch when owls do cry.
On the bat's back I do fly
After Summer, merrily.
Merrily, merrily shall I live now
Under the blossom that hangs on the bough.
(*The Tempest. Act 5. Scene 1. Ariel singing.*)

MISTRESS PAGE   I mean it not. I seek you a better husband.
MISTRESS QUICKLY That's my master, Master Doctor.
ANNE PAGE   Alas ! I had rather be set quick i' the earth
                 And bowled to death with turnips.
(*The Merry Wives of Windsor. Act 3. Scene 4.*)

If it should come to the ear of the court how I have been transformed,
   and how my transformation hath been washed and cudgelled, they
   would melt me out of my fat drop by drop and liquor fishermen's
   boots with me. I warrant they would whip me with their fine wits
   till I were as crest-fallen as a dried pear.
(*The Merry Wives of Windsor. Act 4. Scene 5. Falstaff speaking.*)

The several chairs of order look you scour
With juice of balm and every precious flower.
(*The Merry Wives of Windsor. Act 5. Scene 5. Anne Page speaking.*)

                    Say that thou overheard'st us,
And bid her steal into the pleached bower
Where honey-suckles, ripened by the sun,
Forbid the sun to enter; like favourites,
Made proud by princes, that advance their pride
Against the power that bred it.
(*Much Ado About Nothing. Act 3. Scene 1. Hero speaking.*)

THE KING   Berowne is like an envious sneaping frost
            That bites the first-born infants of the Spring.
BEROWNE   Well, say I am: why should proud Summer boast
            Before the birds have any cause to sing?
            Why should I joy in an abortive birth?
            At Christmas I no more desire a rose
            Than wish a snow in May's new-fangled mirth;
            But like of each thing that in season grows.
(*Love's Labour's Lost. Act 1. Scene 1.*)

Oft have I heard of you, my lord Berowne,
Before I saw you; and the world's large tongue
Proclaims you for a man replete with mocks,
Full of comparisons and wounding flouts,
Which you on all estates will execute
That lie within the mercy of your wit.
To weed this wormwood from your fruitful brain
And therewithal to win me, if you please . . .
Without the which I am not to be won . . .
You shall this twelve-month term, from day to day,
Visit the speechless sick. . . .

(*Love's Labour's Lost. Act 5. Scene 2. Rosaline speaking.*)

Wormwood: this herb was greatly esteemed in Tudor times for its medicinal
    properties. It was also employed for expelling fleas from living
    rooms: hence Rosaline's gibe.

When daisies pied and violets blue
And lady-smocks all silver-white
And cuckoo-buds of yellow hue
Do paint the meadows with delight. . . .
(*Love's Labour's Lost. Act 5. Scene 2. 'Spring' singing.*)

Therefore, fair Hermia, question your desires:
Know of your youth, examine well your blood,
Whether, if you yield not to your father's choice,
You can endure the livery of a nun;
For aye to be in shady cloister mewed,
To live a barren sister all your life,
Chanting faint hymns to the cold fruitless moon.
Thrice blessed they that master so their blood
To undergo such maiden pilgrimage;
But earthlier happy is the rose distilled
Than that which withering on the virgin thorn
Grows, lives and dies, in single blessedness.

(*A Midsummer-Night's Dream. Act 1. Scene 1. Theseus speaking.*)

LYSANDER   How now, my love! Why is your cheek so pale?
            How chance the roses there do fade so fast?

HERMIA   Belike for want of rain, which I could well
            Beteem them from the tempest of mine eyes.

(*A Midsummer-Night's Dream. Act 1. Scene 1.*)

The cowslips tall her pensioners be;
In their gold coats spots you see.
Those be rubies, fairy favours,
In their freckles live their savours.

(*A Midsummer-Night's Dream. Act 2. Scene 1. A fairy speaking.*)
The pensioners at Queen Elizabeth's court were selected from the best-
looking and tallest young men of the nobility.   They wore gold coats
with ruby-coloured 'favours.'

But I might see young Cupid's fiery shaft
Quenched in the chaste beams of the watery moon;
And the imperial votaress passed on
In maiden meditation, fancy-free.
Yet marked I where the bolt of Cupid fell:
It fell upon a little Western flower,
Before milk-white, now purple with love's wound;
And maidens call it Love-in-Idleness.

(*A Midsummer-Night's Dream. Act 2. Scene 1. Oberon speaking.*)
Love-in-Idleness: i.e. Love-in-Vain.   Shakespeare is referring to the pansy.

I know a bank whereon the wild thyme blows,
Where oxlips and the nodding violet grows;
Quite over-canopied with luscious woodbine,
With sweet musk-roses and with eglantine.

(*A Midsummer-Night's Dream. Act 2. Scene 1. Oberon speaking.*)
Eglantine: Shakespeare refers to the sweet briar rose.

BOTTOM   Are we all met?
QUINCE   Pat, pat.   And here's a marvellous convenient place for our
     rehearsal.   This green plot shall be our stage, this hawthorn-brake
     our tiring-house; and we will do it in action, as we will do it before
     the duke.

(*A Midsummer-Night's Dream. Act 3. Scene 1.*)

Be kind and courteous to this gentleman.
Hop in his walks and gambol in his eyes;
Feed him with apricocks and dewberries,
With purple grapes, green figs and mulberries.

(*A Midsummer-Night's Dream. Act 3. Scene 1. Titania speaking.*)

Good Master Mustard-Seed, I know your patience well: that same cowardly,
     giant-like ox-beef hath devoured many a gentleman of your house.
     I promise you, your kindred hath made my eyes water ere now.

(*A Midsummer-Night's Dream. Act 3. Scene 1. Bottom speaking.*)

Come, wait upon him; lead him to my bower.
The moon, methinks, looks with a watery eye;
And when she weeps, weeps every little flower,
Lamenting some enforced chastity.

(*A Midsummer-Night's Dream. Act 3. Scene 1. Titania speaking.*)

Oh, how ripe in show
Thy lips, those kissing cherries, tempting grow!

(*A Midsummer-Night's Dream. Act 3. Scene 2. Demetrius speaking.*)

Come, sit thee down upon this flowery bed,
While I thy amiable cheeks do coy
And stick musk-roses in thy sleek smooth head
And kiss thy fair large ears, my gentle joy.

(*A Midsummer-Night's Dream. Act 4. Scene 1. Titania speaking.*)

TITANIA   I have a venturous fairy that shall seek
           The squirrel's hoard, and fetch thee thence new nuts.
BOTTOM   I had rather have a handful or two of dried pease.   But I pray
          you, let none of your people stir me: I have an exposition of sleep
          come upon me.

(*A Midsummer-Night's Dream. Act 4. Scene 1.*)

So doth the woodbine the sweet honeysuckle
Gently entwist; the female ivy so
Enrings the barky fingers of the elm.
Oh, how I love thee!   How I dote on thee!

(*A Midsummer-Night's Dream. Act 4. Scene 1. Titania speaking.*)

I'll hold thee any wager,
When we are both accoutred like young men
I'll prove the prettier fellow of the two,
And wear my dagger with the braver grace,
And speak between the change of man and boy
With a reed voice. . . .

(*The Merchant of Venice. Act 3. Scene 4. Portia speaking.*)

Oh, Rosalind!   These trees shall be my books
And in their barks my thoughts I'll character;
That every eye which in this forest looks
Shall see thy virtue witnessed everywhere.

(*As You Like It. Act 3. Scene 2. Orlando speaking.*)

ROSALIND   Peace, you dull fool! I found them on a tree.
TOUCHSTONE   Truly, the tree yields bad fruit.
ROSALIND   I'll graff it with you, and then I shall graff it with a medlar.
        Then it will be the earliest fruit i' the country; for you'll be rotten ere
        you be half ripe, and that's the right virtue of the medlar.
(*As You Like It. Act* 3. *Scene* 2.)
Graff: graft.

Lo, what befell! He threw his eye aside,
And mark what object did present itself:
Under an oak, whose boughs were mossed with age
And high top bald with dry antiquity,
A wretched ragged man, o'ergrown with hair,
Lay sleeping on his back.
(*As You Like It. Act* 4. *Scene* 3. *Oliver speaking.*)

Dost thou love pictures? We will fetch thee straight
Adonis painted by a running brook
And Cytherea all in sedges hid,
Which seem to move and wanton with her breath
Even as the waving sedges play with wind.
(*The Taming of the Shrew. Induction. Scene* 2. *Second Servant speaking.*)

And do you tell me of a woman's tongue
That gives not half so great a blow to hear
As will a chestnut in a farmer's fire?
(*The Taming of the Shrew. Act* 1. *Scene* 2. *Petruchio speaking.*)

Say that she rail; why then I'll tell her plain
She sings as sweetly as a nightingale.
Say that she frown; I'll say she looks as clear
As morning roses newly washed with dew.
(*The Taming of the Shrew. Act* 2. *Scene* 1. *Petruchio speaking.*)

BERTRAM   It may be you have mistaken him, my lord.
LAFEU   And shall do so ever, though I took him at his prayers.
        Fare you well, my lord; and believe this of me: there can be no kernel
        in this light nut, the soul of this man is in his clothes.
(*All's Well That Ends Well. Act* 2. *Scene* 5.)

LAFEU   'Twas a good lady, 'twas a good lady. We may pick a thousand
                salads ere we light on such another herb.
CLOWN   Indeed, sir, she was the sweet marjoram of the salad, or, rather,
                the herb of grace.
LAFEU   They are not salad herbs, you knave; they are nose herbs.
CLOWN   I am no great Nebuchadnezzar, sir. I have not much skill in
                grass.
(*All's Well That Ends Well. Act* 4. *Scene* 5.)
Herb of grace: rue.

ORSINO   Then let thy love be younger than thyself,
              Or thy affection cannot hold the bent;
              For women are as roses, whose fair flower
              Being once displayed doth fall that very hour.
VIOLA   And so they are: alas, that they are so!
              To die, even when they to perfection grow!
(Twelfth Night. Act 2. Scene 4.)

When daffodils begin to peer,
With heigh, the doxy over the dale!
Why, then comes in the sweet o' the year;
For the red blood reigns in the Winter's pale.
(The Winter's Tale. Act 4. Scene 2. . . . Temple Shakespeare. Act 4.
Scene 3. Autolycus singing.)

I must have saffron, to colour the warden pies.
(The Winter's Tale. Act 4. Scene 2. . . . Temple Shakespeare. Act 4.
Scene 3. The Clown speaking.)
Saffron: used by Shakespeare to describe any crocus. Saffron is obtained
    from crocus sativus.
Warden pies: this refers to the Warden pear, believed to have originated
    at the Cistercian Monastery of Warden in Bedfordshire.

Reverend sirs,
For you there's rosemary and rue; these keep
Seeming and savour all the Winter long.
(The Winter's Tale. Act 4. Scene 3. . . . Temple Shakespeare. Act 4.
Scene 4. Perdita speaking.)

Sir, the year growing ancient,
Not yet on Summer's death nor on the birth
Of trembling Winter, the fairest flowers o' the season
Are our carnations and streaked gillyvors. . . .
(The Winter's Tale. Act 4. Scene 3. . . . Temple Shakespeare. Act 4.
Scene 4. Perdita speaking.)
Gillyvors: a variety of the carnation, of which there was a great number
    even in Shakespeare's day.

Here's flowers for you:
Hot lavender, mints, savory, marjoram;
The marigold, that goes to bed with the sun
And with him rises weeping. These are flowers
Of middle Summer and I think they are given
To men of middle age. You're very welcome.
(The Winter's Tale. Act 4. Scene 3. . . . Temple Shakespeare. Act 4.
Scene 4. Perdita speaking.)

Daffodils
That come before the swallow dares, and take
The winds of March with beauty; violets dim,
But sweeter than the lids of Juno's eyes
Or Cytherea's breath; pale prime-roses
That die unmarried, ere they can behold
Bright Phœbus in his strength, a malady
Most incident to maids; bold oxlips and
The crown imperial; lilies of all kinds,
The flower-de-luce being one.
(*The Winter's Tale.   Act* 4.   *Scene* 3. . . .   *Temple Shakespeare.   Act* 4.
   Scene 4.   *Perdita speaking.*)
The flower-de-luce: in this instance Shakespeare includes it in the lily family;
   but it is sometimes used to denote an iris.

But thou art fair; and at thy birth, dear boy,
Nature and Fortune joined to make thee great.
Of Nature's gifts thou mayst with lilies boast
And with the half-blown rose.   But Fortune, oh,
She is corrupted, changed, and won from thee!
(*King John.   Act* 3.   *Scene* 1.   *Constance speaking.*)

Feed not thy sovereign's foe, my gentle earth,
Nor with thy sweets comfort his ravenous sense;
But let thy spiders, that suck up thy venom,
And heavy-gaited toads lie in their way,
Doing annoyance to the treacherous feet
Which with usurping steps do trample thee.
Yield stinging nettles to mine enemies;
And when they from thy bosom pluck a flower,
Guard it, I pray thee, with a lurking adder,
Whose double tongue may with a mortal touch
Throw death upon thy sovereign's enemies.
(*Richard the Second.   Act* 3.   *Scene* 2.   *Richard speaking.*)

Go, bind thou up yon dangling apricocks,
Which, like unruly children, make their sire
Stoop with oppression of their prodigal weight:
Give some supportance to the bending twigs.
Go thou, and like an executioner
Cut off the heads of too fast-growing sprays
That look too lofty in our commonwealth.
All must be even in our government.
(*Richard the Second.   Act* 3.   *Scene* 4.   *A Gardener speaking.*)

Oh, what pity is it
That he hath not so trimmed and dressed his land
As we this garden! We at time of year
Do wound the bark, the skin of our fruit trees,
Lest, being over-proud with sap and blood,
With too much riches it confound itself.
(*Richard the Second. Act 3. Scene 4. A Gardener speaking.*)

THE QUEEN   Gardener, for telling me these news of woe,
             Pray God the plants thou graft'st may never grow!
GARDENER   Poor queen! So that thy state might be no worse,
             I would my skill were subject to thy curse.
             Here did she fall a tear; here, in this place,
             I'll set a bank of rue, sour herb of grace.
             Rue, even for ruth, here shortly shall be seen
             In the remembrance of a weeping queen.
(*Richard the Second. Act 3. Scene 4.*)

'The purpose you undertake is dangerous. . . .'
Why, that's certain: 'tis dangerous to take a cold, to sleep, to drink; but
    I tell you, my lord fool, out of this nettle, danger, we pluck this flower,
    safety.
(*Henry the Fourth. Part One. Act 2. Scene 3. Hotspur, reading at first
    a letter.*)

Why, my skin hangs about me like an old lady's loose gown; I am
    withered like an old apple-john.
(*Henry the Fourth. Part One. Act 3. Scene 3. Falstaff speaking.*)
Apple-john: a shrivelled-up Winter apple.

The strawberry grows underneath the nettle,
And wholesome berries thrive and ripen best
Neighboured by fruit of baser quality:
And so the prince obscured his contemplation
Under the veil of wildness; which, no doubt,
Grew like the Summer grass, fastest by night.
(*Henry the Fifth. Act 1. Scene 1. The Bishop of Ely speaking.*)

. . . a' parted even just between twelve and one, even at the turning o'
    the tide: for after I saw him fumble with the sheets and play with
    flowers and smile upon his fingers' ends, I knew there was but one
    way; for his nose was as sharp as a pen, and a' babbled of green fields.
(*Henry the Fifth. Act 2. Scene 3. Hostess of The Boar's Head—Mistress
    Quickly—describing the death of Falstaff.*)

Covering discretion with a coat of folly,
As gardeners do with ordure hide those roots
That shall first spring and be most delicate.
(*Henry the Fifth.   Act 2.   Scene 4.   The Constable of France speaking.*)

For, though I speak it to you, I think the king is but a man, as I am.   The
violet smells to him as it doth to me.
(*Henry the Fifth.   Act 4.   Scene 1.   The King speaking.*)

Alas, she hath from France too long been chased,
And all her husbandry doth lie on heaps
Corrupting in its own fertility.
Her vine, the merry cheerer of the heart,
Unpruned dies: her hedges, even-pleached,
Like prisoners wildly overgrown with hair
Put forth disordered twigs; her fallow leas
The darnel, hemlock and rank fumitory
Doth root upon, while that the coulter rusts
That should deracinate such savagery.
(*Henry the Fifth.   Act 5.   Scene 2.   Burgundy speaking.*)
Coulter: plough-share.

Awake, awake, English nobility!
Let not sloth dim your honours new-begot.
Cropped are the flower-de-luces in your arms;
Of England's coat one half is cut away.
(*Henry the Sixth.   Part One.   Act 1.   Scene 1.   A Messenger speaking.*)
Flower-de-luces: fleur-de-lys, the French emblem.

VERNON   Then for the truth and plainness of the case
          I pluck this pale and maiden blossom here,
          Giving my verdict on the white rose side.
SOMERSET Prick not your finger as you pluck it off;
          Lest, bleeding, you do paint the white rose red
          And fall on my side so, against your will.
(*Henry the Sixth.   Part One.   Act 2.   Scene 4.   The historical quarrel in the
Temple Garden.*)

Now 'tis the Spring, and weeds are shallow-rooted;
Suffer them now and they'll o'ergrow the garden
And choke the herbs for want of husbandry.
(*Henry the Sixth.   Part Two.   Act 3.   Scene 1.   Queen Margaret speaking.*)

And for myself, foe as he was to me,
Might liquid tears or heart-offending groans
Or blood-consuming sighs recall his life,
I would be blind with weeping, sick with groans,
Look pale as primrose with blood-drinking sighs,
And all to have the noble duke alive.
(*Henry the Sixth. Part Two. Act 3. Scene 2. Queen Margaret speaking.*)

Gives not the hawthorn bush a sweeter shade
To shepherds, looking on their silly sheep,
Than doth a rich embroidered canopy
To kings that fear their subjects' treachery?
Oh, yes, it doth; a thousand-fold it doth!
(*Henry the Sixth. Part Three. Act 2. Scene 5. The King speaking.*)

Alas, poor wenches, where are now your fortunes?
Shipwrecked upon a kingdom, where no pity,
No friends, no hope, no kindred weep for me;
Almost no grave allowed me.   Like the lily,
That once was mistress of the field and flourished,
I'll hang my head and perish.
(*Henry the Eighth. Act 3. Scene 1. Queen Katharine speaking.*)

                    Princes,
What grief hath set the jaundice on your cheeks?
The ample proposition that hope makes,
In all designs begun on earth below,
Fails in the promised largeness: checks and disasters
Grow in the veins of actions highest reared;
As knots, by the conflux of meeting sap,
Infect the sound pine and divert his grain
Tortive and errant from his course of growth.
(*Troilus and Cressida. Act 1. Scene 3. Agamemnon speaking.*)
Tortive: twisted.

We have some old crab-trees here at home that will not
Be grafted to your relish.   Yet, welcome, warriors!
We call a nettle but a nettle, and
The faults of fools but folly.
(*Coriolanus. Act 2. Scene 1. Menenius speaking.*)

BENVOLIO   Tut, man, one fire burns out another's burning;
             One pain is lessened by another's anguish;
             Turn giddy, and be holp by backward turning;
             One's desperate grief cures with another's languish.
             Take thou some new infection to thy eye
             And the rank poison of the old will die.

ROMEO   Your plantain leaf is excellent for that.

BENVOLIO For what, I pray thee?

ROMEO   For your broken shin.

(*Romeo and Juliet. Act* 1. *Scene* 2.)

Plantain: this weed was usually called 'waybroad.' Chaucer and
    Shakespeare are the only two early writers who name it 'plantain';
    and Shakespeare sometimes refers to it as 'plantage.' It was highly
    valued for its medicinal qualities.

BENVOLIO Come, knock and enter, and no sooner in
          But every man betake him to his legs.

ROMEO   A torch for me.   Let wantons light of heart
          Tickle the senseless rushes with their heels;
          For I am proverbed with a grandsire phrase:
          I'll be a candle-holder and look on.

(*Romeo and Juliet. Act* 1. *Scene* 4.)

Shakespeare frequently refers in his plays to the custom of strewing rushes
    on the floor.

                    Oh, be some other name!
What's in a name?   That which we call a rose
By any other name would smell as sweet.
So Romeo would, were he not Romeo called,
Retain that dear perfection which he owes
Without that title.

(*Romeo and Juliet. Act* 2. *Scene* 2. *Juliet speaking.*)

Owes: owns.

Wilt thou be gone?   It is not yet near day:
It was the nightingale and not the lark
That pierced the fearful hollow of thine ear;
Nightly she sings on yond pomegranate-tree.
Believe me, love, it was the nightingale.

(*Romeo and Juliet. Act* 3. *Scene* 5. *Juliet speaking.*)

                    Oh, God! God!
How weary, stale, flat and unprofitable
Seem to me all the uses of this world.
Fie on't!   Ah, fie!   'Tis an unweeded garden
That grows to seed; things rank and gross in nature
Possess it merely.

(*Hamlet. Act* 1. *Scene* 2. *Hamlet speaking.*)

For Hamlet and the trifling of his favour,
Hold it a fashion and a toy in blood;
A violet in the youth of primy nature,
Forward, not permanent, sweet, not lasting,
The perfume and suppliance of a minute:
No more.
(*Hamlet. Act 1. Scene 3. Laertes speaking.*)

OPHELIA   There's rosemary, that's for remembrance: pray you, love,
          remember. And there is pansies: that's for thoughts.

LAERTES   A document in madness; thoughts and remembrance fitted!

OPHELIA   There's fennel for you, and columbines. There's rue for you;
          and here's some for me. We may call it herb of grace o'
          Sundays. Oh, you must wear your rue with a difference!
          There's a daisy. I would give you some violets, but they
          withered all when my father died.

(*Hamlet. Act 4. Scene 5.*)
The columbine was popular in Tudor times; but being deficient in medicinal
    properties was regarded as a 'thankless flower.'

There is a willow grows aslant a brook,
That shows his hoar leaves in the glassy stream.
There with fantastic garlands did she come,
Of crow-flowers, nettles, daisies, and long purples
That liberal shepherds give a grosser name
But our cold maids do dead-men's-fingers call them.
(*Hamlet. Act 4. Scene 7. The Queen speaking.*)

                    Lay her i' the earth;
And from her fair and unpolluted flesh
May violets spring! I tell thee, churlish priest,
A ministering angel shall my sister be
When thou liest howling.
(*Hamlet. Act 5. Scene 1. Laertes speaking.*)

                    How fearful
And dizzy 'tis to cast one's eyes so low!
The crows and choughs that wing the midway air
Show scarce so gross as beetles. Halfway down
Hangs one that gathers samphire. Dreadful trade!
(*King Lear. Act 4. Scene 6. Edgar speaking.*)
Samphire: generally found by the sea; and used as an ingredient for salads
    and pickles.

Our bodies are gardens, to the which our wills are gardeners; so that if we
    will plant nettles or sow lettuce, set hyssop and weed up thyme, supply
    it with one gender of herbs or distract it with many, either to have it
    sterile with idleness or manured with industry, why, the power and
    corrigible authority of this lies in our wills.
(*Othello. Act* 1. *Scene* 3. *Iago speaking.*)

                                When I have plucked the rose,
I cannot give it vital growth again.
It must needs wither.
(*Othello. Act* 5. *Scene* 2. *Othello speaking.*)

SOOTHSAYER   You shall outlive the lady whom you serve.
CHARMIAN   Oh, excellent! I love long life better than figs.
(*Antony and Cleopatra. Act* 1. *Scene* 2.)

And winking Mary-buds begin
To ope their golden eyes.
With everything that pretty is
My lady sweet, arise.
Arise, arise!
(*Cymbeline. Act* 2. *Scene* 3. *Song.*)

                            With fairest flowers,
While Summer lasts and I live here, Fidele,
I'll sweeten thy sad grave.   Thou shalt not lack
The flower that's like thy face, pale primrose, nor
The azured hare-bell, like thy veins, no, nor
The leaf of eglantine, whom not to slander,
Out-sweetened not thy breath.
(*Cymbeline. Act* 4. *Scene* 2. *Arviragus speaking.*)

No, I will rob Tellus of her weed,
To strew thy green with flowers; the yellows, blues,
The purple violets and marigolds
Shall as a carpet hang upon thy grave
While Summer days do last.
(*Pericles. Act* 4. *Scene* 1. *Marina speaking.*)

When I do count the clock that tells the time
And see the brave day sunk in hideous night;
When I behold the violet past prime
And sable curls, all silvered o'er with white;
When lofty trees I see barren of leaves
Which erst from heat did canopy the herd,
And Summer's green all girded up in sheaves,
Borne on the bier with white and bristly beard;
Then of thy beauty do I question make,
That thou among the wastes of time must go. . . .
(*Sonnet* 12.)

Great princes' favourites their fair leaves spread,
But as the marigold at the sun's eye;
And in themselves their pride lies buried,
For at a frown they in their glory die.
(*Sonnet* 25.)

No more be grieved at that which thou hast done:
Roses have thorns and silver fountains mud;
Clouds and eclipses stain both moon and sun,
And loathsome canker lives in sweetest bud.
(*Sonnet* 35.)

The Summer's flower is to the Summer sweet,
Though to itself it only live and die;
But if that flower with base infection meet,
The basest weed outbraves his dignity.
For sweetest things turn sourest by their deeds:
Lilies that fester smell far worse than weeds.
(*Sonnet* 94.)

How sweet and lovely dost thou make the shame
Which, like a canker in the fragrant rose,
Doth spot the beauty of thy budding name!
(*Sonnet* 95.)

Nor did I wonder at the lily's white,
Nor praise the deep vermilion in the rose;
They were but sweet, but figures of delight,
Drawn after you, you pattern of all those.
(*Sonnet* 98.)

The forward violet thus did I chide:
Sweet thief, whence didst thou steal thy sweet that smells,
If not from my love's breath?   The purple pride
Which on thy soft cheek for complexion dwells
In my love's veins thou hast too grossly dyed.
The lily I condemnèd for thy hand
And buds of marjoram had stol'n thy hair;
The roses fearfully on thorns did stand,
One blushing shame, another white despair,
A third, nor red nor white, had stol'n of both,
And to his robbery had annexed thy breath;
But, for his theft, in pride of all his growth
A vengeful canker ate him up to death.
More flowers I noted, yet I none could see
But sweet or colour it had stol'n from thee.
(*Sonnet* 99.)

Section IV

LIFE AND DEATH

Now would I give a thousand furlongs of sea for an acre of barren ground,
long heath, brown furze . . . anything. The wills above be done!
But I would fain die a dry death.
(*The Tempest. Act 1. Scene 1. Gonzalo speaking.*)

Full fathom five thy father lies;
Of his bones are coral made,
Those are pearls that were his eyes.
Nothing of him that doth fade,
But doth suffer a sea-change
Into something rich and strange.
Sea-nymphs hourly ring his knell:
Ding-dong, ding-dong, bell.
(*The Tempest. Act 1. Scene 2. Ariel singing.*)

CLAUDIO   I have hope to live, and am prepared to die.
THE DUKE   Be absolute for death; either death or life
           Shall thereby be the sweeter.
(*Measure For Measure. Act 3. Scene 1.*)

Dar'st thou die?
The sense of death is most in apprehension;
And the poor beetle, that we tread upon,
In corporal sufferance finds a pang as great
As when a giant dies.
(*Measure For Measure. Act 3. Scene 1. Isabella speaking.*)

If I must die,
I will encounter darkness as a bride
And hug it in mine arms.
(*Measure For Measure. Act 3. Scene 1. Claudio speaking.*)

The weariest and most loathed worldly life
That age, ache, penury and imprisonment
Can lay on nature is a paradise
To what we fear of death.
(*Measure For Measure. Act 3. Scene 1. Claudio speaking.*)

Therefore let Benedick, like covered fire,
Consume away in sighs, waste inwardly.
It were a better death than die with mocks,
Which is as bad as die with tickling.
(*Much Ado About Nothing. Act 3. Scene 1. Hero speaking.*)

Oh, Fate, take not away thy heavy hand!
Death is the fairest cover for her shame
That may be wished for.
(*Much Ado About Nothing. Act 4. Scene 1. Leonato speaking.*)

Let fame, that all hunt after in their lives,
Live registered upon our brazen tombs
And then grace us in the disgrace of death;
When, spite of cormorant devouring Time,
The endeavour of this present breath may buy
That honour which shall bate his scythe's keen edge
And make us heirs of all eternity.
(*Love's Labour's Lost. Act 1. Scene 1. The King speaking.*)

I am a tainted wether of the flock,
Meetest for death. The weakest kind of fruit
Drops earliest to the ground; and so let me.
You cannot better be employed, Bassanio,
Than to live still and write mine epitaph.
(*The Merchant of Venice. Act 4. Scene 1. Antonio speaking.*)

Antonio, I am married to a wife,
Which is as dear to me as life itself;
But life itself, my wife, and all the world
Are not with me esteemed above thy life:
I would lose all, ay, sacrifice them all
Here to this devil to deliver you!
(*The Merchant of Venice. Act 4. Scene 1. Bassanio speaking.*)

Nay, take my life and all; pardon not that.
You take my house when you do take the prop
That doth sustain my house. You take my life
When you do take the means whereby I live.
(*The Merchant of Venice. Act 4. Scene 1. Shylock speaking.*)

Sit, Jessica. Look how the floor of heaven
Is thick inlaid with patines of bright gold.
There's not the smallest orb which thou behold'st
But in his motion like an angel sings,
Still quiring to the young-eyed cherubins.

Such harmony is in immortal souls;
But, whilst this muddy vesture of decay
Doth grossly close it in, we cannot hear it.
(*The Merchant of Venice. Act 5. Scene 1. Lorenzo speaking.*)

This young gentlewoman had a father . . . oh, that 'had'! How sad a
passage 'tis! . . . whose skill was almost as great as his honesty; had
it stretched so far, would have made nature immortal and death should
have play for lack of work.
(*All's Well That Ends Well. Act 1. Scene 1. The Countess of Rousillon
speaking.*)

Moderate lamentation is the right of the dead; excessive grief the enemy
to the living.
(*All's Well That Ends Well. Act 1. Scene 1. Lafeu speaking.*)

ORSINO   Then let thy love be younger than thyself,
    Or thy affection cannot hold the bent.
    For women are as roses, whose fair flower
    Being once displayed doth fall that very hour.
VIOLA   And so they are. Alas, that they are so!
    To die, even when they to perfection grow!
(*Twelfth Night. Act 2. Scene 4.*)

Come away, come away, death,
And in sad cypress let me be laid.
(*Twelfth Night. Act 2. Scene 4. Feste singing.*)
Cypress: either refers to a kind of mourning crape, or to a coffin of cypress
wood.

And I, most jocund, apt, and willingly,
To do you rest a thousand deaths would die.
(*Twelfth Night. Act 5. Scene 1. Viola speaking.*)

There is a plot against my life, my crown;
All's true that is mistrusted.
(*The Winter's Tale. Act 2. Scene 1. Leontes speaking.*)

     Oh, Hermione,
As every present time doth boast itself
Above a better gone, so must thy grave
Give way to what's seen now!
(*The Winter's Tale. Act 5. Scene 1. Paulina speaking.*)

Prithee, no more. Cease. Thou know'st
He dies to me again when talked of.
(*The Winter's Tale. Act 5. Scene 1. Leontes speaking.*)

Ha, majesty! How high thy glory towers,
When the rich blood of kings is set on fire!
Oh, now doth Death line his dead chaps with steel.
The swords of soldiers are his teeth, his fangs;
And now he feasts, mousing the flesh of men,
In undetermined differences of kings.
(*King John. Act 2. Scene 1. The Bastard speaking.*)

Here's a stay
That shakes the rotten carcase of old Death
Out of his rags!
(*King John. Act 2. Scene 1. The Bastard speaking.*)

KING JOHN   Hubert, throw thine eye
On yon young boy. I'll tell thee what, my friend:
He is a very serpent in my way;
And wheresoe'er this foot of mine doth tread,
He lies before me. Dost thou understand me?
Thou art his keeper.
HUBERT   And I'll keep him so
That he shall not offend your majesty.
KING JOHN Death.
HUBERT My lord?
KING JOHN A grave.
HUBERT He shall not live.
(*King John. Act 3. Scene 3.*)

Death, death! Oh, amiable, lovely death!
Thou odoriferous stench! Sound rottenness!
(*King John. Act 3. Scene 4. Constance speaking.*)

There's nothing in this world can make me joy:
Life is as tedious as a twice-told tale,
Vexing the dull ear of a drowsy man.
(*King John. Act 3. Scene 4. Lewis speaking.*)

They burn in indignation. I repent:
There is no sure foundation set on blood,
No certain life achieved by others' death.
(*King John. Act 4. Scene 2. King John speaking*)

Ay, marry, now my soul hath elbow-room:
It would not out at windows nor at doors.
(*King John. Act 5. Scene 7. King John speaking.*)

Ross   We see the very wrack that we must suffer;
                         And unavoided is the danger now,
                         For suffering so the causes of our wrack.
NORTHUMBERLAND   Not so: even through the hollow eyes of death
                         I see life peering.
(*Richard the Second.   Act* 2.   *Scene* 1.)

                    For within the hollow crown
That rounds the mortal temples of a king,
Keeps Death his court; and there the antick sits,
Scoffing his state and grinning at his pomp.
(*Richard the Second.   Act* 3.   *Scene* 2.   *Richard speaking.*)

                    I am sworn brother, sweet,
To grim Necessity; and he and I
Will keep a league till death.
(*Richard the Second.   Act* 5.   *Scene* 1.   *Richard speaking.*)

                    Now let not nature's hand
Keep the wild flood confined !   Let order die !
And let this world no longer be a stage
To feed contention in a lingering act;
But let one spirit of the first-born, Cain,
Reign in all bosoms, that, each heart being set
On bloody courses, the rude scene may end
And darkness be the burier of the dead !
(*Henry the Fourth.   Part Two.   Act* 1.   *Scene* 1.   *Northumberland speaking.*)

If you will needs say I am an old man, you should give me rest. I would
     to God my name were not so terrible to the enemy as it is: I were
     better to be eaten to death with rust than to be scoured to nothing
     with perpetual motion.
(*Henry the Fourth.   Part Two.   Act* 1.   *Scene* 2.   *Falstaff speaking.*)

Awake remembrance of these valiant dead,
And with your puissant arm renew their feats.
(*Henry the Fifth.   Act* 1.   *Scene* 2.   *Bishop of Ely speaking.*)

We mourn in black: why mourn we not in blood?
Henry is dead and never shall revive.
Upon a wooden coffin we attend;
And death's dishonourable victory
We with·our stately presence glorify,
Like captives bound to a triumphant car.
(*Henry the Sixth.   Part One.   Act* 1.   *Scene* 1.   *Exeter speaking.*)

But now the arbitrator of despairs,
Just death, kind umpire of men's miseries,
With sweet enlargement doth dismiss me hence.
(*Henry the Sixth. Part One. Act 2. Scene 5. Mortimer speaking.*)

SUFFOLK   I go.
QUEEN MARGARET   And take my heart with thee.
SUFFOLK   A jewel, locked into the woefull'st cask
                 That ever did contain a thing of worth.
                 Even as a splitted bark, so sunder we:
                 This way fall I to death.
(*Henry the Sixth. Part Two. Act 3. Scene 2.*)

Ah, what a sign it is of evil life
Where death's approach is seen so terrible.
(*Henry the Sixth. Part Two. Act 3. Scene 3. The King speaking.*)

My blood, my want of strength, my sick heart shows
That I must yield my body to the earth;
And by my fall, the conquest to my foe.
Thus yields the cedar to the axe's edge,
Whose arms gave shelter to the princely eagle;
Under whose shade the ramping lion slept,
Whose top branch overpeered Jove's spreading tree
And kept low shrubs from Winter's powerful wind.
(*Henry the Sixth. Part Three. Act 5. Scene 2. Warwick speaking.*)

And when I am forgotten, as I shall be,
And sleep in dull cold marble, where no mention
Of me more must be heard of, say, I taught thee;
Say, Wolsey, that once trod the ways of glory
And sounded all the depths and shoals of honour,
Found thee a way, out of his wreck, to rise in.
(*Henry the Eighth. Act 3. Scene 2. Wolsey speaking.*)

Ah, that this sight should make so deep a wound,
And yet detested life not shrink thereat!
That ever death should let life bear his name,
Where life hath no more interest but to breathe!
(*Titus Andronicus. Act 3. Scene 1. Lucius speaking.*)

                 Is she a Capulet?
Oh, dear account! My life is my foe's debt.
(*Romeo and Juliet. Act 1. Scene 5. Romeo speaking.*)

JULIET   I would not for the world they saw thee here.
ROMEO   I have night's cloak to hide me from their eyes;
          And but thou love me, let them find me here:
          My life were better ended by their hate,
          Than death prorogued, wanting of thy love.
(*Romeo and Juliet.   Act 2.   Scene 2.*)

Some word there was, worser than Tybalt's death,
That murdered me.   I would forget it, fain;
But, oh, it presses to my memory
Like damnèd guilty deeds to sinners' minds:
'Tybalt is dead, and Romeo banishèd.'
That 'banishèd,' that one word 'banishèd,'
Hath slain ten thousand Tybalts.
(*Romeo and Juliet.   Act 3.   Scene 2.   Juliet speaking.*)

                    'Romeo is banishèd.'
There is no end, no limit, measure, bound,
In that word's death.   No words can that woe sound.
(*Romeo and Juliet.   Act 3.   Scene 2.   Juliet speaking.*)

                    Oh, give me thy hand,
One writ with me in sour misfortune's book!
I'll bury thee in a triumphant grave.
A grave?   Oh, no, a lantern, slaughtered youth;
For here lies Juliet, and her beauty makes
This vault a feasting presence full of light.
Death, lie thou there, by a dead man interred.
(*Romeo and Juliet.   Act 5.   Scene 3.   Romeo speaking.*)

                    Oh, here
Will I set up my everlasting rest,
And shake the yoke of inauspicious stars
From this world-wearied flesh.   Eyes, look your last!
Arms, take your last embrace!   And lips, oh you
The doors of breath, seal with a righteous kiss
A dateless bargain to engrossing death!
Come, bitter conduct!   Come, unsavoury guide!
Thou desperate pilot, now at once run on
The dashing rocks thy sea-sick weary bark.
(*Romeo and Juliet.   Act 5.   Scene 3.   Romeo speaking.*)

I know where I will wear this dagger then:
Cassius from bondage will deliver Cassius.
Therein, ye gods, you make the weak most strong;
Therein, ye gods, you tyrants do defeat:

Nor stony tower, nor walls of beaten brass,
Nor airless dungeon, nor strong links of iron,
Can be retentive to the strength of spirit;
But life, being weary of those worldly bars,
Never lacks power to dismiss itself.
If I know this, know all the world besides,
That part of tyranny that I do bear
I can shake off at pleasure.
(*Julius Cæsar. Act 1. Scene 3. Cassius speaking.*)

Cowards die many times before their deaths,
The valiant never taste of death but once.
Of all the wonders that I yet have heard,
It seems to me most strange that men should fear;
Seeing that death, a necessary end,
Will come when it will come.
(*Julius Cæsar. Act 2. Scene 2. Cæsar speaking.*)

BRUTUS Fates, we will know your pleasures:
That we shall die, we know; 'tis but the time,
And drawing days out, that men stand upon.
CASSIUS Why, he that cuts off twenty years of life
Cuts off so many years of fearing death.
BRUTUS Grant that, and then is death a benefit.
(*Julius Cæsar. Act 3. Scene 1.*)

MALCOLM Nothing in his life
Became him like the leaving it: he died
As one that had been studied in his death,
To throw away the dearest thing he owned
As 'twere a careless trifle.
DUNCAN There's no art
To find the mind's construction in the face:
He was a gentleman on whom I built
An absolute trust.
(*Macbeth. Act 1. Scene 4.*)

That which hath made them drunk hath made me bold;
What hath quenched them hath given me fire.
Hark! Peace!
It was the owl that shrieked, the fatal bellman
Which gives the stern'st good-night. He is about it.
The doors are open, and the surfeited grooms
Do mock their charge with snores: I have drugged their possets,
That death and nature do contend about them
Whether they live or die.
(*Macbeth. Act 2. Scene 2. Lady Macbeth speaking.*)

MACBETH   I'll go no more:
                I am afraid to think what I have done;
                Look on't again I dare not.
LADY MACBETH   Infirm of purpose!
                Give me the daggers.   The sleeping and the dead
                Are but as pictures: 'tis the eye of childhood
                That fears a painted devil.
(*Macbeth.   Act 2.   Scene 2.*)

Confusion now hath made his masterpiece.
Most sacrilegious murder hath broke ope
The Lord's anointed temple, and stole thence
The life o' the building.
(*Macbeth.   Act 2.   Scene 3.   Macduff speaking.*)

Had I but died an hour before this chance,
I had lived a blessèd time; for from this instant
There's nothing serious in mortality.
All is but toys: renown and grace is dead;
The wine of life is drawn, and the mere lees
Is left this vault to brag of.
(*Macbeth.   Act 2.   Scene 3.   Macbeth speaking.*)

But let the frame of things disjoint, both the worlds suffer,
Ere we will eat our meal in fear and sleep
In the affliction of these terrible dreams
That shake us nightly.   Better be with the dead,
Whom we, to gain our peace, have sent to peace,
Than on the torture of the mind to lie
In restless ecstasy.
(*Macbeth.   Act 3.   Scene 2.   Macbeth speaking.*)

                        Out, out, brief candle!
Life's but a walking shadow; a poor player
That struts and frets his hour upon the stage
And then is heard no more.   It is a tale
Told by an idiot, full of sound and fury,
Signifying nothing.
(*Macbeth.   Act 5.   Scene 5.   Macbeth speaking.*)

For what we know must be, and is as common
As any the most vulgar thing to sense,
Why should we in our peevish opposition
Take it to heart?   Fie!   'Tis a fault to heaven,
A fault against the dead, a fault to nature;

To reason most absurd, whose common theme
Is death of fathers, and who still hath cried,
From the first corse till he that died to-day,
'This must be so.'
(*Hamlet. Act* I. *Scene* 2. *The King speaking.*)

That it should come to this!
But two months dead! Nay, not so much, not two.
So excellent a king; that was, to this,
Hyperion to a satyr. So loving to my mother,
That he might not beteem the winds of heaven
Visit her face too roughly.
(*Hamlet. Act* I. *Scene* 2. *Hamlet speaking.*)

Oh, answer me!
Let me not burst in ignorance, but tell
Why thy canonized bones, hearsed in death,
Have burst their cerements; why the sepulchre,
Wherein we saw thee quietly inurned,
Hath oped his ponderous and marble jaws
To cast thee up again. What may this mean,
That thou, dead corse, again, in complete steel,
Revisit'st thus the glimpses of the moon,
Making night hideous; and we fools of nature
So horridly to shake our disposition
With thoughts beyond the reaches of our souls?
Say, why is this? Wherefore? What should we do?
(*Hamlet. Act* I. *Scene* 4. *Hamlet speaking.*)

Why, what should be the fear?
I do not set my life at a pin's fee;
And for my soul, what can it do to that,
Being a thing immortal as itself?
It waves me forth again. I'll follow it.
(*Hamlet. Act* I. *Scene* 4. *Hamlet speaking.*)

There's the respect
That makes calamity of so long life;
For who would bear the whips and scorns of time,
The oppressor's wrong, the proud man's contumely,
The pangs of despised love, the law's delay,
The insolence of office, and the spurns
That patient merit of the unworthy takes,
When he himself might his quietus make
With a bare bodkin?
(*Hamlet. Act* 3. *Scene* I. *Hamlet speaking.*)

Oh, heavens! Die two months ago, and not forgotten yet?
Then there's hope a great man's memory may outlive his life half a year.
(*Hamlet. Act 3. Scene 2. Hamlet speaking.*)

HAMLET   Oh, I die, Horatio!
          The potent poison quite o'er-crows my spirit.
          I cannot live to hear the news from England,
          But I do prophesy the election lights
          On Fortinbras. He has my dying voice.
          So tell him, with the occurrents, more and less,
          Which have solicited. The rest is silence.
HORATIO   Now cracks a noble heart. Good night, sweet prince,
          And flights of angels sing thee to thy rest!
(*Hamlet. Act 5. Scene 2.*)

This quarry cries on havoc. Oh, proud death!
What feast is toward in thine eternal cell,
That thou so many princes at a shot
So bloodily hast struck?
(*Hamlet. Act 5. Scene 2. Fortinbras speaking.*)

Meantime we shall express our darker purpose.
Give me the map there. Know we have divided
In three our kingdom: and 'tis our fast intent
To shake all cares and business from our age,
Conferring them on younger strengths, while we
Unburthened crawl toward death.
(*King Lear. Act 1. Scene 1. Lear speaking.*)

And yet I know not how conceit may rob
The treasury of life, when life itself
Yields to the theft: had he been where he thought,
By this had thought been past.
(*King Lear. Act 4. Scene 6. Edgar speaking.*)
Conceit: imagination.

Is wretchedness deprived that benefit,
To end itself by death? 'Twas yet some comfort,
When misery could beguile the tyrant's rage
And frustrate his proud will.
(*King Lear. Act 4. Scene 6. Gloucester speaking.*)

LEAR   Thou must be patient; we came crying hither.
            Thou know'st, the first time that we smell the air,
            We wawl and cry. I will preach to thee. Mark.
GLOUCESTER Alack! Alack, the day!

LEAR   When we are born, we cry that we are come
        To this great stage of fools.
(*King Lear. Act 4. Scene 6.*)
Wawl: wail.

                    Oh, our lives' sweetness,
That we the pain of death would hourly die
Rather than die at once!
(*King Lear. Act 5. Scene 3. Edgar speaking.*)

Vex not his ghost. Oh, let him pass! He hates him
That would upon the rack of this tough world
Stretch him out longer.
(*King Lear. Act 5. Scene 3. Kent speaking.*)

It is silliness to live, when to live is torment. And then have we a
    prescription to die, when death is our physician.
(*Othello. Act 1. Scene 3. Roderigo speaking.*)

                    If it were now to die,
'Twere now to be most happy; for I fear
My soul hath her content so absolute
That not another comfort like to this
Succeeds in unknown fate.
(*Othello. Act 2. Scene 1. Othello speaking.*)

                    Unkindness may do much;
And his unkindness may defeat my life,
But never taint my love.
(*Othello. Act 4. Scene 2. Desdemona speaking.*)

I kissed thee ere I killed thee. No way but this:
Killing myself, to die upon a kiss.
(*Othello. Act 5. Scene 2. Othello speaking.*)

Things that are past are done with me. 'Tis thus:
Who tells me true, though in his tale lay death,
I hear him as he flattered.
(*Antony and Cleopatra. Act 1. Scene 2. Antony speaking.*)

ENOBARBUS Cleopatra, catching but the least noise of this, dies instantly;
            I have seen her die twenty times upon far poorer moment.
            I do think there is mettle in death which commits some
            loving act upon her, she hath such a celerity in dying.
ANTONY   She is cunning past man's thought.
(*Antony and Cleopatra. Act 1. Scene 2.*)

Know, my hearts,
I hope well of to-morrow; and will lead you
Where rather I'll expect victorious life
Than death and honour. Let's to supper. Come,
And drown consideration.

(*Antony and Cleopatra. Act 4. Scene 2. Antony speaking.*)

Oh, sovereign mistress of true melancholy,
The poisonous damp of night disponge upon me,
That life, a very rebel to my will,
May hang no longer on me.

(*Antony and Cleopatra. Act 4. Scene 9. Enobarbus, addressing the moon.*)

Thou art sworn, Eros,
That, when the exigent should come . . . which now
Is come indeed . . . when I should see behind me
The inevitable prosecution of
Disgrace and horror, that, on my command,
Thou then wouldst kill me. Do it. The time is come.
Thou strik'st not me: 'tis Cæsar thou defeat'st.
Put colour in thy cheeks.

(*Antony and Cleopatra. Act 4. Scene 14. Antony speaking. Scene 12:
The Oxford Shakespeare.*)

Thrice-nobler than myself!
Thou teachest me, oh valiant Eros, what
I should, and thou couldst not. My queen and Eros
Have by their brave instruction got upon me
A nobleness in record; but I will be
A bridegroom in my death, and run into't
As to a lover's bed. Come, then! And, Eros,
Thy master dies thy scholar: to do thus
I learned of thee. (*Falls on his sword.*)

(*Antony and Cleopatra. Act 4. Scene 14. Antony speaking. Scene 12:
The Oxford Shakespeare.*)

I am dying, Egypt, dying; only
I here importune death awhile, until
Of many thousand kisses the poor last
I lay upon thy lips.

(*Antony and Cleopatra. Act 4. Scene 15. Antony speaking. Scene 13:
The Oxford Shakespeare.*)

Oh, come, come, come!
And welcome, welcome!   Die where thou hast lived.
Quicken with kissing: had my lips that power,
Thus would I wear them out.

(*Antony and Cleopatra. Act* 4. *Scene* 15. *Cleopatra speaking. Scene* 13:
The Oxford Shakespeare.)

Noblest of men, wouldst die?
Hast thou no care of me?   Shall I abide
In this dull world, which in thy absence is
No better than a sty?   Oh, see, my women!
The crown o' the earth doth melt.   My lord!
Oh, withered is the garland of the war,
The soldier's pole is fall'n; young boys and girls
Are level now with men; the odds is gone
And there is nothing left remarkable
Beneath the visiting moon.

(*Antony and Cleopatra. Act* 4. *Scene* 15. *Cleopatra speaking. Scene* 13:
The Oxford Shakespeare.)

All's but nought;
Patience is sottish, and impatience does
Become a dog that's mad.   Then is it sin
To rush into the secret house of death,
Ere death dare come to us?

(*Antony and Cleopatra. Act* 4. *Scene* 15. *Cleopatra speaking. Scene* 13:
The Oxford Shakespeare)

Our lamp is spent.   It's out.   Good sirs, take heart.
We'll bury him; and then, what's brave, what's noble,
Let's do it after the high Roman fashion,
And make death proud to take us.   Come, away;
This case of that huge spirit now is cold.
Ah, women, women!   Come; we have no friend
But resolution and the briefest end.

(*Antony and Cleopatra. Act* 4. *Scene* 15. *Cleopatra speaking. Scene* 13:
The Oxford Shakespeare.)

The breaking of so great a thing should make
A greater crack; the round world
Should have shook lions into civil streets,
And citizens to their dens.   The death of Antony
Is not a single doom; in the name lay
A moiety of the world.

(*Antony and Cleopatra. Act* 5. *Scene* 1. *Octavius Cæsar speaking.*)

Where art thou, death?
Come hither, come! Come, come, and take a queen
Worth many babes and beggars!
(*Antony and Cleopatra. Act 5. Scene 2. Cleopatra speaking.*)

This mortal house I'll ruin,
Do Cæsar what he can. Know, sir, that I
Will not wait pinioned at your master's court,
Nor once be chastised with the sober eye
Of dull Octavia. Shall they hoist me up
And show me to the shouting varletry
Of censuring Rome? Rather a ditch in Egypt
Be gentle grave unto me! Rather on Nilus' mud
Lay me stark nak'd, and let the water-flies
Blow me into abhorring! Rather make
My country's high pyramides my gibbet
And hang me up in chains!
(*Antony and Cleopatra. Act 5. Scene 2. Cleopatra speaking.*)

Give me my robe, put on my crown; I have
Immortal longings in me. Now no more
The juice of Egypt's grape shall moist this lip.
(*Antony and Cleopatra. Act 5. Scene 2. Cleopatra speaking.*)

Come, thou mortal wretch,
With thy sharp teeth this knot intrinsicate
Of life at once untie. Poor, venomous fool,
Be angry and dispatch. Oh, couldst thou speak,
That I might hear thee call great Cæsar ass
Unpolicied!
(*Antony and Cleopatra. Act 5. Scene 2. Cleopatra speaking.*)

So, fare thee well.
Now boast thee, death, in thy possession lies
A lass unparalleled. Downy windows, close;
And golden Phœbus never be beheld
Of eyes again so royal! Your crown's awry;
I'll mend it, and then play.
(*Antony and Cleopatra. Act 5. Scene 2. Charmian speaking.*)

There cannot be a pinch in death
More sharp than this is.
(*Cymbeline. Act 1. Scene 1. Imogen speaking.*)

I know not why
I love this youth; and I have heard you say
Love's reason's without reason. The bier at door
And a demand who is't shall die, I'ld say
'My father, not this youth.'
(*Cymbeline. Act 4. Scene 2. Arviragus speaking.*)

If you, born in these latter times,
When wit's more ripe, accept my rhymes,
And that to hear an old man sing
May to your wishes pleasure bring,
I life would wish, and that I might
Waste it for you like taper-light.
(*Pericles. Act 1. Gower speaking, as Chorus.*)

Antiochus, I thank thee, who hath taught
My frail mortality to know itself,
And by those fearful objects to prepare
This body, like to them, to what I must;
For death remembered should be like a mirror,
Who tells us life's but breath, to trust it error.
(*Pericles. Act 1. Scene 1. Pericles speaking.*)

Ten times thyself were happier than thou art,
If ten of thine ten times re-figured thee;
Then what could death do, if thou shouldst depart,
Leaving thee living in posterity?
Be not self-willed, for thou art much too fair
To be death's conquest and make worms thine heir.
(*Sonnet 6.*)

Thou art the grave where buried love doth live,
Hung with the trophies of my lovers gone;
Who all their parts of me to thee did give,
That due of many now is thine alone:
Their images I loved I view in thee,
And thou . . . all they . . . hast all the all of me.
(*Sonnet 31.*)

Ruin hath taught me thus to ruminate:
That Time will come and take my love away.
This thought is as a death, which cannot choose
But weep to have that which it fears to lose.
(*Sonnet 64.*)

But be contented: when that fell arrest
Without all bail shall carry me away,
My life hath in this line some interest
Which for memorial still with thee shall stay.
(*Sonnet* 74.)

You still shall live . . . such virtue hath my pen . . .
Where breath most breathes: even in the mouths of men.
(*Sonnet* 81.)

Section V

SAILORS AND SHIPS

BOATSWAIN Cheerly, good hearts! Out of our way, I say. (*Exit.*)
GONZALO   I have great comfort from this fellow: methinks he hath no
    drowning mark upon him; his complexion is perfect gallows. Stand
    fast, good Fate, to his hanging! Make the rope of his destiny our
    cable, for our own doth little advantage! If he be not born to be
    hanged, our case is miserable.
(*The Tempest. Act* 1. *Scene* 1.)

. . . where they prepared
A rotten carcass of a butt, not rigged,
Nor tackle, sail, nor mast.   The very rats
Instinctively have quit it.
(*The Tempest. Act* 1. *Scene* 2. *Prospero speaking.*)

Your mind is tossing on the ocean;
There, where your argosies with portly sail,
Like signiors and rich burghers on the flood,
Or as it were the pageants of the sea,
Do overpeer the petty traffickers
That curtsy to them, do them reverence,
As they fly by them with their woven wings.
(*The Merchant of Venice. Act* 1. *Scene* 1. *Salarino speaking.*)

I should not see the sandy hour-glass run
But I should think of shallows and of flats,
And see my wealthy Andrew docked in sand
Vailing her high-top lower than her ribs
To kiss her burial.   Should I go to church
And see the holy edifice of stone,

And not bethink me straight of dangerous rocks
Which touching but my gentle vessel's side
Would scatter all her spices on the stream,
Enrobe the roaring waters with my silks;
And, in a word, but even now worth this
And now worth nothing?
(*The Merchant of Venice. Act 1. Scene 1. Salarino speaking.*)

But ships are but boards, sailors but men: there be land-rats and water-rats,
land-thieves and water-thieves . . . I mean pirates . . . and then
there is the peril of waters, winds, and rocks.
(*The Merchant of Venice. Act 1. Scene 3. Shylock speaking.*)

How like a younker or a prodigal
The scarfèd bark puts from her native bay,
Hugged and embracèd by the strumpet wind!
How like the prodigal doth she return,
With over-weathered ribs and ragged sails,
Lean, rent, and beggared by the strumpet wind!
(*The Merchant of Venice. Act 2. Scene 6. Gratiano speaking.*)
Younker: a stripling.

Gremio, 'tis known my father hath no less
Than three great argosies; besides two galliasses,
And twelve tight galleys.
(*The Taming of the Shrew. Act 2. Scene 1. Tranio speaking.*)
Argosies: merchant ships.
Galliasses: large galleys.

MARIA Will you hoist sail, sir? Here lies your way.
VIOLA No, good swabber; I am to hull here a little longer.
(*Twelfth Night. Act 1. Scene 5.*)
Hull: to float.

Oh, the most piteous cry of the poor souls! Sometimes to see 'em, and
not to see 'em; now the ship boring the moon with her main-mast,
and anon swallowed with yest and froth, as you'd thrust a cork into
a hogs-head.
(*The Winter's Tale. Act 3. Scene 3. Clown speaking.*)

Suppose that you have seen
The well-appointed king at Hampton pier
Embark his royalty; and his brave fleet
With silken streamers the young Phœbus fanning:
Play with your fancies, and in them behold
Upon the hempen tackle ship-boys climbing;

Hear the shrill whistle which doth order give
To sounds confused; behold the threaden sails,
Borne with the invisible and creeping wind,
Draw the huge bottoms through the furrowed sea,
Breasting the lofty surge.   Oh, do but think
You stand upon the rivage and behold
A city on the inconstant billows dancing;
For so appears this fleet majestical,
Holding due course to Harfleur.
(*Henry the Fifth.   Act 3.   Chorus.*)

Some troops pursue the bloody-minded queen,
That led calm Henry, though he were a king;
As doth a sail, filled with a fretting gust,
Command an argosy to stem the waves.
(*Henry the Sixth.   Part Three.   Act 2.   Scene 6.   Edward, Earl of March,
    afterwards Edward the Fourth, speaking.*)

Oh, behold!
The riches of the ship is come on shore.
Ye men of Cyprus, let her have your knees.
Hail to thee, lady!   And the grace of heaven,
Before, behind thee, and on every hand,
Enwheel thee round!
(*Othello.   Act 2.   Scene 1.   Cassio, greeting Desdemona.*)

Oh, my soul's joy!
If after every tempest come such calms,
May the winds blow till they have wakened death!
And let the labouring bark climb hills of seas
Olympus-high, and duck again as low
As hell's from heaven!
(*Othello.   Act 2.   Scene 1.   Othello speaking.*)

I will tell you:
The barge she sat in, like a burnished throne,
Burned on the water.   The poop was beaten gold.
Purple the sails, and so perfumèd that
The winds were love-sick with them.   The oars were silver,
Which to the tune of flutes kept stroke, and made
The water which they beat to follow faster,
As amorous of their strokes.
(*Antony and Cleopatra.   Act 2.   Scene 2.   Enobarbus speaking.*)

She once being loofed,
The noble ruin of her magic, Antony,
Claps on his sea-wing; and, like a doting mallard,
Leaving the fight in height, flies after her.
I never saw an action of such shame.
(*Antony and Cleopatra. Act 3. Scene 10. Scarus speaking. Scene 8., The Oxford Shakespeare.*)
Loofed: brought close to the wind.

The swiftest harts have posted you by land,
And winds of all the corners kissed your sails
To make your vessel nimble.
(*Cymbeline. Act 2. Scene 4. Posthumus speaking.*)

Section VI

COMPLIMENTS, COURTESIES AND THEIR OPPOSITES

SILVIA   His worth is warrant for his welcome hither,
          If this be he you oft have wished to hear from.
VALENTINE   Mistress, it is. Sweet lady, entertain him
          To be my fellow-servant to your ladyship.
SILVIA   Too low a mistress for so high a servant.
(*The Two Gentlemen of Verona. Act 2. Scene 4.*)

Thou art the Mars of malcontents. I second thee; troop on.
(*The Merry Wives of Windsor. Act 1. Scene 3. Pistol speaking.*)

FORD   You are a gentleman of excellent breeding, admirable
          discourse, of great admittance, authentic in your place
          and person, generally allowed for your many war-like,
          court-like, and learned preparations.
FALSTAFF   Oh, sir!
(*The Merry Wives of Windsor. Act 2. Scene 2.*)

The hand that hath made you fair hath made you good. The goodness
that is cheap in beauty makes beauty brief in goodness; but grace,
being the soul of your complexion, shall keep the body of it ever fair.
(*Measure For Measure. Act 3. Scene 1. Vincentio, the Duke, speaking.*)

It is thyself, mine own self's better part;
Mine eye's clear eye, my dear heart's dearer heart;
My food, my fortune, and my sweet hope's aim;
My sole earth's heaven, and my heaven's claim.
(*The Comedy of Errors. Act 3. Scene 2. Antipholus of Syracuse speaking.*)

But manhood is melted into courtesies, valour into compliment; and men are only turned into tongue, and trim ones too.
(*Much Ado About Nothing. Act 4. Scene 1. Beatrice speaking.*)

THE KING (*reading*)   There did I see that low-spirited swain, that base
                         minnow of thy mirth . . .
COSTARD   Me.
THE KING   That unlettered, small-knowing soul . . .
COSTARD   Me.
THE KING   That shallow vessel . . .
COSTARD   Still me.
(*Love's Labour's Lost. Act 1. Scene 1.*)

Oh, happy fair!
Your eyes are lode-stars and your tongue's sweet air
More tuneable than lark to shepherd's ear,
When wheat is green, when hawthorn buds appear.
(*A Midsummer-Night's Dream. Act 1. Scene 1. Helena speaking.*)

You can play no part but Pyramus; for Pyramus is a sweet-faced man, a proper man as one shall see in a Summer's day.
(*A Midsummer-Night's Dream. Act 1. Scene 2. Quince speaking.*)

Captain of our fairy band,
Helena is here at hand;
And the youth, mistook by me,
Pleading for a lover's fee.
Shall we their fond pageant see?
Lord, what fools these mortals be!
(*A Midsummer-Night's Dream. Act 3. Scene 2. Puck speaking.*)

Gratiano speaks an infinite deal of nothing, more than any man in all Venice. His reasons are as two grains of wheat hid in two bushels of chaff: you shall seek all day ere you find them; and when you have them, they are not worth the search.
(*The Merchant of Venice. Act 1. Scene 1. Bassanio speaking.*)

God made him, and therefore let him pass for a man.
(*The Merchant of Venice. Act 1. Scene 2. Portia speaking.*)

NERISSA   How like you the young German, the Duke of Saxony's nephew?
PORTIA   Very vilely in the morning, when he is sober; and most vilely
            in the afternoon, when he is drunk. When he is best, he
            is a little worse than a man; and when he is worst, he is
            little better than a beast.
(*The Merchant of Venice. Act 1. Scene 2.*)

I am glad that this parcel of wooers are so reasonable, for there is not one among them but I dote on his very absence.
(*The Merchant of Venice.   Act* 1.   *Scene* 2.   *Portia speaking.*)

Sir, you are very welcome to our house.
It must appear in other ways than words,
Therefore I scant this breathing courtesy.
(*The Merchant of Venice.   Act* 5.   *Scene* 1.   *Portia speaking.*)

Hereafter, in a better world than this,
I shall desire more love and knowledge of you.
(*As You Like It.   Act* 1.   *Scene* 2.   *Le Beau speaking.*)

Oh, good old man!   How well in thee appears
The constant service of the antique world,
When service sweat for duty, not for meed!
Thou art not for the fashion of these times,
Where none will sweat but for promotion;
And having that do choke their service up
Even with the having.   It is not so with thee.
(*As You Like It.   Act* 2.   *Scene* 3.   *Orlando speaking.*)

HORTENSIO   And tell me now, sweet friend, what happy gale
Blows you to Padua here from old Verona?
PETRUCHIO   Such wind as scatters young men through the world
To seek their fortunes farther than at home,
Where small experience grows.
   The Taming of the Shrew.   Act 1.   *Scene* 2.)

FESTE   Beshrew me, the knight's in admirable fooling.
SIR ANDREW   Ay, he does well enough if he be disposed;   and so do I
too.   He does it with a better grace, but I do it more
natural.
(*Twelfth Night.   Act* 2.   *Scene* 3.)

When you do dance, I wish you
A wave o' the sea, that you might ever do
Nothing but that.
(*The Winter's Tale.   Act* 4.   *Scene* 3. . . . *Temple Shakespeare: Act* 4.
Scene 4.   *Florizel speaking.*)

I count myself in nothing else so happy
As in a soul remembering my good friends.
(*Richard the Second.   Act* 2.   *Scene* 3.   *Bolingbroke speaking.*)

Oh, thou hast damnable iteration and art, indeed, able to corrupt a saint. Thou hast done much harm upon me, Hal. God forgive thee for it! Before I knew thee, Hal, I knew nothing; and now am I, if a man should speak truly, little better than one of the wicked.
(*Henry the Fourth. Part One. Act* 1. *Scene* 2. *Falstaff speaking.*)

Why, what a candy deal of courtesy
This fawning greyhound then did proffer me!
Look 'when his infant fortune came to age,'
And 'gentle Harry Percy,' and 'kind cousin.'
Oh, the devil take such cozeners!
(*Henry the Fourth. Part One. Act* 1. *Scene* 3. *Hotspur speaking.*)

There is a devil haunts thee in the likeness of a fat old man; a tun of man is thy companion. Why dost thou converse with that trunk of humours, that bolting-hutch of beastliness, that swollen parcel of dropsies, that huge bombard of sack . . . that reverend vice, that grey iniquity, that father ruffian, that vanity in years?
(*Henry the Fourth. Part One. Act* 2. *Scene* 4. *Prince Henry, referring to Falstaff.*)

Come, brother John; full bravely hast thou fleshed
Thy maiden sword.
(*Henry the Fourth. Part One. Act* 5. *Scene* 4. *Prince Henry speaking.*)

Let him be damned like the glutton! May his tongue be hotter! A whoreson Achitophel! A rascally 'yea-forsooth' knave, to bear a gentleman in hand and then stand upon security!
(*Henry the Fourth. Part Two. Act* 1. *Scene* 2. *Falstaff speaking.*)

Blunt not his love,
Nor lose the good advantage of his grace
By seeming cold or careless of his will;
For he is gracious if he be observed.
He hath a tear for pity and a hand
Open as day for melting charity.
(*Henry the Fourth. Part Two. Act* 4. *Scene* 4. *The King speaking.*)

GLOUCESTER   Sweet saint, for charity, be not so curst.
ANNE   Foul devil, for God's sake hence and trouble us not;
                     For thou hast made the happy earth thy hell,
                     Filled it with cursing cries and deep exclaims.
(*Richard the Third. Act* 1. *Scene* 2.)

The fairest hand I ever touched! Oh, beauty,
Till now I never knew thee!
(*Henry the Eighth. Act* 1. *Scene* 4. *The King, speaking to Anne Bullen.*)

A good digestion to you all; and once more
I shower a welcome on ye.   Welcome all!
(*Henry the Eighth.   Act 1.   Scene 4.   Wolsey speaking.*)

Ladies, a general welcome from his Grace
Salutes ye all.   This night he dedicates
To fair content and you.   None here, he hopes,
In all this noble bevy, has brought with her
One care abroad; he would have all as merry
As, first, good company, good wine, good welcome,
Can make good people.
(*Henry the Eighth.   Act 1.   Scene 4.   Guildford speaking.*)

You're welcome, my fair guests.   That noble lady
Or gentleman that is not freely merry
Is not my friend.   This, to confirm my welcome;
And to you all, good health.   (*Drinks.*)
(*Henry the Eighth.   Act 1.   Scene 4.   Wolsey speaking.*)

By heaven, she is a dainty one.   Sweetheart,
I were unmannerly to take you out
And not to kiss you.
(*Henry the Eighth.   Act 1.   Scene 4.   The King, speaking to Anne Bullen.*)

You bear a gentle mind, and heavenly blessings
Follow such creatures.
(*Henry the Eighth.   Act 2.   Scene 3.   Lord Chamberlain speaking.*

The elephant hath joints, but none for courtesy: his legs are legs for
   necessity, not for flexure.
(*Troilus and Cressida.   Act 2.   Scene 3.   Ulysses speaking.*)

This was the noblest Roman of them all.
All the conspirators, save only he,
Did that they did in envy of great Cæsar;
He only, in a general honest thought
And common good to all, made one of them.
His life was gentle, and the elements
So mixed in him that Nature might stand up
And say to all the world 'This was a man!'
(*Julius Cæsar.   Act 5.   Scene 5.   Antony speaking.*)

                    Nothing in his life
Became him like the leaving it: he died
As one that had been studied in his death
To throw away the dearest thing he owned
As 'twere a careless trifle.
(*Macbeth.   Act 1.   Scene 4.   Malcolm speaking.*)

The devil damn thee black, thou cream-faced loon!
Where got'st thou that goose look?
(*Macbeth. Act 5. Scene 3. Macbeth speaking.*)

Oh, there be players that I have seen play and heard others praise, and that
   highly, not to speak it profanely, that neither having the accent of
   Christians, nor the gait of Christian, pagan, nor man, have so strutted
   and bellowed that I have thought some of nature's journeymen had
   made men, and not made them well, they imitated humanity so
   abominably.
(*Hamlet. Act 3. Scene 2. Hamlet speaking.*)

A plague upon you, murderers, traitors all!
I might have saved her; now she's gone for ever.
Cordelia, Cordelia! Stay a little. Ha!
What is't thou say'st? Her voice was ever soft,
Gentle and low; an excellent thing in woman.
I killed the slave that was a-hanging thee.
(*King Lear. Act 5. Scene 3. Lear speaking.*)

How courtesy would seem to cover sin,
When what is done is like a hypocrite!
The which is good in nothing but in sight.
(*Pericles. Act I. Scene I. Pericles speaking.*)

SECTION VII

CLIMATE AND THE ELEMENTS

BOATSWAIN Do you not hear him? You mar our labour. Keep your
                cabins; you do assist the storm.
GONZALO   Nay, good, be patient.
BOATSWAIN When the sea is. Hence! What care these roarers for the
                name of king? To cabin. Silence! Trouble us not.
(*The Tempest. Act I. Scene I.*)

If by your art, my dearest father, you have
Put the wild waters in this roar, allay them.
The sky, it seems, would pour down stinking pitch,
But that the sea, mounting to the welkin's cheek,
Dashes the fire out.
(*The Tempest. Act I. Scene 2. Miranda speaking.*)

There they hoist us,
To cry to the sea that roared to us; to sigh
To the winds, whose pity, sighing back again,
Did us but loving wrong.
(*The Tempest. Act* 1. *Scene* 2. *Prospero speaking.*)

PROSPERO   Hast thou, spirit,
            Performed to point the tempest that I bade thee?
ARIEL   To every article.
            I boarded the king's ship; now on the beak,
            Now in the waist, the deck, in every cabin,
            I flamed amazement.   Sometime I'ld divide
            And burn in many places; on the topmast,
            The yards and bowsprit, would I flame distinctly,
            Then meet and join.   Jove's lightnings, the precursors
            O' the dreadful thunder-claps, more momentary
            And sight-outrunning were not: the fire and cracks
            Of sulphurous roaring the most mighty Neptune
            Seem to besiege, and make his bold waves tremble;
            Yea, his dread trident shake.
(*The Tempest. Act* 1. *Scene* 2.)
The beak: the bow of the ship.

PROSPERO   Dost thou forget
            From what a torment I did free thee?
ARIEL   No.
PROSPERO Thou dost, and think'st it much to tread the ooze
            Of the salt deep,
            To run upon the sharp wind of the North,
            To do me business in the veins o' the earth
            When it is baked with frost.
(*The Tempest. Act* 1. *Scene* 2.)

            Oh, it is monstrous, monstrous!
Methought the billows spoke and told me of it;
The winds did sing it to me; and the thunder,
That deep and dreadful organ-pipe, pronounced
The name of Prosper.
(*The Tempest. Act* 3. *Scene* 3. *Alonso speaking.*)

. . . I have bedimmed
The noontide sun, called forth the mutinous winds,
And 'twixt the green sea and the azured vault
Set roaring water.
(*The Tempest. Act* 5. *Scene* 1. *Prospero speaking.*)

Thus have I shunned the fire for fear of burning,
And drenched me in the sea; where I am drowned.
(*The Two Gentlemen of Verona. Act* 1. *Scene* 3. *Proteus speaking.*)

What tempest, I trow, threw this whale, with so many tuns of oil in his
    belly, ashore at Windsor?
(*The Merry Wives of Windsor. Act* 2. *Scene* 1. *Mistress Ford, referring to
    Falstaff.*)

. . . the moon, like to a silver bow,
New-bent in heaven.
(*A Midsummer-Night's Dream. Act* 1. *Scene* 1. *Hippolyta speaking.*)

Brief as the lightning in the collied night
That, in a spleen, unfolds both heaven and earth,
And ere a man hath power to say, 'Behold!'
The jaws of darkness do devour it up:
So quick bright things come to confusion.
(*A Midsummer-Night's Dream. Act* 1. *Scene* 1. *Lysander speaking.*)
Collied: sooty, black.

The moon, methinks, looks with a watery eye.
(*A Midsummer-Night's Dream. Act* 3. *Scene* 1. *Titania speaking.*)

There may as well be amity and life
'Tween snow and fire, as treason and my love.
(*The Merchant of Venice. Act* 3. *Scene* 2. *Bassanio speaking.*)

I pray you, think you question with the Jew:
You may as well go stand upon the beach
And bid the main flood bate his usual height;
You may as well use question with the wolf
Why he hath made the ewe bleat for the lamb;
You may as well forbid the mountain pines
To wag their high tops and to make no noise
When they are fretted with the gusts of heaven.
(*The Merchant of Venice. Act* 4. *Scene* 1. *Antonio speaking.*)

You foolish shepherd, wherefore do you follow her,
Like foggy South, puffing with wind and rain?
(*As You Like It. Act* 3. *Scene* 5. *Rosalind speaking.*)

. . . though she chide as loud
As thunder when the clouds in Autumn crack.
(*The Taming of the Shrew. Act* 1. *Scene* 2. *Petruchio speaking.*)

Think you a little din can daunt mine ears?
Have I not in my time heard lions roar?
Have I not heard the sea, puffèd up with winds,
Rage like an angry boar chafèd with sweat?
Have I not heard great ordnance in the field,
And heaven's artillery thunder in the skies?

. . . .

And do you tell me of a woman's tongue,
That gives not half so great a blow to hear
As will a chestnut in a farmer's fire?
Tush! Tush! Fear boys with bugs.
(*The Taming of the Shrew. Act 1. Scene 2. Petruchio speaking.*)
Bugs: bogeys.

And where two raging fires meet together,
They do consume the thing that feeds their fury:
Though little fire grows great with little wind,
Yet extreme gusts will blow out fire and all.
(*The Taming of the Shrew. Act 2. Scene 1. Petruchio speaking.*)

SIR TOBY   Does not our life consist of the four elements?
SIR ANDREW   Faith, so they say; but *I* think it rather consists of eating
             and drinking.
(*Twelfth Night. Act 2. Scene 3.*)

Foolery, sir, does walk about the orb like the sun. It shines everywhere.
(*Twelfth Night. Act 3. Scene 1. Feste speaking.*)

Oh, that my tongue were in the thunder's mouth!
Then with a passion would I shake the world.
(*King John. Act 3. Scene 4. Constance speaking.*)

His rash fierce blaze of riot cannot last,
For violent fires soon burn out themselves;
Small showers last long, but sudden storms are short.
(*Richard the Second. Act 2. Scene 1. Gaunt speaking.*)

Methinks King Richard and myself should meet
With no less terror than the elements
Of fire and water, when their thundering shock
At meeting tears the cloudy cheeks of heaven.
Be he the fire, I'll be the yielding water:
The rage be his, while on the earth I rain
My waters; on the earth, and not on him.
(*Richard the Second. Act 3. Scene 3. Bolingbroke speaking.*)

I know you all, and will awhile uphold
The unyoked humour of your idleness.
Yet herein will I imitate the sun,
Who doth permit the base contagious clouds
To smother up his beauty from the world,
That when he please again to be himself,
Being wanted, he may be more wondered at
By breaking through the foul and ugly mists
Of vapours that did seem to strangle him.
(*Henry the Fourth. Part One. Act 1. Scene 2. Prince Henry speaking.*)

GLENDOWER I say the earth did shake when I was born.

HOTSPUR   And *I* say the earth was not of *my* mind,
            If you suppose as fearing you it shook.

GLENDOWER The heavens were all on fire, the earth did tremble.

HOTSPUR   Oh, then the earth shook to see the heavens on fire
            And not in fear of your nativity.
(*Henry the Fourth. Part One. Act 3. Scene 1.*)

Open your ears, for which of you will stop
The vent of hearing when loud Rumour speaks?
I, from the Orient to the drooping West,
Making the wind my post-horse, still unfold
The acts commencèd on this ball of earth.
(*Henry the Fourth. Part Two. Induction. Rumour speaking.*)

Dieu de battailes! Where have they this mettle?
Is not their climate foggy, raw and dull;
On whom, as in despite, the sun looks pale,
Killing their fruit with frowns?
(*Henry the Fifth. Act 3. Scene 5. The Constable of France speaking.*)

When heaven doth weep, doth not the earth o'erflow?
If the winds rage, doth not the sea wax mad,
Threat'ning the welkin with his big-swoln face?
(*Titus Andronicus. Act 3. Scene 1. Titus speaking.*)
Welkin: the firmament.

ROMEO   Peace, peace, Mercutio, peace!
            Thou talk'st of nothing.

MERCUTIO   True, I talk of dreams,
            Which are the children of an idle brain,
            Begot of nothing but vain fantasy;

Which is as thin of substance as the air
And more inconstant than the wind, who woos
Even now the frozen bosom of the North
And, being angered, puffs away from thence,
Turning his face to the dew-dropping South.
(*Romeo and Juliet. Act* 1. *Scene* 4.)

Although I joy in thee,
I have no joy of this contract to-night:
It is too rash, too unadvised, too sudden,
Too like the lightning, which doth cease to be
Ere one can say 'It lightens.'
(*Romeo and Juliet. Act* 2. *Scene* 2. *Juliet speaking.*)

My bounty is as boundless as the sea,
My love as deep; the more I give to thee
The more I have, for both are infinite.
(*Romeo and Juliet. Act* 2. *Scene* 2. *Juliet speaking.*)

The fault, dear Brutus, is not in our stars
But in ourselves, that we are underlings.
(*Julius Cæsar. Act* 1. *Scene* 2. *Cassius speaking.*)

Are not you moved, when all the sway of earth
Shakes like a thing unfirm?   Oh, Cicero,
I have seen tempests, when the scolding winds
Have rived the knotty oaks, and I have seen
The ambitious ocean swell and rage and foam,
To be exalted with the threatening clouds.
(*Julius Cæsar. Act* 1. *Scene* 3. *Casca speaking.*)

CASCA   Who ever knew the heavens menace so?
CASSIUS   Those that have known the earth so full of faults.
          For my part, I have walked about the streets,
          Submitting me unto the perilous night;
          And thus unbraced, Casca, as you see,
          Have bared my bosom to the thunder-stone;
          And when the cross blue lightning seemed to open
          The breast of heaven, I did present myself
          Even in the aim and very flash of it.
(*Julius Cæsar. Act* 1. *Scene* 3.)

Those that with haste will make a mighty fire
Begin it with weak straws.
(*Julius Cæsar. Act* 1. *Scene* 3. *Cassius speaking.*)

When beggars die, there are no comets seen;
The heavens themselves blaze forth the death of princes.
(*Julius Cæsar. Act 2. Scene 2. Calpurnia speaking.*)

But I am constant as the northern star,
Of whose true-fixed and resting quality
There is no fellow in the firmament.
The skies are painted with unnumbered sparks;
They are all fire and every one doth shine;
But there's but one in all doth hold his place:
So, in the world.
(*Julius Cæsar. Act 3. Scene 1. Cæsar speaking.*)

MACBETH   Say from whence
              You owe this strange intelligence? Or why
              Upon this blasted heath you stop our way
              With such prophetic greeting? Speak, I charge you.
                  (*The Witches vanish.*)
BANQUO   The earth hath bubbles as the water has,
              And these are of them. Whither are they vanished?
MACBETH   Into the air; and what seemed corporal melted
              As breath into the wind. Would they had stayed!
(*Macbeth. Act 1. Scene 3.*)
Owe: own.

                  Thou losest labour:
As easy may'st thou the intrenchant air
With thy keen sword impress, as make me bleed.
(*Macbeth. Act 5.   Scene 8. Macbeth speaking.   Scene 7. The Oxford
     Shakespeare.*)

MARCELLUS   Shall I strike at it with my partisan?
HORATIO   Do, if it will not stand.
BERNADO   'Tis here!
HORATIO   'Tis here! (*Exit Ghost.*)
MARCELLUS   'Tis gone
              We do it wrong, being so majestical,
              To offer it the show of violence;
              For it is, as the air, invulnerable,
              And our vain blows malicious mockery.
(*Hamlet. Act 1. Scene 1.*)

I have of late, but wherefore I know not, lost all my mirth, forgone all
     custom of exercises; and indeed it goes so heavily with my disposition
     that this goodly frame, the earth, seems to me a sterile promontory;
     this most excellent canopy, the air, look you, this brave o'er-hanging
     firmament, this majestical roof fretted with golden fire, why, it appears
     no other thing to me than a foul and pestilent congregation of vapours.
(*Hamlet. Act 2. Scene 2. Hamlet speaking.*)

But as we often see, against some storm,
A silence in the heavens, the rack stand still,
The bold winds speechless and the orb below
As hush as death, anon the dreadful thunder
Doth rend the region. . . .
(*Hamlet. Act 2. Scene 2. First Player speaking.*)
Rack: clouds in motion.

KENT   I know you. Where's the king?
GENTLEMAN   Contending with the fretful elements:
            Bids the wind blow the earth into the sea,
            Or swell the curled waters 'bove the main,
            That things might change or cease; tears his white hair,
            Which the impetuous blasts, with eyeless rage,
            Catch in their fury and make nothing of;
            Strives in his little world of man to out-scorn
            The to-and-fro-conflicting wind and rain.
(*King Lear. Act 3. Scene 1.*)

Blow winds, and crack your cheeks! Rage! Blow!
You cataracts and hurricanoes, spout
Till you have drenched our steeples, drowned the cocks!
You sulphurous and thought-executing fires,
Vaunt-couriers to oak-cleaving thunderbolts,
Singe my white head! And thou, all-shaking thunder,
Smite flat the thick rotundity o' the world!
Crack nature's moulds; all germins spill at once
That make ingrateful man!
(*King Lear. Act 3. Scene 2. Lear speaking.*)
Vaunt-couriers: forerunners.
Germins: evil germs.

                Spit fire! Spout rain!
Nor rain, wind, thunder, fire, are my daughters.
I tax not you, you elements, with unkindness:
I never gave you kingdom, called you children,
You owe me no subscription.
(*King Lear. Act 3. Scene 2. Lear speaking.*)

                Oh, my soul's joy!
If after every tempest come such calms,
May the winds blow till they have wakened death!
And let the labouring bark climb hills of seas
Olympus-high, and duck again as low
As hell's from heaven!
(*Othello. Act 2. Scene 1. Othello speaking.*)

The city cast
Her people out upon her, and Antony,
Enthroned i' the market-place, did sit alone,
Whistling to the air; which, but for vacancy,
Had gone to gaze on Cleopatra too
And make a gap in nature.
(*Antony and Cleopatra. Act 2. Scene 2. Enobarbus speaking.*)

Farewell, my dearest sister, fare thee well.
The elements be kind to thee, and make
Thy spirits all of comfort! Fare thee well.
(*Antony and Cleopatra. Act 3. Scene 2. Octavius Cæsar speaking.*)

Now he'll outstare the lightning. To be furious
Is to be frighted out of fear, and in that mood
The dove will peck the estridge; and I see still,
A diminution in our captain's brain
Restores his heart. When valour preys on reason
It eats the sword it fights with.
(*Antony and Cleopatra. Act 3. Scene 13. Enobarbus speaking. Scene 11:*
The Oxford Shakespeare.)

Husband, I come.
Now to that name my courage prove my title!
I am fire and air; my other elements
I give to baser life.
(*Antony and Cleopatra. Act 5. Scene 2. Cleopatra speaking.*)

The king, he takes the babe
To his protection; calls him Posthumus Leonatus;
Breeds him and makes him of his bedchamber;
Puts to him all the learnings that his time
Could make him the receiver of; which he took
As we do air, fast as 'twas ministered,
And in's Spring became a harvest.
(*Cymbeline. Act 1. Scene 1. First Gentleman speaking.*)

His majesty bids you welcome. Make pastime with us a day or two, or
    longer; if you seek us afterwards in other terms, you shall find us in
    our salt-water girdle. If you beat us out of it, it is yours. If you fall
    in the adventure, our crows shall fare the better for you; and there's
    an end.
(*Cymbeline. Act 3. Scene 1. Cloten speaking.*)

Fear no more the heat o' the sun,
Nor the furious Winter's rages;
Thou thy worldly task hast done,
Home art gone and ta'en thy wages.
Golden lads and girls all must,
As chimney-sweepers, come to dust.
(*Cymbeline. Act 4. Scene 2. Guiderius speaking.*)

                    I am ashamed
To look upon the holy sun, to have
The benefit of his blessed beams, remaining
So long a poor unknown.
(*Cymbeline. Act 4. Scene 4. Arviragus speaking.*)

Yet cease your ire, you angry stars of heaven!
Wind, rain, and thunder, remember earthly man
Is but a substance that must yield to you;
And I, as fits my nature, do obey you.
(*Pericles. Act 2. Scene 1. Pericles speaking.*)

Why didst thou promise such a beauteous day
And make me travel forth without my cloak,
To let base clouds o'ertake me in my way,
Hiding thy bravery in their rotten smoke?
'Tis not enough that through the cloud thou break,
To dry the rain on my storm-beaten face,
For no man well of such a salve can speak
That heals the wound and cures not the disgrace.
(*Sonnet 34.*)

But, ah! Thought kills me that I am not thought,
To leap large lengths of miles when thou art gone,
But that, so much of earth and water wrought,
I must attend time's leisure with my moan;
Receiving nought by elements so slow
But heavy tears, badges of either's woe.
(*Sonnet 44.*)

The other two, slight air and purging fire,
Are both with thee, wherever I abide;
The first my thought, the other my desire,
These present-absent with swift motion slide.
(*Sonnet 45.*)

SECTION VIII

THE ANIMAL KINGDOM

I prithee, let me bring thee where crabs grow;
And I with my long nails will dig thee pig-nuts,
Show thee a jay's nest and instruct thee how
To snare the nimble marmozet.   I'll bring thee
To clustering filberts, and sometimes I'll get thee
Young scamels from the rock.   Wilt thou go with me?
(*The Tempest. Act 2. Scene 2. Caliban speaking.*)
Scamel: a sort of bird; possibly a sea-mew.

STEPHANO	Here; swear, then, how thou escapedst.
TRINCULO	Swam ashore, man, like a duck: I can swim like a duck, I'll be sworn.
STEPHANO	Here, kiss the book. Though thou canst swim like ɐ duck, thou art made like a goose.

(*The Tempest. Act 2. Scene 2.*)

Pray you, tread softly, that the blind mole may not
Hear a footfall.
(*The Tempest. Act 4. Scene 1. Caliban speaking.*)

I think Crab, my dog, be the sourest-natured dog that lives: my mother
    weeping, my father wailing, my sister crying, our maid howling,
    our cat wringing her hands, and all our house in a great perplexity;
    yet did not this cruel-hearted cur shed one tear! He is a stone, a very
    pebble stone, and has no more pity in him than a dog.
(*The Two Gentlemen of Verona. Act 2. Scene 3. Launce speaking.*)

SLENDER	Why do your dogs bark so? Be there bears i' the town?
ANNE PAGE	I think there are, sir; I heard them talked of.
SLENDER	I love the sport well; but I shall as soon quarrel at it as any man in England. You are afraid if you see the bear loose, are you not?
ANNE PAGE	Ay, indeed, sir.
SLENDER	That's meat and drink to me, now: I have seen Sackerson loose twenty times, and have taken him by the chain; but I warrant you, the women have so cried and shrieked at it that it passed. But women, indeed, cannot abide 'em; they are very ill-favoured, rough things.

(*The Merry Wives of Windsor. Act 1. Scene 1.*)
Sackerson: Bear-baiting was a favourite sport in Tudor times. 'Sackerson'
    was the name of a famous bear at Paris Garden, a pleasure-resort on
    the Bankside.

For look where Beatrice, like a lapwing, runs
Close by the ground, to hear our conference.
(*Much Ado About Nothing. Act 3. Scene 1. Hero speaking.*)

The pleasant'st angling is to see the fish
Cut with her golden oars the silver stream,
And greedily devour the treacherous bait:
So angle we for Beatrice.
(*Much Ado About Nothing. Act 3. Scene 1. Ursula speaking.*)

The time, when? About the sixth hour; when beasts most graze, birds
best peck, and men sit down to that nourishment which is called
supper. So much for the time when.
(*Love's Labour's Lost. Act 1. Scene 1. The King, reading aloud a letter
from Don Armado.*)

This side is Hiems, Winter; this Ver, the Spring. The one maintained by
the owl, the other by the cuckoo. Ver, begin.
(*Love's Labour's Lost. Act 5. Scene 2. Don Armado speaking.*)

When shepherds pipe on oaten straws
And merry larks are ploughmen's clocks;
When turtles tread, and rooks, and daws,
And maidens bleach their Summer smocks;
The cuckoo then, on every tree,
Mocks married men, for thus sings he: 'Cuckoo!
Cuckoo! Cuckoo!' Oh, word of fear;
Unpleasing to a married ear!
(*Love's Labour's Lost. Act 5. Scene 2. 'Spring' singing.*)

When all aloud the wind doth blow
And coughing drowns the parson's saw;
And birds sit brooding in the snow
And Marian's nose looks red and raw;
When roasted crabs hiss in the bowl,
Then nightly sings the staring owl: 'Tu-who!
Tu-whit! Tu-who!' A merry note!
While greasy Joan doth keel the pot.
(*Love's Labour's Lost. Act 5. Scene 2. 'Winter' singing.*)
The parson's saw: the parson's words.
Keel: to cool; or perhaps to skim.

SNUG   Have you the lion's part written? Pray you, if it be, give it
me, for I am slow of study.
QUINCE   You may do it extempore, for it is nothing but roaring.
(*A Midsummer-Night's Dream. Act 1. Scene 2.*)

I grant you, friends, if that you should fright the ladies out of their wits
　　they would have no more discretion but to hang us. But I will
　　aggravate my voice so that I will roar you as gently as any sucking
　　dove; I will roar you as 'twere any nightingale.
(*A Midsummer-Night's Dream. Act* 1. *Scene* 2. *Bottom speaking.*)

Come, now a roundel and a fairy song.
Then, for the third of a minute, hence;
Some to kill cankers in the musk-rose buds,
Some war with rere-mice for their leathern wings
To make my small elves coats, and some keep back
The clamorous owl that nightly hoots and wonders
At our quaint spirits.
(*A Midsummer-Night's Dream. Act* 2. *Scene* 2. *Titania speaking.*)

You spotted snakes with double tongue,
Thorny hedge-hogs, be not seen;
Newts and blind-worms, do no wrong.
Come not near our fairy queen. . . .
Weaving spiders, come not here;
Hence, you long-legged spinners, hence!
Beetles black, approach not near;
Worm nor snail, do no offence.
(*A Midsummer-Night's Dream. Act* 2. *Scene* 2. *Song.*)
Rere-mice: bats.

What thou seest when thou dost wake,
Do it for thy true love take;
Love and languish for his sake.
Be it ounce, or cat, or bear,
Pard, or boar with bristled hair
In thy eye that shall appear,
When thou wak'st, it is thy dear.
Wake when some vile thing is near!
(*A Midsummer-Night's Dream. Act* 2. *Scene* 2. *Oberon speaking.*)
Ounce: the snow-leopard; but possibly used by Shakespeare to denote
　　the lynx.
Pard: leopard.

Content with Hermia! No. I do repent
The tedious minutes I with her have spent.
Not Hermia, but Helena I love:
Who will not change a raven for a dove?
(*A Midsummer-Night's Dream. Act* 2. *Scene* 2. *Lysander speaking.*)

Masters, you ought to consider with yourselves: to bring in . . . God shield us! . . . a lion among ladies, is a most dreadful thing; for there is not a more fearful wild-fowl than your lion living, and we ought to look to it.

(*A Midsummer-Night's Dream. Act 3. Scene 1. Bottom speaking.*)

I see their knavery: this is to make an ass of me; to fright me, if they could. But I will not stir from this place, do what they can. I will walk up and down here and I will sing, that they shall hear I am not afraid.

> The ousel-cock, so black of hue,
>   With orange-tawny bill,
> The throstle with his note so true,
>   The wren with little quill.

(*A Midsummer-Night's Dream. Act 3. Scene 1. Bottom speaking . . . and singing.*)

Ousel-cock: blackbird.

Throstle: thrush.

> When they him spy,
> As wild geese that the creeping fowler eye,
> Or russet-pated choughs, many in sort,
> Rising and cawing at the gun's report,
> Sever themselves and madly sweep the sky;
> So, at his sight, away his fellows fly. . . .

(*A Midsummer-Night's Dream. Act 3. Scene 2. Puck speaking.*)

Chough: a bird of the crow family, found by the sea.

> My hounds are bred out of the Spartan kind,
> So flewed, so sanded; and their heads are hung
> With ears that sweep away the morning dew;
> Crook-kneed and dew-lapped like Thessalian bulls;
> Slow in pursuit, but matched in mouth like bells
> Each under each.

(*A Midsummer-Night's Dream. Act 4. Scene 1. Theseus speaking.*)

Flewed: deep-mouthed.

Sanded: of a sandy colour.

NERISSA First, there is the Neapolitan prince.

PORTIA Ay, that's a colt indeed, for he doth nothing but talk of his horse; and he makes it a great appropriation to his own good parts that he can shoe him himself.

(*The Merchant of Venice. Act 1. Scene 2.*)

Well, then, it now appears you need my help.
Go to, then; you come to me and you say
'Shylock, we would have moneys.' You say so!
You that did void your rheum upon my beard
And foot me as you spurn a stranger cur
Over your threshold! Moneys is your suit.
What should I say to you? Should I not say
'Hath a dog money? Is it possible
A cur can lend three thousand ducats?'
(*The Merchant of Venice. Act 1. Scene 3. Shylock speaking.*)

OLD GOBBO   What a beard hast thou got! Thou hast got more hair
             on thy chin than Dobbin, my thill-horse, has on his tail.
LAUNCELOT   It should seem then that Dobbin's tail grows backward:
             I am sure he had more hair on his tail than I have on
             my face when I last saw him.
(*The Merchant of Venice. Act 2. Scene 2.*)
Thill-horse: a shaft-horse.

SHYLOCK   What says that fool of Hagar's offspring, ha?
JESSICA   His words were 'Farewell, mistress.' Nothing else.
SHYLOCK   The patch is kind enough, but a huge feeder;
           Snail-slow in profit, and he sleeps by day
           More than the wild cat. Drones hive not with me;
           Therefore I part with him, and part with him
           To one that I would have him help to waste
           His borrowed purse.
(*The Merchant of Venice. Act 2. Scene 5.*)

As there is no firm reason to be rendered
Why he cannot abide a gaping pig;
Why he, a harmless necessary cat;
Why he, a wauling bagpipe, but of force
Must yield to such inevitable shame
As to offend, himself being offended;
So can I give no reason, nor I will not,
More than a lodged hate and a certain loathing
I bear Antonio, that I follow thus
A losing suit against him. Are you answered?
(*The Merchant of Venice. Act 4. Scene 1. Shylock speaking.*)

BASSANIO Every offence is not a hate at first.
SHYLOCK   What! Wouldst thou have a serpent sting thee twice?
(*The Merchant of Venice. Act 4. Scene 1.*)

I am a tainted wether of the flock,
Meetest for death. The weakest kind of fruit
Drops earliest to the ground; and so let me.
You cannot better be employed, Bassanio,
Than to live still and write mine epitaph.
(*The Merchant of Venice. Act 4. Scene 1. Antonio speaking.*)

The crow doth sing as sweetly as the lark
When neither is attended; and I think
The nightingale, if she should sing by day
When every goose is cackling, would be thought
No better a musician than the wren.
How many things by season seasoned are
To their right praise and true perfection!
(*The Merchant of Venice. Act 5. Scene 1. Portia speaking.*)

BANISHED DUKE   But what said Jaques?
                Did he not moralise this spectacle?
FIRST LORD   Oh, yes; into a thousand similes.
                First, for his weeping into the needless stream:
                'Poor deer,' quoth he, 'thou mak'st a testament
                As worldlings do, giving thy sum of more
                To that which had too much.' Then, being there alone,
                Left and abandoned by his velvet friends:
                ' 'Tis right,' quoth he; 'thus misery doth part
                The flux of company.' Anon a careless herd,
                Full of the pasture, jumps along by him
                And never stays to greet him. 'Ay,' quoth Jaques,
                'Sweep on, you fat and greasy citizens;
                'Tis just the fashion. Wherefore do you look
                Upon that poor and broken bankrupt there?'
                Thus most invectively he pierceth through
                The body of the country, city, court,
                Yea, and of this our life, swearing that we
                Are mere usurpers, tyrants and what's worse,
                To fright the animals and to kill them up
                In their assigned and native dwelling place.
(*As You Like It. Act 2. Scene 1.*)

                I have five hundred crowns,
The thrifty hire I saved under your father,
Which I did store to be my foster-nurse
When service should in my old limbs lie lame
And unregarded age in corners thrown.
Take that; and He that doth the ravens feed
Yea, providently caters for the sparrow,
Be comfort to my age!
(*As You Like It. Act 2. Scene 3. Adam speaking.*)

About his neck
A green and gilded snake had wreathed itself,
Who, with her head nimble in threats, approached
The opening of his mouth; but suddenly,
Seeing Orlando, it unlinked itself
And with indented glides did slip away
Into a bush.   Under which bush's shade
A lioness, with udders all drawn dry,
Lay couching, head on ground, with catlike watch,
When that the sleeping man should stir; for 'tis
The royal disposition of that beast
To prey on nothing that doth seem as dead. .
(*As You Like It.   Act* 4.   *Scene* 3.   *Oliver speaking.*)

The ambition in my love thus plagues itself:
The hind that would be mated by the lion
Must die for love.
(*All's Well That Ends Well.   Act* 1.   *Scene* 1.   *Helena speaking.*)

SIR TOBY	He shall think, by the letters that thou wilt drop, that they come from my niece and that she's in love with him.
MARIA	My purpose is, indeed, a horse of that colour.
SIR ANDREW	And your horse now would make him an ass.
MARIA	Ass, I doubt not.

(*Twelfth Night.   Act* 2.   *Scene* 3.)

MARIA	How do you, Malvolio?
MALVOLIO	At your request ! Yes; nightingales answer daws.

(*Twelfth Night.   Act* 3.   *Scene* 4.)

The lark that tirra-lirra chants,
With heigh, with heigh, the thrush and the jay,
Are Summer songs for me and my aunts
While we lie tumbling in the hay.
(*The Winter's Tale.   Act* 4.   *Scene* 2. . . . *Temple Shakespeare: Act* 4.
   Scene 3.   *Autolycus singing.*)

Here's a stay,
That shakes the rotten carcase of old Death
Out of his rags !   Here's a large mouth, indeed,
That spits forth death and mountains, rocks and seas,
Talks as familiarly of roaring lions
As maids of thirteen do of puppy-dogs !
(*King John.   Act* 2.   *Scene* 1.   *The Bastard speaking.*)

Thou cold-blooded slave,
Hast thou not spoke like thunder on my side?
Been sworn my soldier, bidding me depend
Upon thy stars, thy fortunes and thy strength?
And dost thou now fall over to my foes?
Thou wear a lion's hide! Doff it for shame
And hang a calf's skin on those recreant limbs.

(*King John. Act 3. Scene 1. Constance speaking.*)

GROOM   Oh, how it yearned my heart when I beheld,
In London streets that coronation day
When Bolingbroke rode on roan Barbary,
That horse that thou so often hast bestrid!
That horse that I so carefully have dressed!

RICHARD   Rode he on Barbary? Tell me, gentle friend,
How went he under him?

GROOM   So proudly as if he disdained the ground.

RICHARD   So proud that Bolingbroke was on his back!
That jade hath ate bread from my royal hand;
This hand hath made him proud with clapping him.
Would he not stumble? Would he not fall down,
Since pride must have a fall, and break the neck
Of that proud man that did usurp his back?
Forgiveness, horse! Why do I rail on thee,
Since thou, created to be awed by man,
Wast born to bear? I was not made a horse;
And yet I bear a burden like an ass,
Spur-galled and tired by jauncing Bolingbroke.

(*Richard the Second. Act 5. Scene 5.*)
Jauncing: using the spurs.

Oh, the blood more stirs
To rouse a lion than to start a hare!

(*Henry the Fourth. Part One. Act 1. Scene 3. Hotspur speaking.*)

He said he would not ransom Mortimer;
Forbade my tongue to speak of Mortimer.
But I will find him when he lies asleep
And in his ear I'll holla 'Mortimer!'
Nay,
I'll have a starling shall be taught to speak
Nothing but 'Mortimer'; and give it him
To keep his anger still in motion.

(*Henry the Fourth. Part One. Act 1. Scene 3. Hotspur speaking.*)

SERVANT   One horse, my lord, he brought even now.
HOTSPUR   What horse? A roan, a crop-ear, is it not?
SERVANT   It is, my lord.
HOTSPUR   That roan shall be my throne.
(*Henry the Fourth. Part One. Act 2. Scene 3.*)

                Out, you mad-headed ape!
A weasel hath not such a deal of spleen
As you are tossed with.

      • • • • • • • •

Come, come, you paraquito, answer me
Directly unto this question that I ask.
(*Henry the Fourth. Part One. Act 2. Scene 3. Lady Percy speaking.*)

I had rather be a kitten and cry mew,
Than one of these same metre ballad-mongers.
(*Henry the Fourth. Part One. Act 3. Scene 1. Hotspur speaking.*)

                Sometimes he angers me
With telling me of the moldwarp and the ant,
Of the dreamer Merlin and his prophecies,
And of a dragon and a finless fish,
A clip-winged griffin and a moulten raven,
A couching lion and a ramping cat,
And such a deal of skimble-skamble stuff
As puts me from my faith.
(*Henry the Fourth. Part One. Act 3. Scene 1. Hotspur speaking.*)
Moldwarp: mole.

                All furnished, all in arms,
All plumed like estridges that wing the wind,
Baited like eagles having lately bathed,
Glittering in golden coats, like images,
As full of spirit as the month of May
And gorgeous as the sun at midsummer;
Wanton as youthful goats, wild as young bulls.
(*Henry the Fourth. Part One. Act 4. Scene 1. Vernon speaking.*)
Estridges: ostriches.

In peace there's nothing so becomes a man
As modest stillness and humility.
But when the blast of war blows in our ears,
Then imitate the action of the tiger,
Stiffen the sinews, summon up the blood,
Disguise fair nature with hard-favoured rage.

      • • • • • • • •

I see you stand like greyhounds in the slips,
Straining upon the start. The game's afoot.
(*Henry the Fifth. Act 3. Scene 1. The King speaking.*)

I will not change my horse with any that treads but on four pasterns. . . .
    When I bestride him, I soar, I am a hawk. He trots the air; the earth
    sings when he touches it; the basest horn of his hoof is more musical
    than the pipe of Hermes.
(*Henry the Fifth. Act 3. Scene 7. The Dauphin speaking.*)
Pasterns: legs.

RAMBURES   That island of England breeds very valiant creatures; their
                mastiffs are of unmatchable courage.
ORLEANS   Foolish curs, that run winking into the mouth of a Russian
                bear and have their heads crushed like rotten apples!
                You may as well say that's a valiant flea that dare eat
                his breakfast on the lip of a lion.
(*Henry the Fifth. Act 3. Scene 7.*)

I pray thee, bear my former answer back:
Bid them achieve me and then sell my bones.
Good God, why should they mock poor fellows thus?
The man that once did sell the lion's skin
While the beast lived, was killed with hunting him.
(*Henry the Fifth. Act 4. Scene 3. The King speaking.*)

DICK   The first thing we do, let's kill all the lawyers.
CADE   Nay, that I mean to do. Is not this a lamentable thing, that of
            the skin of an innocent lamb should be made parchment?
            That parchment, being scribbled o'er, should undo a man?
            Some say the bee stings, but I say 'tis the bee's wax; for I
            did but seal once to a thing and I was never mine own man
            since.
(*Henry the Sixth. Part Two. Act 4. Scene 2.*)

My gracious liege, this too much lenity
And harmful pity must be laid aside.
To whom do lions cast their gentle looks?
Not to the beast that would usurp their den.
Whose hand is that the forest bear both lick?
Not his that spoils her young before her face.
Who 'scapes the lurking serpent's mortal sting?
Not he that sets his foot upon her back.
The smallest worm will turn, being trodden on;
And doves will peck in safeguard of their brood.
(*Henry the Sixth. Part Three. Act 2. Scene 2. Clifford speaking.*)

I cannot tell: the world is grown so bad
That wrens make prey where eagles dare not perch;
Since every Jack became a gentleman,
There's many a gentle person made a Jack.
(*Richard the Third. Act* 1. *Scene* 3. *Gloucester, afterwards Richard the Third, speaking.*)

RICHARD   A horse! A horse! My kingdom for a horse!
CATESBY   Withdraw, my lord. I'll help you to a horse.
RICHARD   Slave, I have set my life upon a cast
            And I will stand the hazard of the die.
            I think there be six Richmonds in the field;
            Five have I slain to-day instead of him.
            A horse! A horse! My kingdom for a horse!
(*Richard the Third. Act* 5. *Scene* 4.)

If you have writ your annals true, 'tis there,
That like an eagle in a dove-cote I
Fluttered your Volscians in Corioli.
Alone I did it.
(*Coriolanus. Act* 5. *Scene* 5. *Coriolanus speaking.*)

King, be thy thoughts imperious like thy name.
Is the sun dimmed, that gnats do fly in it?
The eagle suffers little birds to sing
And is not careful what they mean thereby,
Knowing that with the shadow of his wings
He can at pleasure stint their melody.
(*Titus Andronicus. Act* 4. *Scene* 4. *Tamora speaking.*)

It was the lark, the herald of the morn.
No nightingale. Look, love, what envious streaks
Do lace the severing clouds in yonder East:
Night's candles are burnt out, and jocund day
Stands tiptoe on the misty mountain tops.
I must be gone and live, or stay and die.
(*Romeo and Juliet. Act* 3. *Scene* 5. *Romeo speaking.*)

                            What, shall one of us
That struck the foremost man of all this world
But for supporting robbers, shall we now
Contaminate our fingers with base bribes
And sell the mighty space of our large honours
For so much trash as may be graspèd thus?
I had rather be a dog and bay the moon
Than such a Roman.
(*Julius Cæsar. Act* 4. *Scene* 3. *Brutus speaking.*)

This guest of Summer,
The temple-haunting martlet, does approve
By his loved mansionry that the heaven's breath
Smells wooingly here: no jutty, frieze,
Buttress, nor coign of vantage, but this bird
Hath made his pendent bed and procreant cradle.
Where they most breed and haunt, I have observed
The air is delicate.
(*Macbeth. Act* 1. *Scene* 6. *Banquo speaking.*)

MACBETH Is't far you ride?
BANQUO As far, my lord, as will fill up the time
'Twixt this and supper. Go not my horse the better,
I must become a borrower of the night
For a dark hour or twain.
(*Macbeth. Act* 3. *Scene* 1.)

We have scotched the snake, not killed it:
She'll close and be herself, whilst our poor malice
Remains in danger of her former tooth.
(*Macbeth. Act* 3. *Scene* 2. *Macbeth speaking.*)

MACBETH Oh, full of scorpions is my mind, dear wife!
Thou know'st that Banquo, and his Fleance, lives.
LADY MACBETH But in them nature's copy's not eterne.
MACBETH There's comfort yet. They are assailable.
Then be thou jocund: ere the bat hath flown
His cloistered flight; ere to black Hecate's summons
The shard-borne beetle with his drowsy hums
Hath wrung night's yawning peal, there shall be done
A deed of dreadful note.
(*Macbeth. Act* 3. *Scene* 2.)
Shard-borne: borne by scaly wing-cases.

FIRST WITCH Thrice the brinded cat hath mewed.
SECOND WITCH Thrice; and once the hedge-pig whined.
(*Macbeth. Act* 4. *Scene* 1.)
Brinded: brindled; streaked.

He loves us not.
He wants the natural touch: for the poor wren,
The most diminutive of birds, will fight,
Her young ones in her nest, against the owl.
(*Macbeth. Act* 4. *Scene* 2. *Lady Macduff speaking.*)

THE KING   How fares our cousin Hamlet?
HAMLET   Excellent, i' faith; of the chameleon's dish. I eat the air,
            promise-crammed. You cannot feed capons so.
(*Hamlet. Act 3. Scene 2.*)

'Tis a knavish piece of work, but what o' that? Your majesty and we that
     have free souls, it touches us not. Let the galled jade wince, our
     withers are unwrung.
(*Hamlet. Act 3. Scene 2. Hamlet speaking.*)
Galled: injured.

Why, let the stricken deer go weep,
The hart ungallèd play;
For some must watch, while some must sleep:
Thus runs the world away.
(*Hamlet. Act 3. Scene 2. Hamlet speaking.*)

HAMLET   Do you see yonder cloud that's almost in the shape of a camel?
POLONIUS   By the mass, and 'tis like a camel indeed.
HAMLET   Methinks it is like a weasel.
POLONIUS   It is backed like a weasel.
HAMLET   Or like a whale?
POLONIUS   Very like a whale.
HAMLET   Then I will come to my mother by and by.
            They fool me to the top of my bent. I will come by and by.
(*Hamlet. Act 3. Scene 2.*)

Hear you, sir:
What is the reason that you use me thus?
I loved you ever. But 'tis no matter.
Let Hercules himself do what he may,
The cat will mew and dog will have his day.
(*Hamlet. Act 5. Scene 1. Hamlet speaking.*)

What have you done?
Tigers, not daughters, what have you performed?
A father and a gracious aged man,
Whose reverence the head-lugged bear would lick,
Most barbarous, most degenerate, have you madded.
(*King Lear. Act 4. Scene 2. Albany speaking.*)

I pardon that man's life. What was thy cause?
Adultery?
Thou shalt not die. Die for adultery! No.
The wren goes to't, and the small gilded fly
Does lecher in my sight.
(*King Lear. Act 4. Scene 6. Lear speaking.*)

LEAR   Thou hast seen a farmer's dog bark at a beggar?
GLOUCESTER Ay, sir.
LEAR   And the creature run from the cur? There thou mightst
          behold the great image of authority: a dog's obeyed in
          office.
(*King Lear. Act 4. Scene 6.*)

          Mine enemy's dog,
Though he had bit me, should have stood that night
Against my fire; and wast thou fain, poor father,
To hovel thee with swine and rogues forlorn
In short and musty straw? Alack, alack!
(*King Lear. Act 4. Scene 7. Cordelia speaking.*)

CORDELIA Shall we not see these daughters and these sisters?
LEAR   No, no, no, no! Come, let's away to prison.
          We two alone will sing like birds i' the cage.
          When thou dost ask me blessing, I'll kneel down
          And ask of thee forgiveness; so we'll live,
          And pray, and sing, and tell old tales, and laugh
          At gilded butterflies, and hear poor rogues
          Talk of court news.
(*King Lear. Act 5. Scene 3.*)

          Oh, Charmian!
Where think'st thou he is now?   Stands he, or sits he,
Or does he walk?   Or is he on his horse?
Oh, happy horse, to bear the weight of Antony!
Do bravely, horse, for wot'st thou whom thou mov'st?
The demi-Atlas of this earth, the arm
And burgonet of men.   He's speaking now,
Or murmuring 'Where's my serpent of old Nile?'
For so he calls me.
(*Antony and Cleopatra. Act 1. Scene 5. Cleopatra speaking.*)
Burgonet: a close-fitting helmet.

Hark, hark!   The lark at heaven's gate sings,
And Phœbus 'gins arise
His steeds to water at those springs
On chaliced flowers that lies.
(*Cymbeline. Act 2. Scene 3. Song.*)

SECTION IX

PSYCHOLOGY

I have considered well his loss of time
And how he cannot be a perfect man,
Not being tried and tutored in the world:
Experience is by industry achieved
And perfected by the swift course of time.
(*The Two Gentlemen of Verona. Act 1. Scene 3. Antonio speaking.*)

DUKE OF MILAN But she did scorn a present that I sent her.
VALENTINE   A woman sometimes scorns what best contents her.
    Send her another, never give her o'er;
    For scorn at first makes after-love the more.
    If she do frown, 'tis not in hate of you,
    But rather to beget more love in you;
    If she do chide, 'tis not to have you gone;
    For, why, the fools are mad if left alone!
    Take no repulse, whatever she doth say;
    For 'get you gone' she doth not mean 'away!'
    Flatter and praise, commend, extol their graces;
    Though ne'er so black, say they have angels' faces.
    That man that hath a tongue, I say, is no man
    If with his tongue he cannot win a woman.
(*The Two Gentlemen of Verona. Act 3. Scene 1.*)

           Could great men thunder
As Jove himself does, Jove would ne'er be quiet;
For every pelting, petty officer
Would use his heaven for thunder, nothing but thunder.
Merciful heaven;
Thou rather with thy sharp and sulphurous bolt
Split'st at the unwedgeable and gnarled oak
Than the soft myrtle; but man, proud man,
Dressed in a little brief authority,
Most ignorant of what he's most assured,
His glassy essence, like an angry ape,
Plays such fantastic tricks before high heaven
As make the angels weep; who, with our spleens,
Would all themselves laugh mortal.
(*Measure For Measure. Act 2. Scene 2. Isabella speaking.*)

They say best men are moulded out of faults;
And, for the most, become much more the better
For being a little bad.
(*Measure For Measure. Act 5. Scene 1. Mariana speaking.*)

Oh, what men dare do! What men may do! What men daily do, not
knowing what they do!
(*Much Ado About Nothing. Act 4. Scene 1. Claudio speaking.*)

For it so falls out
That what we have we prize not to the worth
Whiles we enjoy it; but being lacked and lost,
Why, then we rack the value, then we find
The virtue that possession would not show us
Whiles it was ours.
(*Much Ado About Nothing. Act 4. Scene 1. Friar Francis speaking.*)

What a pretty thing man is, when he goes in his doublet and hose and
leaves off his wit!
(*Much Ado About Nothing. Act 5. Scene 1. Don Pedro speaking.*)

Lovers and madmen have such seething brains,
Such shaping fantasies, that apprehend
More than cool reason ever comprehends.
The lunatic, the lover and the poet
Are of imagination all compact:
One sees more devils than vast hell can hold;
That is the madman. The lover, all as frantic,
Sees Helen's beauty in a brow of Egypt.
The poet's eye, in a fine frenzy rolling,
Doth glance from heaven to earth, from earth to heaven;
And, as imagination bodies forth
The forms of things unknown, the poet's pen
Turns them to shapes and gives to airy nothing
A local habitation and a name.
(*A Midsummer-Night's Dream. Act 5. Scene 1. Theseus speaking.*)

There are a sort of men whose visages
Do cream and mantle like a standing pond,
And do a wilful stillness entertain
With purpose to be dressed in an opinion
Of wisdom, gravity, profound conceit;
As who should say 'I am Sir Oracle,
And when I ope my lips let no dog bark!'

Oh, my Antonio, I do know of these
That therefore are reputed wise
For saying nothing; when, I am very sure,
If they should speak would almost damn those ears
Which, hearing them, would call their brothers fools.
(*The Merchant of Venice. Act* 1. *Scene* 1. *Gratiano speaking.*)

She's beautiful, and therefore to be wooed;
She is a woman, therefore to be won.
(*Henry the Sixth. Part One. Act* 5. *Scene* 3. *Suffolk speaking.*)

Things won are done; joy's soul lies in the doing:
That she beloved knows nought that knows not this:
Men prize the thing ungained more than it is:
That she was never yet, that ever knew
Love got so sweet as when desire did sue.
Therefore this maxim out of love I teach:
Achievement is command; ungained, beseech.
(*Troilus and Cressida. Act* 1. *Scene* 2. *Cressida speaking.*)

What! Am I poor of late?
'Tis certain, greatness, once fallen out with fortune,
Must fall out with men, too. What the declined is
He shall as soon read in the eyes of others
As feel in his own fall; for men, like butterflies,
Show not their mealy wings but to the Summer.
(*Troilus and Cressida. Act* 3. *Scene* 3. *Achilles speaking.*)

I should fear those that dance before me now
Would one day stamp upon me. It has been done:
Men shut their doors against a setting sun.
(*Timon of Athens. Act* 1. *Scene* 2. *Apemantus speaking.*)

Men at some time are masters of their fates:
The fault, dear Brutus, is not in our stars
But in ourselves that we are underlings.
(*Julius Cæsar. Act* 1. *Scene* 2. *Cassius speaking.*)

HAMLET   My excellent good friends! How dost thou, Guildenstern?
                     Ah, Rosencrantz! Good lads, how do you both?
ROSENCRANTZ As the indifferent children of the earth.
GUILDENSTERN Happy, in that we are not over-happy:
                     On Fortune's cap we are not the very button.
HAMLET   Nor the soles of her shoe?
ROSENCRANTZ Neither, my lord.
(*Hamlet. Act* 2. *Scene* 2.)

What a piece of work is a man! How noble in reason! How infinite
in faculty! In form and moving, how express and admirable! In
action, how like an angel! In apprehension, how like a god! The
beauty of the world! The paragon of animals!
(*Hamlet. Act 2. Scene 2. Hamlet speaking.*)

HAMLET Good, my lord, will you see the players well bestowed? Do
you hear, let them be well used, for they are the abstract
and brief chronicles of the time: after your death you were
better have a bad epitaph than their ill report while you live.
POLONIUS My lord, I will use them according to their desert.
HAMLET God's bodykins, man, much better! Use every man after his
desert, and who shall 'scape whipping?
(*Hamlet. Act 2. Scene 2.*)

How all occasions do inform against me
And spur my dull revenge! What is a man,
If his chief good and market of his time
Be but to sleep and feed? A beast, no more.
Sure, He that made us with such large discourse,
Looking before and after, gave us not
That capability and god-like reason
To fust in us unused.
(*Hamlet. Act 4. Scene 4. Hamlet speaking.*)

What, are men mad? Hath nature given them eyes
To see this vaulted arch and the rich crop
Of sea and land, which can distinguish 'twixt
The fiery orbs above and the twinned stones
Upon the numbered beach, and can we not
Partition make with spectacles so precious
'Twixt fair and foul?
(*Cymbeline. Act 1. Scene 6. Iachimo speaking.*)

Some glory in their birth, some in their skill,
Some in their wealth, some in their body's force;
Some in their garments, though new-fangled ill;
Some in their hawks and hounds, some in their horse;
And every humour hath his adjunct pleasure,
Wherein it finds a joy above the rest.
(*Sonnet 91.*)

SECTION X

BRITAIN AND THE BRITISH

Go, bear him in thine arms.
I am amazed, methinks, and lose my way
Among the thorns and dangers of this world.
How easy dost thou take all England up!
From forth this morsel of dead royalty,
The life, the right and truth of all this realm
Is fled to heaven; and England now is left
To tug and scamble and to part by the teeth
The unowed interest of proud-swelling state.
(*King John. Act 4. Scene 3. The Bastard speaking.*)

Oh, let us pay the time but needful woe,
Since it hath been beforehand with our griefs.
This England never did, nor never shall,
Lie at the proud foot of a conqueror
But when it first did help to wound itself.
Now these her princes are come home again,
Come the three corners of the world in arms
And we shall shock them.   Nought shall make us rue,
If England to itself do rest but true.
(*King John. Act 5. Scene 7. The Bastard speaking.*)

Lo, as at English feasts, so I regreet
The daintiest last, to make the end most sweet.
(*Richard the Second. Act 1. Scene 3. Bolingbroke speaking.*)

MOWBRAY   I am too old to fawn upon a nurse;
            Too far in years to be a pupil now.
            What is thy sentence then but speechless death,
            Which robs my tongue from breathing native breath?
RICHARD   It boots thee not to be compassionate:
            After our sentence, plaining comes too late.
MOWBRAY   Then thus I turn me from my country's light,
            To dwell in solemn shades of endless night.
(*Richard the Second. Act 1. Scene 3.*)

Then, England's ground, farewell; sweet soil, adieu:
My mother and my nurse, that bears me yet.
Where'er I wander, boast of this I can:
Though banished, yet a true-born Englishman.
(*Richard the Second. Act 1. Scene 3. Bolingbroke speaking.*)

This royal throne of kings, this sceptred isle,
This earth of majesty, this seat of Mars,
This other Eden, demi-paradise;
This fortress, built by nature for herself
Against infection and the hand of war;
This happy breed of men, this little world,
This precious stone set in the silver sea,
Which serves it in the office of a wall
Or as a moat defensive to a house
Against the envy of less happier lands;
This blessed plot, this earth, this realm, this England.
(*Richard the Second. Act 2. Scene 1. John of Gaunt speaking.*)

England, bound in with the triumphant sea,
Whose rocky shore beats back the envious siege
Of watery Neptune, is now bound in with shame,
With inky blots and rotten parchment bonds:
That England, that was wont to conquer others,
Hath made a shameful conquest of itself.
(*Richard the Second. Act 2. Scene 1. John of Gaunt speaking.*)

Why, cousin, wert thou regent of the world,
It were a shame to let this land by lease;
But for thy world enjoying but this land,
Is it not more than shame to shame it so?
Landlord of England art thou now, not king.
(*Richard the Second. Act 2. Scene 1. John of Gaunt speaking.*)

Myself, a prince by fortune of my birth,
Near to the king in blood, and near in love
Till you did make him misinterpret me,
Have stooped my neck under your injuries
And sighed my English breath in foreign clouds
Eating the bitter bread of banishment.
(*Richard the Second. Act 3. Scene 1. Bolingbroke speaking.*)

Tell Bolingbroke, for yond methinks he is,
That every stride he makes upon my land
Is dangerous treason: he is come to open
The purple testament of bleeding war.
But ere the crown he looks for live in peace,
Ten thousand bloody crowns of mothers' sons
Shall ill become the flower of England's face,
Change the complexion of her maid-pale peace
To scarlet indignation, and bedew
Her pastures' grass with faithful English blood.
(*Richard the Second. Act 3. Scene 3. Richard speaking.*)

Two stars keep not their motion in one sphere,
Nor can one England brook a double reign
Of Harry Percy and the Prince of Wales.
(*Henry the Fourth. Part One. Act 5. Scene 4. Prince Henry speaking.*)

But it was always yet the trick of our English nation, if they have a good
  thing, to make it too common.
(*Henry the Fourth. Part Two. Act 1. Scene 2. Falstaff speaking.*)

Harry the Fifth is crowned. Up, vanity!
Down, royal state! All you sage counsellors, hence!
And to the English court assemble now,
From every region, apes of idleness!
Now, neighbour confines, purge you of your scum:
Have you a ruffian that will swear, drink, dance,
Revel the night, rob, murder, and commit
The oldest sins the newest kind of ways?
Be happy, he will trouble you no more:
England shall double gild his treble guilt.
England shall give him office, honour, might;
For the fifth Harry from curbed licence plucks
The muzzle of restraint, and the wild dog
Shall flesh his tooth in every innocent.
(*Henry the Fourth. Part Two. Act 4. Scene 5. The King speaking.*)

Now all the youth of England are on fire
And silken dalliance in the wardrobe lies;
Now thrive the armourers, and honour's thought
Reigns solely in the breast of every man.

   . . . .

Oh, England! Model to thy inward greatness,
Like little body with a mighty heart!
What mightst thou do, that honour would thee do,
Were all thy children kind and natural?
(*Henry the Fifth. Act 2. Chorus speaking.*)

    Follow, follow!
Grapple your minds to sternage of this navy
And leave your England, as dead midnight still,
Guarded with grandsires, babies and old women. . . .
(*Henry the Fifth. Act 3. Chorus speaking.*)

    For, to say the sooth,
Though 'tis no wisdom to confess so much
Unto an enemy of craft and vantage,
My people are with sickness much enfeebled,

My numbers lessened, and those few I have
Almost no better than so many French;
Who when they were in health, I tell thee, herald,
I thought upon one pair of English legs
Did march three Frenchmen.
(*Henry the Fifth. Act 3. Scene 6. The King speaking.*)

Assigned am I to be the English scourge:
This night the siege assuredly I'll raise.
Expect Saint Martin's Summer, halcyon days,
Since I have entered into these wars.
(*Henry the Sixth. Part One. Act 1. Scene 2. Joan of Arc speaking.*)

MACDUFF   Stands Scotland where it did?
ROSS   Alas, poor country!
          Almost afraid to know itself! It cannot
          Be called our mother, but our grave, where nothing,
          But who knows nothing, is once seen to smile;
          Where sighs and groans and shrieks that rend the air
          Are made, not marked; where violent sorrow seems
          A modern ecstasy. The dead man's knell
          Is there scarce asked for who; and good men's lives
          Expire before the flowers in their caps,
          Dying or ere they sicken.
(*Macbeth. Act 4. Scene 3.*)

PISANIO   If not at court,
          Then not in Britain must you bide.
IMOGEN   Where, then?
          Hath Britain all the sun that shines? Day, night,
          Are they not, but in Britain? I' the world's volume
          Our Britain seems as of it, but not in't:
          In a great pool, a swan's nest. Prithee, think
          There's livers out of Britain.
(*Cymbeline. Act 3. Scene 4.*)

SECTION XI

FAMILY RELATIONSHIPS

PROSPERO   Mark his condition, and the event; then tell me
           If this might be a brother.
MIRANDA   I should sin
           To think but nobly of my grandmother:
           Good wombs have borne bad sons.
(*The Tempest. Act 1. Scene 2.*)

Bring me a father that so loved his child,
Whose joy of her is overwhelmed like mine,
And bid him speak of patience.
(*Much Ado About Nothing. Act 5. Scene 1. Leonato speaking.*)

. . . but oh, methinks, how slow
This old moon wanes! She lingers my desires,
Like to a step-dame, or a dowager,
Long withering out a young man's revenue.
(*A Midsummer-Night's Dream. Act 1. Scene 1. Theseus speaking.*)

I have a widow aunt, a dowager
Of great revenue, and she hath no child.
From Athens is her house remote seven leagues;
And she respects me as her only son.
(*A Midsummer-Night's Dream. Act 1. Scene 1. Lysander speaking.*)

Alack, what heinous sin is it in me
To be ashamed to be my father's child!
But though I am a daughter to his blood,
I am not to his manners. Oh, Lorenzo!
If thou keep promise I shall end this strife,
Become a Christian and thy loving wife.
(*The Merchant of Venice. Act 2. Scene 3. Jessica speaking.*)

The courtesy of nations allows you my better in that you are the first-born;
but the same tradition takes not away my blood, were there twenty
brothers betwixt us: I have as much of my father in me as you.
(*As You Like It. Act 1. Scene 1. Orlando speaking.*)

He was my father, and he is thrice a villain that says such a father begot
villains.
(*As You Like It. Act 1. Scene 1. Orlando speaking.*)

The spirit of my father grows strong in me.
(*As You Like It. Act 1. Scene 1. Orlando speaking.*)

. . . whose loves
Are dearer than the natural bond of sisters.
(*As You Like It. Act 1. Scene 2. Le Beau speaking.*)

Wilt thou change fathers? I will give thee mine.
(*As You Like It. Act 1. Scene 3. Celia speaking.*)

Come, madam wife, sit by my side and let the world slip: we shall ne'er
be younger.
(*The Taming of the Shrew. Induction. Scene 2. Sly speaking.*)

But for my bonny Kate, she must with me.
Nay, look not big, nor stamp, nor stare, nor fret;
I will be master of what is mine own:
She is my goods, my chattels; she is my house,
My household stuff, my field, my barn,
My horse, my ox, my ass, my anything.
And here she stands, touch her whoever dare.
(*The Taming of the Shrew. Act 3. Scene 2. Petruchio speaking.*)

Oh, she that had a heart of that fine frame
To pay this debt of love but to a brother,
How will she love when the rich golden shaft
Hath killed the flock of all affections else
That live in her?   When liver, brain and heart,
These sovereign thrones, are all supplied, and filled
Her sweet perfections with one self king !
(*Twelfth Night. Act 1. Scene 1. Orsino speaking.*)

POLIXENES   Have you a father?
FLORIZEL   I have.   But what of him?
POLIXENES   Knows he of this?
FLORIZEL   He neither does nor shall.
POLIXENES   Methinks a father
Is at the nuptial of his son a guest
That best becomes the table.
(*The Winter's Tale. Act 4. Scene 4. The Oxford Shakespeare: Act 4. Scene 3.*)

Reason, my son,
Should choose himself a wife; but as good reason,
The father, all whose joy is nothing else
But fair posterity, should hold some counsel
In such a business.
(*The Winter's Tale. Act 4. Scene 4. Polixenes speaking. The Oxford Shakespeare: Act 4. Scene 3.*)

Your mother was most true to wedlock, prince;
For she did print your royal father off,
Conceiving you.   Were I but twenty-one,
Your father's image is so hit in you,
His very air, that I should call you brother,
As I did him.
(*The Winter's Tale. Act 5. Scene 1. Leontes speaking.*)

Madam, an if my brother had my shape,
And I had his, Sir Robert his, like him;
And if my legs were two such riding-rods,
My arms such eel-skins stuffed, my face so thin
That in mine ear I durst not stick a rose
Lest men should say 'Look, where three-farthings goes!'
And, to his shape, were heir to all this land,
Would I might never stir from off this place.
I would give it every foot to have this face.
(*King John. Act* I. *Scene* I. *The Bastard speaking.*)
'*Look, where three-farthings goes!*' : three-farthing pieces of silver were coined
in 1561 (discontinued 1582). They were very thin, and were
distinguished from the silver pence by an impression of the queen's
profile, with a rose behind her ear.

Brother by the mother's side, give me your hand.
My father gave me honour, *yours* gave land.
Now blessèd be the hour, by night or day,
When I was got, Sir Robert was away!
(*King John. Act* I. *Scene* I. *The Bastard speaking.*)

He that perforce robs lions of their hearts
May easily win a woman's. Ay, my mother,
With all my heart I thank thee for my father!
Who lives and dares but say thou didst not well
When I was got, I'll send his soul to hell.
Come, lady, I will show thee to my kin;
And they shall say, when Richard me begot,
If thou hadst said him nay, it had been sin.
(*King John. Act* I. *Scene* I. *The Bastard speaking.*)

QUEEN ELINOR   Out, insolent! Thy bastard shall be king
That thou may'st be a queen, and check the world.
CONSTANCE   My bed was ever to thy son as true
As thine was to thy husband, and this boy
Liker in feature to his father Geoffrey
Than thou and John in manners; being as like
As rain to water, or devil to his dam.
(*King John. Act* 2. *Scene* I.)

Yea, there thou mak'st me sad, and mak'st me sin
In envy that my Lord Northumberland
Should be the father to so blest a son;
A son who is the theme of honour's tongue:
Amongst a grove, the very straightest plant.
(*Henry the Fourth. Part One. Act* I. *Scene* I. *The King speaking.*)

Most subject is the fattest soil to weeds;
And he, the noble image of my youth,
Is overspread with them.
(*Henry the Fourth. Part Two. Act 4. Scene 4. The King, referring to his son, Prince Henry.*)

COMINIUS   I offered to awaken his regard
           For's private friends: his answer to me was,
           He could not stay to pick them in a pile
           Of noisome musty chaff. He said 'twas folly,
           For one poor grain or two, to leave unburnt
           And still to nose the offence.
MENENIUS   For one poor grain or two!
           I am one of those. His mother, wife, his child,
           And this brave fellow too, we are the grains;
           You are the musty chaff, and you are smelt
           Above the moon. We must be burnt for you.
(*Coriolanus. Act 5. Scene 1.*)

                This last old man,
Whom with a cracked heart I have sent to Rome,
Loved me above the measure of a father;
Nay, godded me indeed.
(*Coriolanus. Act 5. Scene 3. Coriolanus, referring to Menenius.*)

My wife comes foremost; then the honoured mould
Wherein this trunk was framed, and in her hand
The grandchild to her blood. But out, affection!
All bond and privilege of nature, break!
Let it be virtuous to be obstinate.
(*Coriolanus. Act 5. Scene 3. Coriolanus speaking.*)

VIRGILIA   My lord and husband!
CORIOLANUS   These eyes are not the same I wore in Rome.
VIRGILIA   The sorrow that delivers us thus changed
           Makes you think so.
CORIOLANUS   Like a dull actor now,
           I have forgot my part; and I am out,
           Even to a full disgrace. Best of my flesh,
           Forgive my tyranny; but do not say
           For that 'Forgive our Romans.' Oh, a kiss
           Long as my exile, sweet as my revenge!
           Now, by the jealous queen of heaven, that kiss
           I carried from thee, dear, and my true lip
           Hath virgined it e'er since. You gods! I prate,

And the most noble mother of the world
Leave unsaluted.   Sink, my knee, i' the earth;
Of thy deep duty more impression show
Than that of common sons.

VOLUMNIA   Oh, stand up blessed,
Whilst, with no softer cushion than the flint,
I kneel before thee; and unproperly
Show duty, as mistaken all this while
Between the child and parent.   (*Kneels.*)

CORIOLANUS   What is this?
Your knees to me!   To your corrected son!
Then let the pebbles on the hungry beach
Fillip the stars; then let the mutinous winds
Strike the proud cedars 'gainst the fiery sun,
Murdering impossibility, to make
What cannot be, slight work.

(*Coriolanus.   Act 5.   Scene 3.*)

Thou hast never in thy life
Showed thy dear mother any courtesy,
When she . . . poor hen, fond of no second brood! . . .
Has clucked thee to the wars and safely home
Loaden with honour.

(*Coriolanus.   Act 5.   Scene 3.   Volumnia speaking.*)

NURSE   Will you speak well of him that killed your cousin?
JULIET   Shall I speak ill of him that is my husband?
Ah, poor my lord, what tongue shall smooth thy name,
When I, thy three-hours wife, have mangled it?
But wherefore, villain, didst thou kill my cousin?

(*Romeo and Juliet.   Act 3.   Scene 2.*)

Wisdom!   To leave his wife, to leave his babes,
His mansion and his titles, in a place
From whence himself does fly?   He loves us not;
He wants the natural touch: for the poor wren,
The most diminutive of birds, will fight,
Her young ones in her nest, against the owl.

(*Macbeth.   Act 4.   Scene 2.   Lady Macduff speaking.*)

ROSENCRANTZ   Then thus she says: your behaviour hath struck her into
amazement and admiration.
HAMLET   Oh, wonderful son that can so astonish a mother!

(*Hamlet.   Act 3.   Scene 2.*)

Oh, my offence is rank! It smells to heaven.
It hath the primal eldest curse upon't:
A brother's murder.
(*Hamlet. Act 3. Scene 3. The King speaking.*)

Now might I do it pat, now he is praying;
And now I'll do't: and so he goes to heaven,
And so am I revenged. That would be scanned:
A villain kills my father; and for that,
I, his sole son, do this same villain send
To heaven.
Oh, this is hire and salary, not revenge!
(*Hamlet. Act 3. Scene 3. Hamlet speaking.*)

HAMLET Now, mother, what's the matter?
THE QUEEN Hamlet, thou hast thy father much offended.
HAMLET Mother, you have my father much offended.
THE QUEEN Come, come! You answer with an idle tongue.
HAMLET Go, go! You question with a wicked tongue.
(*Hamlet. Act 3. Scene 4.*)

THE QUEEN Have you forgot me?
HAMLET No, by the rood, not so:
        You are the queen, your husband's brother's wife;
        And . . . would it were not so! . . . you are my mother.
(*Hamlet. Act 3. Scene 4.*)

HAMLET (*To the King*) Farewell, dear mother.
THE KING Thy loving father, Hamlet.
HAMLET My mother: father and mother is man and wife; man and
        wife is one flesh, and so, my mother.
(*Hamlet. Act 4. Scene 3.*)

Why have my sisters husbands, if they say
They love you, all? Haply, when I shall wed,
That lord, whose hand must take my plight, shall carry
Half my love with him, half my care and duty.
Sure, I shall never marry, like my sisters,
To love my father all.
(*King Lear. Act 1. Scene 1. Cordelia speaking.*)

Ingratitude, thou marble-hearted fiend,
More hideous when thou show'st thee in a child
Than the sea-monster!
(*King Lear. Act 1. Scene 4. Lear speaking.*)

Turn all her mother's pains and benefits
To laughter and contempt, that she may feel
How sharper than a serpent's tooth it is
To have a thankless child!
(*King Lear*. *Act* 1. *Scene* 4. *Lear speaking.*)

I prithee, daughter, do not make me mad.
I will not trouble thee, my child; farewell.
We'll no more meet, no more see one another.
But yet thou art my flesh, my blood, my daughter;
Or rather a disease that's in my flesh,
Which I must needs call mine.
(*King Lear*. *Act* 2. *Scene* 4. *Lear speaking.*)

Oh, treason of the blood!
Fathers, from hence trust not your daughters' minds
By what you see them act.
(*Othello*. *Act* 1. *Scene* 1. *Brabantio speaking.*)

My noble father,
I do perceive here a divided duty:
To you I am bound for life and education.
My life and education both do learn me
How to respect you. You are the lord of duty;
I am hitherto your daughter. But here's my husband;
And so much duty as my mother showed
To you, preferring you before her father,
So much I challenge that I may profess
Due to the Moor, my lord.
(*Othello*. *Act* 1. *Scene* 3. *Desdemona speaking.*)

God be with you! I have done.
Please it your grace, on to the state-affairs:
I had rather to adopt a child than get it.
Come hither, Moor.
I here do give thee that with all my heart
Which, but thou hast already, with all my heart
I would keep from thee. (*To Desdemona*) For your sake, jewel,
I am glad at soul I have no other child;
For thy escape would teach me tyranny,
To hang clogs on them. I have done, my lord.
(*Othello*. *Act* 1. *Scene* 3. *Brabantio speaking.*)

Look to her, Moor, if thou hast eyes to see:
She has deceived her father, and may thee.
(*Othello*. *Act* 1. *Scene* 3. *Brabantio speaking.*)

Desdemona comes.
If she be false, oh, then heaven mocks itself!
I'll not believe it.
(*Othello. Act 3. Scene 3. Othello speaking.*)

My wife! My wife! What wife? I have no wife.
Oh, insupportable! Oh, heavy hour!
Methinks it should be now a huge eclipse
Of sun and moon, and that the affrighted globe
Should yawn at alteration.
(*Othello. Act 5. Scene 2. Othello speaking.*)

No, be assured you shall not find me, daughter,
After the slander of most step-mothers,
Evil-eyed unto you. You're my prisoner, but
Your gaoler shall deliver you the keys
That lock up your restraint.
(*Cymbeline. Act 1. Scene 1. The Queen speaking.*)

Oh, dissembling courtesy! How fine this tyrant
Can tickle where she wounds. My dearest husband,
I something fear my father's wrath, but nothing,
Always reserved my holy duty, what
His rage can do on me. You must be gone;
And I shall here abide the hourly shot
Of angry eyes, not comforted to live,
But that there is this jewel in the world
That I may see again.
(*Cymbeline. Act 1. Scene 1. Imogen speaking.*)

Or ere I could
Give him that parting kiss which I had set
Betwixt two charming words, comes in my father;
And like the tyrannous breathing of the North,
Shakes all our buds from growing.
(*Cymbeline. Act 1. Scene 3. Imogen speaking.*)

Why, good fellow,
What shall I do the while? Where bide? How live?
Or in my life what comfort, when I am
Dead to my husband?
(*Cymbeline. Act 3. Scene 4. Imogen speaking.*)

My dearest wife was like this maid, and such a one
My daughter might have been: my queen's square brows;
Her stature to an inch; as wand-like straight;

As silver-voiced; her eyes as jewel-like,
And cased as richly; in pace another Juno;
Who starves the ears she feeds, and makes them hungry
The more she gives them speech.
(*Pericles. Act 5. Scene 1. Pericles speaking.*)

Mark how one string, sweet husband to another,
Strikes each in each by mutual ordering;
Resembling sire and child and happy mother,
Who, all in one, one pleasing note do sing:
Whose speechless song, being many, seeming one,
Sings this to thee: 'Thou, single, wilt prove none.'
(*Sonnet 8.*)

Who lets so fair a house fall to decay,
Which husbandry in honour might uphold
Against the stormy gusts of Winter's day
And barren rage of death's eternal cold?
Oh, none but unthrifts. Dear my love, you know
You had a father: let your son say so.
(*Sonnet 13.*)

SECTION XII

MUSIC AND MUSICAL INSTRUMENTS

Be not afeard; the isle is full of noises,
Sounds and sweet airs that give delight and hurt not.
Sometimes a thousand twangling instruments
Will hum about mine ears; and sometimes voices,
That, if I then had waked after long sleep,
Will make me sleep again.
(*The Tempest. Act 3. Scene 2. Caliban speaking.*)

This will prove a brave kingdom to me, where I shall have my music for
    nothing.
(*The Tempest. Act 3. Scene 2. Stephano speaking.*)

                    But this rough magic
I here abjure; and when I have required
Some heavenly music, which even now I do,
To work mine end upon their senses that
This airy charm is for, I'll break my staff,
Bury it certain fathoms in the earth,
And deeper than did ever plummet sound
I'll drown my book.
(*The Tempest. Act 5. Scene 1. Prospero speaking.*)

The current that with gentle murmur glides,
Thou knowest, being stopped, impatiently doth rage;
But when his fair course is not hindered
He makes sweet music with the enamelled stones,
Giving a gentle kiss to every sedge
He overtaketh in his pilgrimage.
(*The Two Gentlemen of Verona.   Act 2.   Scene 7.   Julia speaking.*)

Except I be by Silvia in the night,
There is no music in the nightingale;
Unless I look on Silvia in the day,
There is no day for me to look upon.
(*The Two Gentlemen of Verona.   Act 3.   Scene 1.   Valentine speaking.*)

MARIANA   I cry you mercy, sir; and well could wish
                    You had not found me here so musical.
                    Let me excuse me, and believe me so:
                    My mirth it much displeased, but pleased my woe.
DUKE   'Tis good; though music oft hath such a charm
                    To make bad good, and good provoke to harm.
(*Measure For Measure.   Act 4.   Scene 1.*)

(*As the music commences*) Now, divine air! Now is his soul ravished!
        Is it not strange that sheeps' guts should hale souls out of men's bodies?
        Well, a horn for my money, when all's done.
(*Much Ado About Nothing.   Act 2.   Scene 3.   Benedick speaking.*)

For valour, is not Love a Hercules,
Still climbing trees in the Hesperides?
Subtle as Sphinx; as sweet and musical
As bright Apollo's lute, strung with his hair;
And when Love speaks, the voice of all the gods
Makes heaven drowsy with the harmony.
(*Love's Labour's Lost.   Act 4.   Scene 3.   Berowne speaking.*)

The words of Mercury are harsh after the songs of Apollo.   You, that way;
        we, this way.
(*Love's Labour's Lost.   Act 5.   Scene 2.   Don Armado speaking.*)

My gentle Puck, come hither.   Thou remember'st
Since once I sat upon a promontory,
And heard a mermaid on a dolphin's back
Uttering such dulcet and harmonious breath
That the rude sea grew civil at her song;
And certain stars shot madly from their spheres
To hear the sea-maid's music.
(*A Midsummer-Night's Dream.   Act 2.   Scene 1.   Oberon speaking.*)

TITANIA   What, wilt thou hear some music, my sweet love?
BOTTOM   I have a reasonable good ear in music: let us have the tongs
               and the bones.
(*A Midsummer-Night's Dream.   Act 4.   Scene 1.*)

What! Are there masques?   Hear you me, Jessica:
Lock up my doors; and when you hear the drum
And the vile squealing of the wry-necked fife,
Clamber not you up to the casements then,
Nor thrust your head into the public street
To gaze on Christian fools with varnished faces.
But stop my house's ears; I mean my casements.
Let not the sound of shallow foppery enter
My sober house.
(*The Merchant of Venice.   Act 2.   Scene 5.   Shylock speaking.*)

Let music sound while he doth make his choice;
Then, if he lose, he makes a swan-like end,
Fading in music.
(*The Merchant of Venice.   Act 3.   Scene 2.   Portia speaking.*)

How sweet the moonlight sleeps upon this bank!
Here will we sit and let the sounds of music
Creep in our ears: soft stillness and the night
Become the touches of sweet harmony.
Sit, Jessica.   Look, how the floor of heaven
Is thick inlaid with patines of bright gold.
There's not the smallest orb which thou behold'st
But in his motion like an angel sings,
Still quiring to the young-eyed cherubins.
Such harmony is in immortal souls;
But whilst this muddy vesture of decay
Doth grossly close it in, we cannot hear it.
(*The Merchant of Venice.   Act 5.   Scene 1.   Lorenzo speaking.*)

I am never merry when I hear sweet music.
(*The Merchant of Venice.   Act 5.   Scene 1.   Jessica speaking.*)

The man that hath no music in himself,
Nor is not moved with concord of sweet sounds,
Is fit for treasons, stratagems and spoils.
The motions of his spirit are dull as night
And his affections dark as Erebus.
Let no such man be trusted.   Mark the music!
(*The Merchant of Venice.   Act 5.   Scene 1.   Lorenzo speaking.*)

Under the greenwood tree,
Who loves to lie with me
And turn his merry note
Unto the sweet bird's throat,
Come hither, come hither, come hither:
Here shall he see
No enemy
But Winter and rough weather.
(*As You Like It. Act 2. Scene 5. Amiens singing.*)

If he, compact of jars, grow musical,
We shall have shortly discord in the spheres.
Go, seek him: tell him I would speak with him.
(*As You Like It. Act 2. Scene 7. The Banished Duke speaking.*)

Meantime, forget this new-fallen dignity
And fall into our rustic revelry.
Play, music! And you, brides and bridegrooms all,
With measure heaped in joy to the measures fall.
(*As You Like It. Act 5. Scene 4. The Banished Duke speaking.*)

Procure me music ready when he wakes,
To make a dulcet and a heavenly sound;
And if he chance to speak, be ready straight
And with a low submissive reverence
Say 'What is it your honour will command?'
(*The Taming of the Shrew. Induction. Scene 1. A Lord speaking.*)

Wilt thou have music? Hark! Apollo plays;
And twenty cagèd nightingales do sing.
(*The Taming of the Shrew. Induction. Scene 2. A Lord speaking.*)

Preposterous ass, that never read so far
To know the cause why music was ordained!
Was it not to refresh the mind of man,
After his studies or his usual pain?
(*The Taming of the Shrew. Act 3. Scene 1. Lucentio speaking.*)

HORTENSIO   Madam, my instrument's in tune.
BIANCA   Let's hear. Oh, fie! The treble jars.
LUCENTIO   Spit in the hole, man, and tune again.
(*The Taming of the Shrew. Act 3. Scene 1.*)

If music be the food of love, play on;
Give me excess of it, that, surfeiting,
The appetite may sicken and so die.

That strain again! It had a dying fall.
Oh, it came o'er my ear like the sweet sound
That breathes upon a bank of violets,
Stealing and giving odour! Enough; no more.
'Tis not so sweet now as it was before.
(*Twelfth Night. Act* 1. *Scene* 1. *Orsino speaking.*)
Sound: sometimes edited as 'south' . . . the South wind.

Fie, that you'll say so! He plays o' the viol-de-gamboys and speaks three
    or four languages word for word without book; and hath all the
    good gifts of nature.
(*Twelfth Night. Act* 1. *Scene* 3. *Sir Toby Belch speaking.*)
Viol-de-gamboys: Sir Toby's error for the viol da gamba. This was a
    popular instrument of the day and closely resembled the modern 'cello.

Give me some music. Now, good morrow, friends.
Now, good Cesario, but that piece of song,
That old and antique song we heard last night.
Methought it did relieve my passion much,
More than light airs and recollected terms
Of these most brisk and giddy-pacèd times.
Come, but one verse.
(*Twelfth Night. Act* 2. *Scene* 4. *Orsino speaking.*)

Oh, fellow, come; the song we had last night.
Mark it, Cesario. It is old and plain.
The spinsters and the knitters in the sun,
And the free maids that weave their thread with bones
Do use to chant it.
(*Twelfth Night. Act* 2. *Scene* 4. *Orsino speaking.*)

VIOLA   Save thee, friend, and thy music. Dost thou live by thy tabor?
FESTE   No, sir, I live by the church.
(*Twelfth Night. Act* 3. *Scene* 1.)
Tabor: a musical instrument used by professional fools.

                    'Tis strange that death should sing.
I am the cygnet to this pale faint swan
Who chants a doleful hymn to his own death,
And from the organ-pipe of frailty sings
His soul and body to their lasting rest.
(*King John. Act* 5. *Scene* 7. *Prince Henry speaking.*)

The language I have learned these forty years,
My native English, now I must forego:

And now my tongue's use is to me no more
Than an unstringed viol or a harp;
Or like a cunning instrument cased up,
Or, being open, put into his hands
That knows no touch to tune the harmony.
(*Richard the Second.   Act 1.   Scene 3.   Mowbray speaking.*)

Oh, but they say the tongues of dying men
Enforce attention like deep harmony.
        . . . .
More are men's ends marked than their lives before:
The setting sun, and music at the close,
As the last taste of sweets, is sweetest last;
Writ in remembrance more than things long past.
(*Richard the Second.   Act 2.   Scene 1.   John of Gaunt speaking.*)

                Music, do I hear?
Ha, ha!   Keep time!   How sour sweet music is
When time is broke and no proportion kept!
So is it in the music of men's lives.
(*Richard the Second.   Act 5.   Scene 5.   Richard speaking.*)

Orpheus, with his lute, made trees
And the mountain tops that freeze
Bow themselves when he did sing.
To his music plants and flowers
Ever sprung, as sun and showers
There had made a lasting Spring.

Every thing that heard him play,
Even the billows of the sea,
Hung their heads and then lay by.
In sweet music is such art,
Killing care and grief of heart
Fall asleep, or hearing, die.
(*Henry the Eighth.   Act 3.   Scene 1.   Song.*)

HAMLET	Will you play upon this pipe?
GUILDENSTERN	My lord, I cannot.
HAMLET	I pray you.
GUILDENSTERN	Believe me, I cannot.
HAMLET	I do beseech you.
GUILDENSTERN	I know no touch of it, my lord.
HAMLET	It is as easy as lying: govern these ventages with your fingers and thumb, give it breath with your mouth and it will discourse most eloquent music. Look you, these are the stops.

GUILDENSTERN But these cannot I command to any utterance of harmony; I have not the skill.

HAMLET   Why, look you now, how unworthy a thing you make of me! You would play upon *me*; you would seem to know *my* stops; you would pluck out the heart of my mystery; you would sound me from my lowest note to the top of my compass. And there is much music, excellent voice, in this little organ; yet cannot you make *it* speak. 'Sblood, do you think I am easier to be played on than a pipe? Call me what instrument you will, though you can fret me yet you cannot play upon me.

(*Hamlet. Act* 3. *Scene* 2.)
Fret: a play upon words. A 'fret' is a stop used for regulating the fingering of stringed instruments.

Music to hear, why hear'st thou music sadly?
Sweets with sweets war not, joy delights in joy:
Why lov'st thou that which thou receiv'st not gladly,
Or else receiv'st with pleasure thine annoy?
If the true concord of well-tuned sounds,
By unions married, do offend thine ear,
They do but sweetly chide thee, who confounds
In singleness the parts that thou should'st bear.
(*Sonnet* 8.)

SECTION XIII

VIRTUE AND VICE

But truer stars did govern Proteus' birth:
His words are bonds, his oaths are oracles,
His love sincere, his thoughts immaculate,
His tears pure messengers sent from his heart,
His heart as far from fraud as heaven from earth.
(*The Two Gentlemen of Verona. Act* 2. *Scene* 7. *Julia speaking.*)

Why, Sir John, do you think, though we would have thrust virtue out of our hearts by the head and shoulders and have given ourselves without scruple to hell, that ever the devil could have made you our delight?
(*The Merry Wives of Windsor. Act* 5. *Scene* 5. *Mistress Page speaking.*)

Heaven doth with us as we with torches do:
Not light them for themselves. For if our virtues
Did not go forth of us, 'twere all alike
As if we had them not.
(*Measure For Measure. Act* 1. *Scene* 1. *The Duke speaking.*)

Well, heaven forgive him, and forgive us all!
Some rise by sin, and some by virtue fall.
(*Measure For Measure. Act 2. Scene 1. Escalus speaking.*)

ISABELLA   Save your honour! (*Exit.*)
ANGELO   From thee. Even from thy virtue!
          What's this? What's this? Is this her fault or mine?
          The tempter or the tempted, who sins most?
(*Measure For Measure. Act 2. Scene 2.*)

Oh, cunning enemy, that, to catch a saint
With saints dost bait thy hook! Most dangerous
Is that temptation that doth goad us on
To sin in loving virtue.
(*Measure For Measure. Act 2. Scene 2. Angelo speaking.*)

Virtue is bold, and goodness never fearful.
(*Measure For Measure. Act 3. Scene 1. The Duke speaking.*)

Oh, what authority and show of truth
Can cunning sin cover itself withal!
Comes not that blood as modest evidence
To witness simple virtue?
(*Much Ado About Nothing. Act 4. Scene 1. Claudio speaking.*)

. . . for it so falls out
That what we have we prize not to the worth
Whiles we enjoy it; but being lacked and lost,
Why, then we rack the value, then we find
The virtue that possession would not show us
Whiles it was ours.
(*Much Ado About Nothing. Act 4. Scene 1. Friar Francis speaking.*)

THE KING   Rebuke me not for that which you provoke:
            The virtue of your eye must break my oath.
PRINCESS   You nick-name virtue; vice you should have spoke,
            For virtue's office never breaks men's troth.
(*Love's Labour's Lost. Act 5. Scene 2.*)

Yet he's gentle; never schooled, and yet learned; full of noble device; of
     all sorts enchantingly beloved; and indeed so much in the heart of the
     world, and especially of my own people, who best know him, that
     I am altogether misprised: but it shall not be so long.
(*As You Like It. Act 1. Scene 1. Oliver speaking.*)

From lowest place when virtuous things proceed,
The place is dignified by the doer's deed.
(*All's Well That Ends Well. Act 2. Scene 3. The King speaking.*)

Anything that's mended is but patched: virtue that transgresses is but
    patched with sin; and sin that amends is but patched with virtue.
(*Twelfth Night. Act 1. Scene 5. Feste speaking.*)

I hate ingratitude more in a man
Than lying, vainness, babbling, drunkenness,
Or any taint of vice whose strong corruption
Inhabits our frail blood.
(*Twelfth Night. Act 3. Scene 4. Viola speaking.*)

Virtue is beauty; but the beauteous evil
Are empty trunks, o'erflourished by the devil.
(*Twelfth Night. Act 3. Scene 4. Antonio speaking.*)
Trunks: a reference to the elaborately carved chests that were very popular
    in Shakespeare's day.

AUTOLYCUS   I cannot tell, good sir, for which of his virtues it was, but he
              was certainly whipped out of the court.
CLOWN   His vices, you would say; there's no virtue whipped out of
              the court. They cherish it to make it stay there, and
              yet it will no more but abide.
(*The Winter's Tale. Act 4. Scene 3. Scene 2, The Oxford Shakespeare.*)

Well, whiles I am a beggar, I will rail
And say there is no sin but to be rich;
And being rich, my virtue then shall be
To say there is no vice but beggary.
(*King John. Act 2. Scene 1. The Bastard speaking.*)

Dost thou hear, Hal? Thou knowest in the state of innocency Adam fell;
    and what should poor Jack Falstaff do in the days of villany? Thou
    seest I have more flesh than another man; and therefore more frailty.
(*Henry the Fourth. Part One. Act 3. Scene 3. Falstaff speaking.*)

Oh, God! What mischiefs work the wicked ones,
Heaping confusion on their own heads thereby.
(*Henry the Sixth. Part Two. Act 2. Scene 1. The King speaking.*)

Noble madam,
Men's evil manners live in brass; their virtues
We write in water.
(*Henry the Eighth. Act 4. Scene 2. Griffith speaking.*)

> Thus to persist
> In doing wrong extenuates not wrong,
> But makes it much more heavy.
> (*Troilus and Cressida. Act 2. Scene 2. Hector speaking.*)

> Oh, let not virtue seek
> Remuneration for the thing it was;
> For beauty, wit,
> High birth, vigour of bone, desert in service,
> Love, friendship, charity, are subjects all
> To envious and calumniating time.
> (*Troilus and Cressida. Act 3. Scene 3. Ulysses speaking.*)

ROMEO   If I profane with my unworthiest hand
       This holy shrine, the gentle fine is this:
       My lips, two blushing pilgrims, ready stand
       To smooth that rough touch with a tender kiss.

JULIET   Good pilgrim, you do wrong your hand too much,
       Which mannerly devotion shows in this;
       For saints have hands that pilgrims' hands do touch,
       And palm to palm is holy palmers' kiss.

ROMEO   Have not saints lips, and holy palmers too?

JULIET   Ay, pilgrim; lips that they must use in prayer.

ROMEO   Oh then, dear saint, let lips do what hands do:
       They pray, grant thou, lest faith turn to despair.

JULIET   Saints do not move, though grant for prayers' sake.

ROMEO   Then move not, while my prayer's effect I take.
       Thus from my lips, by thine my sin is purged.   (*Kissing her.*)

JULIET   Then have *my* lips the sin that they have took.

ROMEO   Sin from my lips?   Oh, trespass sweetly urged!
       Give me my sin again.

JULIET   You kiss by the book.
(*Romeo and Juliet. Act 1. Scene 5.*)

> For nought so vile that on the earth doth live,
> But to the earth some special good doth give;
> Nor aught so good, but, strained from that fair use,
> Revolts from true birth, stumbling on abuse:
> Virtue itself turns vice, being misapplied,
> And vice sometime's by action dignified.
> (*Romeo and Juliet. Act 2. Scene 3. Friar Laurence speaking.*)

MERCHANT   Oh, 'tis a worthy lord!

JEWELLER   Nay, that's most fixed.

MERCHANT   A most incomparable man, breathed as it were,
       To an untirable and continuate goodness.
(*Timon of Athens. Act 1. Scene 1.*)

Oh, he sits high in all the people's hearts;
And that which would appear offence in us,
His countenance, like richest alchemy,
Will change to virtue and to worthiness.
(*Julius Cæsar.   Act 1.   Scene 3.   Casca speaking.*)

Come, seeling night,
Scarf up the tender eye of pitiful day,
And with thy bloody and invisible hand
Cancel and tear to pieces that great bond
Which keeps me pale! Light thickens, and the crow
Makes wing to the rooky wood:
Good things of day begin to droop and drowse,
Whiles night's black agents to their preys do rouse.
Thou marvell'st at my words.   But hold thee still;
Things bad begun make strong themselves by ill.
(*Macbeth.   Act 3.   Scene 2.   Macbeth speaking.*)

THE QUEEN   What have I done, that thou darest wag thy tongue
                         In noise so rude against me?
HAMLET   Such an act
                         That blurs the grace and blush of modesty,
                         Calls virtue hypocrite, takes off the rose
                         From the fair forehead of an innocent love
                         And sets a blister there.
(*Hamlet.   Act 3.   Scene 4.*)

Rebellious hell,
If thou canst mutine in a matron's bones,
To flaming youth let virtue be as wax
And melt in her own fire!
(*Hamlet.   Act 3.   Scene 4.   Hamlet speaking.*)

Forgive me this my virtue;
For in the fatness of these pursy times
Virtue itself of vice must pardon beg,
Yea, curb and woo for leave to do him good.
(*Hamlet.   Act 3.   Scene 4.   Hamlet speaking.*)

Assume a virtue if you have it not.
That monster, custom, who all sense doth eat,
Of habits devil, is angel yet in this:
That to the use of actions fair and good
He likewise gives a frock or livery,
That aptly is put on.
(*Hamlet.   Act 3.   Scene 4.   Hamlet speaking.*)

Behold yond simpering dame,
Whose face between her forks presages snow,
That minces virtue and does shake the head
To hear of pleasure's name.
(*King Lear. Act 4. Scene 6. Lear speaking.*)

Through tattered clothes small vices do appear;
Robes and furred gowns hide all. Plate sin with gold,
And the strong lance of justice hurtless breaks;
Arm it in rags, a pigmy's straw does pierce it.
(*King Lear. Act 4. Scene 6. Lear speaking.*)

The gods are just, and of our pleasant vices
Make instruments to plague us.
(*King Lear. Act 5. Scene 3. Edgar speaking.*)

And till she come, as truly as to heaven
I do confess the vices of my blood,
So justly to your grave ears I'll present
How I did thrive in this fair lady's love
And she in mine.
(*Othello. Act 1. Scene 3. Othello speaking.*)

You see this fellow that is gone before?
He is a soldier fit to stand by Cæsar
And give direction. And do but see his vice:
'Tis to his virtue a just equinox,
The one as long as the other. 'Tis pity of him.
(*Othello. Act 2. Scene 3. Iago speaking.*)

And then for her
To win the Moor, were't to renounce his baptism,
All seals and symbols of redeemèd sin,
His soul is so enfettered to her love
That she may make, unmake, do what she list.
(*Othello. Act 2. Scene 3. Iago speaking.*)

Divinity of hell!
When devils will the blackest sins put on,
They do suggest at first with heavenly shows;
As I do now.
(*Othello. Act 2. Scene 3. Iago speaking.*)

So will I turn her virtue into pitch;
And out of her own goodness make the net
That shall enmesh them all.
(*Othello. Act 2. Scene 3. Iago speaking.*)

Utter my thoughts?   Why, say they are vile and false;
As where's that palace whereinto foul things
Sometimes intrude not?   Who has a breast so pure,
But some uncleanly apprehensions
Keep leets and law-days, and in session sit
With meditations lawful?
(*Othello.   Act* 3.   *Scene* 3.   *Iago speaking.*)

DESDEMONA   Wouldst thou do such a deed for all the world?
EMILIA   The world's a huge thing: it is a great price for a small vice.
(*Othello.   Act* 4.   *Scene* 3.)

                    I must not think there are
Evils enow to darken all his goodness.
His faults in him seem as the spots of heaven,
More fiery by night's blackness; hereditary
Rather than purchased; what he cannot change
Than what he chooses.
(*Antony and Cleopatra.   Act* 1.   *Scene* 4.   *Lepidus speaking.*)

                    Lord of lords!
Oh, infinite virtue!   Com'st thou smiling from
The world's great snare uncaught?
(*Antony and Cleopatra.   Act* 4.   *Scene* 8.   *Cleopatra speaking.*)

                    The love I bear him
Made me to fan you thus; but the gods made you,
Unlike all others, chaffless.   Pray, your pardon.
(*Cymbeline.   Act* 1.   *Scene* 6.   *Iachimo speaking.*)

See where she comes, apparelled like the Spring;
Graces her subjects, and her thoughts the king
Of every virtue gives renown to men!
(*Pericles.   Act* 1.   *Scene* 1.   *Pericles speaking.*)

                    Great king,
Few love to hear the sins they love to act;
'Twould braid yourself too near for me to tell it.
Who has a book of all that monarchs do,
He's more secure to keep it shut than shown;
For vice repeated is like the wandering wind:
Blows dust in others' eyes to spread itself.
And yet the end of all is bought thus dear:
The breath is gone, and the sore eyes see clear
To stop the air would hurt them.
(*Pericles.   Act* 1.   *Scene* 1.   *Pericles speaking.*)

Kings are earth's gods; in vice their law's their will.
And if Jove stray, who dares say Jove doth ill?
(*Pericles. Act* 1. *Scene* 1. *Pericles speaking.*)

One sin, I know, another doth provoke;
Murder's as near to lust as flame to smoke.
Poison and treason are the hands of sin,
Ay, and the targets, to put off the shame.
(*Pericles. Act* 1. *Scene* 1. *Pericles speaking.*)

Peace! Peace! And give experience tongue.
They do abuse the king that flatter him;
For flattery is the bellows blows up sin.
(*Pericles. Act* 1. *Scene* 2. *Helicanus speaking.*)

No visor does become black villany
So well as soft and tender flattery.
(*Pericles. Act* 4. *Scene* 4. *Gower, as Chorus, speaking.*)

Yet what of thee thy poet doth invent
He robs thee of, and pays it thee again.
He lends thee virtue, and he stole that word
From thy behaviour; beauty doth he give,
And found it in thy cheek. He can afford
No praise to thee but what in thee doth live.
(*Sonnet* 79.)

Oh, what a mansion have those vices got
Which for their habitation chose out thee;
Where beauty's veil doth cover every blot,
And all things turn to fair that eyes can see!
Take heed, dear heart, of this large privilege:
The hardest knife, ill-used, doth lose his edge.
(*Sonnet* 95.)

Section XIV

QUESTIONS AND ANSWERS

What seest thou else
In the dark backward and abysm of time?
(*The Tempest. Act* 1. *Scene* 2. *Prospero speaking.*)

What! Have I 'scaped love-letters in the holiday-time of my beauty, and
am I now a subject for them?
(*The Merry Wives of Windsor. Act* 2. *Scene* 1. *Mistress Page speaking.*)

ISABELLA   I have a brother is condemned to die.
                 I do beseech you, let it be his fault
                 And not my brother.
PROVOST (aside) Heaven give thee moving graces!
ANGELO   Condemn the fault and not the actor of it?
                 Why, every fault's condemned ere it be done:
                 Mine were the very cipher of a function,
                 To fine the faults whose fine stands in record
                 And let go by the actor.
(*Measure For Measure. Act 2. Scene 2.*)

ANTIPHOLUS OF SYRACUSE   Shall I tell you why?
DROMIO OF SYRACUSE   Ay, sir, and wherefore; for they say every
                         why hath a wherefore.
(*The Comedy of Errors. Act 2. Scene 2.*)

BEATRICE   I wonder that you will still be talking, Signior Benedick:
            nobody marks you.
BENEDICK   What, my dear Lady Disdain! Are you yet living?
BEATRICE   Is it possible disdain should die while she hath such meet food
            to feed it as Signior Benedick? Courtesy itself must
            convert to disdain, if you come in her presence.
(*Much Ado About Nothing. Act 1. Scene 1.*)

DON PEDRO   Will you have me, lady?
BEATRICE   No, my lord, unless I might have another for working days:
            your Grace is too costly to wear every day. But I
            beseech your Grace, pardon me: I was born to speak all
            mirth and no matter.
DON PEDRO   Your silence most offends me, and to be merry best becomes
            you; for, out of question, you were born in a merry hour.
BEATRICE   No, sure, my lord, my mother cried; but then there was a
            star danced, and under that was I born.
(*Much Ado About Nothing. Act 2. Scene 1.*)

Shall quips and sentences and these paper bullets of the brain awe a man
    from the career of his humour? No; the world must be peopled.
    When I said I would die a bachelor, I did not think I should live till
    I were married.
(*Much Ado About Nothing. Act 2. Scene 3. Benedick speaking.*)

DON PEDRO   Hath any man seen him at the barber's?
CLAUDIO   No, but the barber's man hath been seen with him; and
            the old ornament of his cheek hath already stuffed
            tennis balls.
(*Much Ado About Nothing. Act 3. Scene 2.*)

DON ARMADO How hast thou purchased this experience?
MOTH   By my penny of observation.
(*Love's Labour's Lost. Act 3. Scene 1.*)

Now, for not looking on a woman's face
You have in that forsworn the use of eyes
And study too, the causer of your vow;
For where is any author in the world
Teaches such beauty as a woman's eye?
(*Love's Labour's Lost. Act 4. Scene 3. Berowne speaking.*)

Why should a man whose blood is warm within
Sit like his grandsire, cut in alabaster;
Sleep when he wakes, and creep into the jaundice
By being peevish?
(*The Merchant of Venice. Act 1. Scene 1. Gratiano speaking.*)

                    Or
Shall I bend low and in a bondman's key,
With bated breath and whispering humbleness,
Say this:
'Fair sir, you spit on me on Wednesday last;
You spurned me such a day; another time
You called me dog; and for these courtesies
I'll lend you thus much moneys.'?
(*The Merchant of Venice. Act 1. Scene 3. Shylock speaking.*

SALARINO   Oh, ten times faster Venus' pigeons fly
           To seal love's bonds new-made, than they are wont
           To keep obligèd faith unforfeited!
GRATIANO   That ever holds: who riseth from a feast
           With that keen appetite that he sits down?
           Where is the horse that doth untread again
           His tedious measures with the unbated fire
           That he did pace them first? All things that are
           Are with more spirit chasèd than enjoyed.
(*The Merchant of Venice. Act 2. Scene 6.*)

Tell me, where is fancy bred,
Or in the heart or in the head?
How begot, how nourishèd?
Reply, reply.
It is engendered in the eyes,
With gazing fed; and fancy dies
In the cradle where it lies.
Let us all ring fancy's knell;
I'll begin it: ding, dong, bell.
(*The Merchant of Venice. Act 3. Scene 2. Song.*)

CELIA   Why, cousin! Why, Rosalind! Cupid have mercy! Not a word?

ROSALIND   Not one to throw at a dog.

CELIA   No, thy words are too precious to be cast away upon curs. Throw some of them at me. Come, lame me with reasons.

(*As You Like It. Act 1. Scene 3.*)

ORLANDO   But forbear, I say: He dies that touches any of this fruit Till I and my affairs are answered.

JAQUES   An you will not be answered with reason, I must die.

BANISHED DUKE What would you have? Your gentleness shall force More than your force move us to gentleness.

(*As You Like It. Act 2. Scene 7.*)

TOUCHSTONE   This is the very false gallop of verses. Why do you infect yourself with them?

ROSALIND   Peace, you dull fool! I found them on a tree.

TOUCHSTONE   Truly, the tree yields bad fruit.

(*As You Like It. Act 3. Scene 2.*)

JAQUES   Rosalind is your love's name?

ORLANDO   Yes, just.

JAQUES   I do not like her name.

ORLANDO   There was no thought of pleasing you when she was christened.

JAQUES   What stature is she of?

ORLANDO   Just as high as my heart.

JAQUES   You are full of pretty answers. Have you not been acquainted with goldsmiths' wives, and conned them out of rings?

(*As You Like It. Act 3. Scene 2.*)

ROSALIND   But come, now I will be your Rosalind in a more coming-on disposition; and ask me what you will, I will grant it.

ORLANDO   Then love me, Rosalind.

ROSALIND   Yes, faith, will I; Fridays and Saturdays and all.

ORLANDO   And wilt thou have me?

ROSALIND   Ay, and twenty such.

ORLANDO   What sayest thou?

ROSALIND   Are you not good?

ORLANDO   I hope so.

ROSALIND   Why then, can one desire too much of a good thing?

(*As You Like It. Act 4. Scene 1.*)

ROSALIND   Now tell me how long you would have her after you have
            possessed her.
ORLANDO   For ever and a day.
ROSALIND   Say 'a day' without the 'ever.'
(*As You Like It. Act 4. Scene 1.*)

TOUCHSTONE Wast born i' the forest here?
WILLIAM   Ay, sir; I thank God.
TOUCHSTONE 'Thank God.' A good answer. Art rich?
WILLIAM   Faith, sir; so so.
TOUCHSTONE 'So so' is good; very good, very excellent good. And
            yet it is not; it is but so so.
(*As You Like It. Act 5. Scene 1.*)

VIOLA   Good madam, let me see your face.
OLIVIA   Have you any commission from your lord to negotiate with my
            face? You are now out of your text; but we will draw the
            curtain and show you the picture. Look you, sir: such a
            one I was this present. Is't not well done? (*Unveiling.*)
VIOLA   Excellently done; if God did all.
(*Twelfth Night. Act 1. Scene 5.*)

OLIVIA   How does he love me?
VIOLA   With adorations, fertile tears,
            With groans that thunder love, with sighs of fire.
                    . . . .
OLIVIA   Why, what would *you*?
VIOLA   Make me a willow cabin at your gate
            And call upon my soul within the house;
            Write loyal cantons of contemnèd love
            And sing them loud, even in the dead of night;
            Halloo your name to the reverberate hills
            And make the babbling gossip of the air
            Cry out 'Olivia!' Oh, you should not rest
            Between the elements of air and earth
            But you should pity me!
(*Twelfth Night. Act 1. Scene 5.*)

MALVOLIO   Is there no respect of place, persons, nor time in you?
SIR TOBY   We did keep time, sir, in our catches. Sneck up!
(*Twelfth Night. Act 2. Scene 3.*)
Sneck up: 'go and be hanged!'

SIR TOBY   Out o' tune, sir: ye lie. Art any more than a steward?
            Dost thou think, because thou art virtuous, there shall
            be no more cakes and ale?

FESTE   Yes, by Saint Anne; and ginger shall be hot i' the mouth, too.
(*Twelfth Night.   Act 2.   Scene 3.*)
Ginger was a favourite spice in Shakespeare's time, being particularly
   popular at christenings.

My kind Antonio,
I can no other answer make but thanks,
And thanks, and ever thanks: and oft good turns
Are shuffled off with such uncurrent pay.
(*Twelfth Night.   Act 3.   Scene 3.   Sebastian speaking.*)

Why do you bend such solemn brows on me?
Think you I bear the shears of destiny?
Have I commandment on the pulse of life?
(*King John.   Act 4.   Scene 2.   The King speaking.*)

Oh, who can hold a fire in his hand
By thinking on the frosty Caucasus?
Or cloy the hungry edge of appetite
By bare imagination of a feast?
Or wallow naked in December snow
By thinking on fantastic Summer's heat?
Oh, no!   The apprehension of the good
Gives but the greater feeling to the worse.
(*Richard the Second.   Act 1.   Scene 3.   Bolingbroke speaking.*)

FALSTAFF   What manner of man is he?
HOSTESS   An old man.
FALSTAFF   What doth gravity out of his bed at midnight?
(*Henry the Fourth.   Part One.   Act 2.   Scene 4.*)

FALSTAFF   What wind blew you hither, Pistol?
PISTOL   Not the ill wind which blows no man to good.
(*Henry the Fourth.   Part Two.   Act 5.   Scene 3.*)

NYM   You'll pay me the eight shillings I won of you at betting?
PISTOL   Base is the slave that pays.
(*Henry the Fifth.   Act 2.   Scene 1.*)

Are these your herd?
Must these have voices, that can yield them now
And straight disclaim their tongues?   What are your offices?
You being their mouths, why rule you not their teeth?
Have you not set them on?
(*Coriolanus.   Act 3.   Scene 1.   Coriolanus speaking.*)

SICINIUS   It is a mind
That shall remain a poison where it is,
Not poison any further.
CORIOLANUS   Shall remain.
Hear you this Triton of the minnows?   Mark you
His absolute 'shall'?
(*Coriolanus.   Act 3.   Scene 1.   Coriolanus speaking.*)

But, soft!   What light through yonder window breaks?
It is the East, and Juliet is the sun!
Arise, fair sun, and kill the envious moon;
Who is already sick and pale with grief
That thou, her maid, are far more fair than she.
(*Romeo and Juliet.   Act 2.   Scene 2.   Romeo speaking.*)

Oh, serpent heart, hid with a flowering face!
Did ever dragon keep so fair a cave?
                    .   .   .   .
Was ever book containing such vile matter
So fairly bound?   Oh, that deceit should dwell
In such a gorgeous palace!
(*Romeo and Juliet.   Act 3.   Scene 2.   Juliet speaking.*)

CÆSAR   Who is it in the press that calls on me?
I hear a tongue, shriller than all the music,
Cry 'Cæsar!'   Speak;. Cæsar is turned to hear.
SOOTHSAYER   Beware the Ides of March.
(*Julius Cæsar.   Act 1.   Scene 2.*)

CALPURNIA   Oh, Cæsar!   These things are beyond all use,
And I do fear them.
CÆSAR   What can be avoided
Whose end is purposed by the mighty gods?
(*Julius Cæsar.   Act 2.   Scene 2.*)

FIRST WITCH   When shall we three meet again?
In thunder, lightning, or in rain?
SECOND WITCH When the hurlyburly's done,
When the battle's lost and won.
(*Macbeth.   Act 1.   Scene 1.*)

Is this a dagger which I see before me,
The handle toward my hand?   Come, let me clutch thee.
I have thee not, and yet I see thee still.
Art thou not, fatal vision, sensible
To feeling as to sight?   Or art thou but
A dagger of the mind, a false creation,
Proceeding from the heat-oppressèd brain?
(*Macbeth.   Act 2.   Scene 1.   Macbeth speaking.*)

But wherefore could not I pronounce 'Amen'?
I had most need of blessing, and 'Amen'
Stuck in my throat.
(*Macbeth. Act 2. Scene 2. Macbeth speaking.*)

How is't with me, when every noise appals me?
What hands are here?   Ha!   They pluck out mine eyes!
Will all great Neptune's ocean wash this blood
Clean from my hand?   No; this my hand will rather
The multitudinous seas incarnadine,
Making the green one red.
(*Macbeth. Act 2. Scene 2. Macbeth speaking.*)
Making the green one red: making the green (seas) completely red.

               Can such things be,
And overcome us like a Summer's cloud,
Without our special wonder?   You make me strange
Even to the disposition that I owe,
When now I think you can behold such sights,
And keep the natural ruby of your cheeks
When mine is blanched with fear.
(*Macbeth. Act 3. Scene 4. Macbeth speaking.*)
Owe: own.

MACBETH   What is the night?
LADY MACBETH   Almost at odds with morning, which is which.
(*Macbeth. Act 3. Scene 4.*)

MACBETH   How now, you secret, black, and midnight hags!
            What is't you do?
WITCHES   A deed without a name.
(*Macbeth. Act 4. Scene 1.*)

Good now, sit down, and tell me, he that knows,
Why this same strict and most observant watch
So nightly toils the subject of the land;
And why such daily cast of brazen cannon,
And foreign mart for implements of war;
Why such impress of shipwrights, whose sore task
Does not divide the Sunday from the week?
What might be toward, that this sweaty haste
Doth make the night joint-labourer with the day?
Who is't that can inform me?
(*Hamlet. Act 1. Scene 1. Marcellus speaking.*)

Heaven and earth!
Must I remember? Why, she would hang on him
As if increase of appetite had grown
By what it fed on; and yet, within a month . . .
Let me not think on't! . . . Frailty, thy name is woman!
(*Hamlet. Act* 1. *Scene* 2. *Hamlet speaking.*)

HAMLET   My father! Methinks I see my father.
HORATIO   Oh, where, my lord?
HAMLET   In my mind's eye, Horatio.
(*Hamlet. Act* 1. *Scene* 2.)

HAMLET   What, looked he frowningly?
HORATIO   A countenance more in sorrow than in anger.
(*Hamlet. Act* 1. *Scene* 2.)

HORATIO   Is it a custom?
HAMLET   Ay, marry, is't!
But to my mind, though I am native here
And to the manner born, it is a custom
More honoured in the breach than the observance.
(*Hamlet. Act* 1. *Scene* 4.)

Why, what should be the fear?
I do not set my life at a pin's fee;
And for my soul, what can it do to that,
Being a thing immortal as itself?
(*Hamlet. Act* 1. *Scene* 4. *Hamlet speaking.*)

POLONIUS   What do you read, my lord?
·HAMLET   Words, words, words.
(*Hamlet. Act* 2. *Scene* 2.)

To be, or not to be: that is the question:
Whether 'tis nobler in the mind to suffer
The slings and arrows of outrageous fortune,
Or to take arms against a sea of troubles
And, by opposing, end them.
(*Hamlet. Act* 3. *Scene* 1. *Hamlet speaking.*)

HAMLET   Madam, how like you this play?
QUEEN   The lady doth protest too much, methinks.
HAMLET   Oh, but *she'll* keep her word.
(*Hamlet. Act* 3. *Scene* 2.)

HAMLET   Has this fellow no feeling of his business, that he sings at
          grave-making?
HORATIO   Custom hath made it in him a property of easiness.
HAMLET   'Tis e'en so: the hand of little employment hath the daintier
          sense.
(*Hamlet.*   *Act 5.*   *Scene 1.*)

LEAR   Now, our joy,
        Although the last, not least, to whose young love
        The vines of France and milk of Burgundy
        Strive to be interess'd, what can you say to draw
        A third more opulent than your sisters?   Speak.
CORDELIA Nothing, my lord.
LEAR   Nothing!
CORDELIA Nothing.
LEAR   Nothing will come of nothing: speak again.
(*King Lear.*   *Act 1.*   *Scene 1.*)

DESDEMONA What wouldst thou write of me, if thou shouldst praise me?
IAGO   Oh, gentle lady, do not put me to't,
        For I am nothing if not critical.
(*Othello.*   *Act 2.*   *Scene 1.*)

IAGO   She that could think and ne'er disclose her mind,
        See suitors following and not look behind;
        She was a wight, if ever such wight were. . . .
DESDEMONA To do what?
IAGO   To suckle fools and chronicle small beer.
(*Othello.*   *Act 2.*   *Scene 1.*)
Wight: a person, either male or female.

DESDEMONA   Mine eyes do itch.
        Doth that bode weeping?
EMILIA   'Tis neither here nor there.
(*Othello.*   *Act 4.*   *Scene 3.*)

Section XV

COURAGE AND COWARDICE

CALIBAN   I'll not serve him; he is not valiant.
TRINCULO   Thou liest, most ignorant monster: I am in case to justle a
        constable. Why, thou deboshed fish, thou, was there
        ever man a coward that hath drunk so much sack as
        I to-day?
(*The Tempest.*   *Act 3.*   *Scene 2.*)

ISABELLA My power? Alas, I doubt. . . .
LUCIO   Our doubts are traitors,
      And make us lose the good we oft might win
      By fearing to attempt.
(*Measure For Measure. Act* 1. *Scene* 4.)

How many cowards, whose hearts are all as false
As stairs of sand, wear yet upon their chins
The beards of Hercules and frowning Mars;
Who, inward searched, have livers white as milk?
(*The Merchant of Venice. Act* 3. *Scene* 2. *Bassanio speaking.*)

             Were it not better,
Because that I am more than common tall,
That I did suit me all points like a man?
A gallant curtle-axe upon my thigh,
A boar-spear in my hand; and . . . in my heart
Lie there what hidden woman's fear there will . . .
We'll have a swashing and a martial outside,
As many other mannish cowards have
That do outface it with their semblances.
(*As You Like It. Act* 1. *Scene* 3. *Rosalind speaking.*)

SIR ANDREW An't be any way, it must be with valour; for policy I hate.
      I had as lief be a Brownist as a politician.
SIR TOBY Why, then, build me thy fortunes upon the basis of valour.
      Challenge me the count's youth to fight with him;
      hurt him in eleven places. My niece shall take note
      of it; and assure thyself, there is no love-broker in the
      world can more prevail in man's commendation with
      woman than report of valour.
(*Twelfth Night. Act* 3. *Scene* 2.)

KING PHILIP How much unlooked for is this expedition!
AUSTRIA By how much unexpected, by so much
      We must awake endeavour for defence;
      For courage mounteth with occasion.
(*King John. Act* 2. *Scene* 1.)

I call thee coward! I'll see thee damned ere I call thee coward; but I
      would give a thousand pound I could run as fast as thou canst.
(*Henry the Fourth. Part One. Act* 2. *Scene* 4. *Falstaff speaking.*)

Why, thou knowest I am as valiant as Hercules. But beware instinct: the
      lion will not touch the true prince. Instinct is a great matter; I was
      a coward on instinct.
(*Henry the Fourth. Part One. Act* 2. *Scene* 4. *Falstaff speaking.*)

The better part of valour is discretion; in the which better part I have saved my life.
(*Henry the Fourth. Part One. Act 5. Scene 4. Falstaff speaking.*)

For Pistol, he hath a killing tongue and a quiet sword; by the means whereof a' breaks words and keeps whole weapons. For Nym, he hath heard that men of few words are the best men; and therefore he scorns to say his prayers, lest a' should be thought a coward.
(*Henry the Fifth. Act 3. Scene 2. The Boy speaking.*)

Oh, coward conscience, how dost thou afflict me!
The lights burn blue. It is now dead midnight.
Cold fearful drops stand on my trembling flesh.
What do I fear? Myself? There's none else by.
(*Richard the Third. Act 5. Scene 3. Richard speaking.*)

The deeds of Coriolanus
Should not be uttered feebly. It is held
That valour is the chiefest virtue and
Most dignifies the haver. If it be,
The man I speak of cannot in the world
Be singly counterpoised.
(*Coriolanus. Act 2. Scene 2. Cominius speaking.*)

He's truly valiant that can wisely suffer
The worst that man can breathe; and make his wrongs
His outsides, to wear them like his raiment, carelessly,
And ne'er prefer his injuries to his heart
To bring it into danger.
(*Timon of Athens. Act 3. Scene 5. First Senator speaking.*)

Cowards die many times before their deaths;
The valiant never taste of death but once.
(*Julius Cæsar. Act 2. Scene 2. Cæsar speaking.*)

The gods do this in shame of cowardice:
Cæsar should be a beast without a heart
If he should stay at home to-day for fear.
No, Cæsar shall not: danger knows full well
That Cæsar is more dangerous than he.
We are two lions littered in one day,
And I the elder and more terrible;
And Cæsar shall go forth.
(*Julius Cæsar. Act 2. Scene 2. Cæsar speaking.*)

LADY MACBETH   Art thou afeard
To be the same in thine own act and valour
As thou art in desire?   Wouldst thou have that
Which thou esteem'st the ornament of life
And live a coward in thine own esteem,
Letting 'I dare not' wait upon 'I would,'
Like the poor cat i' the adage?

MACBETH   Prithee, peace!
I dare do all that may become a man;
Who dares do more is none.

(Macbeth.   Act 1.   *Scene* 7.)
Like the poor cat i' the adage: 'The cat would eat fyshe, and would not wet
her feete.'   (Heywood's 'Proverbs.')

MACBETH   If we should fail?
LADY MACBETH   We fail!
But screw your courage to the sticking-place
And we'll not fail.

(Macbeth.   Act 1.   *Scene* 7.)

ROSS   You must have patience, madam.
LADY MACDUFF   He had none.
His flight was madness: when our actions do not,
Our fears do make us traitors.

(Macbeth.   Act 4.   *Scene* 2.)

I have almost forgot the taste of fears.
The time has been my senses would have cooled
To hear a night-shriek, and my fell of hair
Would at a dismal treatise rouse and stir
As life were in't.   I have supped full with horrors:
Direness, familiar to my slaughterous thoughts,
Cannot once start me.
(Macbeth.   Act 5.   *Scene* 5.   *Macbeth speaking.*)
Fell: scalp.

Am I a coward?
Who calls me villain?   Breaks my pate across?
Plucks off my beard and blows it in my face?
Tweaks me by the nose?   Gives me the lie *i'* the throat
As deep as to the lungs?   Who does me this?
Ha!
'Swounds, I should take it: for it cannot be
But I am pigeon-livered and lack gall
To make oppression bitter, or ere this
I should have fatted all the region kites
With this slave's offal.
(Hamlet.   Act 2.   *Scene* 2.   *Hamlet speaking.*)

Thus conscience does make cowards of us all,
And thus the native hue of resolution
Is sicklied o'er with the pale cast of thought;
And enterprises of great pitch and moment
With this regard their currents turn awry
And lose the name of action.
(*Hamlet. Act 3. Scene 1. Hamlet speaking.*)

Section XVI

LOVE   AND   FRIENDSHIP

MIRANDA   My husband, then?
FERDINAND   Ay, with a heart as willing
                      As bondage e'er of freedom: here's my hand.
MIRANDA   And mine, with my heart in't.
(*The Tempest. Act 3. Scene 1.*)

VALENTINE   Love is your master, for he masters you;
                      And he that is so yoked by a fool,
                      Methinks should not be chronicled for wise.
PROTEUS   Yet writers say, as in the sweetest bud
                      The eating canker dwells, so eating love
                      Inhabits in the finest wits of all.
VALENTINE   And writers say, as the most forward bud
                      Is eaten by the canker ere it blow,
                      Even so by love the young and tender wit
                      Is turned to folly; blasting in the bud,
                      Losing his verdure even in the prime,
                      And all the fair effects of future hopes.
(*The Two Gentlemen of Verona. Act 1. Scene 1.*)

Oh, how this Spring of love resembleth
The uncertain glory of an April day,
Which now shows all the beauty of the sun
And by and by a cloud takes all away!
(*The Two Gentlemen of Verona. Act 1. Scene 3. Proteus speaking.*)

VALENTINE   Why, lady, Love hath twenty pairs of eyes.
THURIO   They say that Love hath not an eye at all.
VALENTINE   To see such lovers, Thurio, as yourself:
                      Upon a homely object Love can wink.
(*The Two Gentlemen of Verona. Act 2. Scene 4.*)

Oh, gentle Proteus! Love's a mighty lord,
And hath so humbled me as I confess
There is no woe to his correction,
Nor to his service no such joy on earth.
Now no discourse, except it be of love.
Now can I break my fast, dine, sup and sleep
Upon the very naked name of love.
(*The Two Gentlemen of Verona. Act 2. Scene 4. Valentine speaking.*)

Why, man, she is mine own,
And I as rich in having such a jewel
As twenty seas, if all their sand were pearl,
The water nectar and the rocks pure gold.
(*The Two Gentlemen of Verona. Act 2. Scene 4. Valentine speaking.*)

Oh, know'st thou not his looks are my soul's food?
Pity the dearth that I have pinèd in,
By longing for that food so long a time.
Didst thou but know the inly touch of love,
Thou wouldst as soon go kindle fire with snow
As seek to quench the fire of love with words.
(*The Two Gentlemen of Verona. Act 2. Scene 7. Julia speaking.*)

But whatsoever I have merited, either in my mind or in my means, meed,
I am sure, I have received none; unless experience be a jewel that I
have purchased at an infinite rate, and that hath taught me to say this:
'Love like a shadow flies when substance love pursues:
Pursuing that that flies, and flying what pursues.'
(*The Merry Wives of Windsor. Act 2. Scene 2. Ford speaking.*)

FALSTAFF Of what quality was your love, then?
FORD Like a fair house built on another man's ground; so that I have
lost my edifice by mistaking the place where I erected it.
(*The Merry Wives of Windsor. Act 2. Scene 2.*)

Friendship is constant in all other things
Save in the office and affairs of love.
Therefore all hearts in love use their own tongues.
Let every eye negotiate for itself
And trust no agent; for beauty is a witch,
Against whose charms faith melteth into blood.
(*Much Ado About Nothing. Act 2. Scene 1. Claudio speaking.*)

I do much wonder that one man, seeing how much another man is a fool
when he dedicates his behaviours to love, will, after he hath laughed
at such shallow follies in others, become the argument of his own
scorn by falling in love.
(*Much Ado About Nothing. Act 2. Scene 3. Benedick speaking.*)

If it prove so, then loving goes by haps:
Some Cupid kills with arrows, some with traps.
(*Much Ado About Nothing. Act 3. Scene 1. Hero speaking.*)

BEATRICE   You have stayed me in a happy hour: I was about to protest
            I loved you.
BENEDICK   And do it, with all thy heart!
BEATRICE   I love you with so much of my heart that none is left to
            protest.
(*Much Ado About Nothing. Act 4. Scene 1.*)

And I, forsooth, in love! I, that have been love's whip;
A very beadle to a humorous sigh;
A critic, nay, a night-watch constable;
A domineering pedant o'er the boy,
Than whom no mortal so magnificent:
This whimpled, whining, purblind, wayward boy,
This senior-junior, giant-dwarf, Dan Cupid!
(*Love's Labour's Lost. Act 3. Scene 1. Berowne speaking.*)

On a day . . . alack the day! . . .
Love, whose month is ever May,
Spied a blossom passing fair
Playing in the wanton air;
Through the velvet leaves, the wind,
All unseen 'gan passage find,
That the lover, sick to death,
Wished himself the heaven's breath.
(*Love's Labour's Lost. Act 4. Scene 3. Dumaine speaking.*)

But love, first learnèd in a lady's eyes,
Lives not alone immurèd in the brain;
But, with the motion of all elements,
Courses as swift as thought in every power
And gives to every power a double power
Above their functions and their offices.
It adds a precious seeing to the eye;
A lover's eyes will gaze an eagle blind;
A lover's ear will hear the lowest sound
When the suspicious head of theft is stopped:
Love's feeling is more soft and sensible
Than are the tender horns of cockled snails.
(*Love's Labour's Lost. Act 4. Scene 3. Berowne speaking.*)

Ay me! For aught that ever I could read,
Could ever hear by tale or history,
The course of true love never did run smooth.
(*A Midsummer-Night's Dream. Act 1. Scene 1. Lysander speaking.*)

Things base and vile, holding no quantity,
Love can transpose to form and dignity.
Love looks not with the eyes, but with the mind;
And therefore is winged Cupid painted blind.
Nor hath Love's mind of any judgment taste.
Wings and no eyes figure unheedy haste;
And therefore Love is said to be a child,
Because in choice he is so oft beguiled.
(*A Midsummer-Night's Dream.   Act 1.   Scene 1.   Helena speaking.*)

You draw me, you hard-hearted adamant;
But yet you draw not iron, for my heart
Is true as steel: leave you your power to draw,
And I shall have no power to follow you.
(*A Midsummer-Night's Dream.   Act 2.   Scene 1.   Helena speaking.*)

Oh, take the sense, sweet, of my innocence:
Love takes the meaning in love's conference.
I mean that my heart unto yours is knit,
So that but one heart we can make of it.
Two bosoms interchainèd with an oath;
So then two bosoms and a single troth.
(*A Midsummer-Night's Dream.   Act 2.   Scene 2.   Lysander speaking.*)

Things growing are not ripe until their season:
So I, being young, till now ripe not to reason.
And touching now the point of human skill,
Reason becomes the marshal to my will
And leads me to your eyes; where I o'erlook
Love's stories written in love's richest book.
(*A Midsummer-Night's Dream.   Act 2.   Scene 2.   Lysander speaking.*)

                    Oh, is it all forgot?
All school-days' friendship, childhood innocence?
We, Hermia, like two artificial gods,
Have with our needles created both one flower,
Both on one sampler, sitting on one cushion,
Both warbling of one song, both in one key;
As if our hands, our sides, voices and minds
Had been incorporate.   So we grew together,
Like to a double cherry, seeming parted,
But yet an union in partition:
Two lovely berries moulded on one stem.
(*A Midsummer-Night's Dream.   Act 3.   Scene 2.   Helena speaking.*)

Lovers and madmen have such seething brains,
Such shaping fantasies that apprehend
More than cool reason ever comprehends.
(*A Midsummer-Night's Dream. Act 5. Scene 1. Theseus speaking.*)

This passion, and the death of a dear friend, would go near to make a man
    look sad.
(*A Midsummer-Night's Dream. Act 5. Scene 1. Theseus speaking.*)

I am as like to call thee so again,
To spit on thee again, to spurn thee too.
If thou wilt lend this money, lend it not
As to thy friends . . . for when did friendship take
A breed for barren metal of his friend! . . .
But lend it rather to thine enemy;
Who, if he break, thou mayest with better face
Exact the penalty.
(*The Merchant of Venice. Act 1. Scene 3. Antonio speaking.*)

I am glad 'tis night, you do not look on me,
For I am much ashamed of my exchange.
But love is blind, and lovers cannot see
The pretty follies that themselves commit;
For if they could, Cupid himself would blush
To see me thus transformèd to a boy!
(*The Merchant of Venice. Act 2. Scene 6. Jessica speaking.*)

PORTIA   Is it your dear friend that is thus in trouble?
BASSANIO   The dearest friend to me, the kindest man,
            The best-conditioned and unwearied spirit
            In doing courtesies; and one in whom
            The ancient Roman honour more appears
            Than any that draws breath in Italy.
(*The Merchant of Venice. Act 3. Scene 2.*)

I never did repent for doing good,
Nor shall not now: for in companions
That do converse and waste the time together,
Whose souls do bear an equal yoke of love,
There must be needs a like proportion
Of lineaments, of manners and of spirit;
Which makes me think that this Antonio,
Being the bosom lover of my lord,
Must needs be like my lord.
(*The Merchant of Venice. Act 3. Scene 4. Portia speaking.*)

Commend me to your honourable wife.
Tell her the process of Antonio's end;
Say how I loved you, speak me fair in death,
And, when the tale is told, bid her be judge
Whether Bassanio had not once a love.
(*The Merchant of Venice. Act 4. Scene 1. Antonio speaking.*)

I was too young that time to value her;
But now I know her. If she be a traitor,
Why so am I! We still have slept together,
Rose at an instant, learned, played, ate together;
And wheresoe'er we went, like Juno's swans
Still we went coupled and inseparable.
(*As You Like It. Act 1. Scene 3. Celia speaking.*)

Oh, thou didst then ne'er love so heartily!
If thou rememberest not the slightest folly
That ever love did make thee run into,
Thou hast not loved.
Or if thou hast not sat as I do now,
Wearing thy hearer in thy mistress' praise,
Thou hast not loved.
Or if thou hast not broke from company
Abruptly, as my passion now makes me,
Thou hast not loved.
(*As You Like It. Act 2. Scene 4. Silvius speaking.*)
Wearing: wearying.

We that are true lovers run into strange capers; but as all is mortal in
    nature, so is all nature in love mortal in folly.
(*As You Like It. Act 2. Scene 4. Touchstone speaking.*)

ROSALIND   But are you so much in love as your rhymes speak?
ORLANDO   Neither rhyme nor reason can express how much.
ROSALIND   Love is merely a madness; and, I tell you, deserves as well a
            dark house and a whip as madmen do. And the reason
            why they are not so punished and cured is that the lunacy
            is so ordinary that the whippers are in love too.
(*As You Like It. Act 3. Scene 2.*)

ROSALIND   Well, in her person, I say I will not have you.
ORLANDO   Then, in mine own person, I die.
ROSALIND   No, faith, die by attorney. The poor world is almost six
            thousand years old, and in all this time there was not
            any man died in his own person, videlicet, in a love-
            cause. . . . Men have died from time to time and
            worms have eaten them, but not for love.
(*As You Like It. Act 4. Scene 1.*)

It was a lover and his lass,
With a hey, and a ho, and a hey nonino,
That o'er the green corn-field did pass
In the Spring time, the only pretty ring time,
When birds do sing, hey ding a ding, ding:
Sweet lovers love the Spring.
(*As You Like It. Act 5. Scene 3. Song.*)

My friends were poor but honest; so's my love.
(*All's Well That Ends Well. Act 1. Scene 3. Helena speaking.*)

Oh, mistress mine, where are you roaming?
Oh, stay and hear; your true love's coming,
That can sing both high and low.
Trip no further, pretty sweeting:
Journeys end in lovers meeting,
Every wise man's son doth know.
(*Twelfth Night. Act 2. Scene 3. Feste singing.*)

ORSINO   Come hither, boy. If ever thou shalt love,
           In the sweet pangs of it remember me;
           For such as I am all true lovers are,
           Unstaid and skittish in all motions else
           Save in the constant image of the creature
           That is beloved. How dost thou like this tune?
VIOLA   It gives a very echo to the seat
           Where love is throned.
(*Twelfth Night. Act 2. Scene 4.*)

ORSINO   And what's her history?
VIOLA   A blank, my lord. She never told her love;
           But let concealment, like a worm i' the bud,
           Feed on her damask cheek. She pined in thought;
           And with a green and yellow melancholy
           She sat like patience on a monument,
           Smiling at grief. Was not this love indeed?
(*Twelfth Night. Act 2. Scene 4.*)

Do not extort thy reasons from this clause,
For that I woo thou therefore hast no cause;
But rather reason thus with reason fetter:
Love sought is good, but given unsought is better.
(*Twelfth Night. Act 3. Scene 1. Olivia speaking.*)

> Besides, you know,
> Prosperity's the very bond of love,
> Whose fresh complexion and whose heart together
> Affliction alters.
>
> (*The Winter's Tale. Act* 4. *Scene* 3. *Act* 4. *Scene* 4 . . . *Temple
> Shakespeare. Camillo speaking.*)

RICHARD   Terrible hell make war
>   Upon their spotted souls for this offence!
SCROOP   Sweet love, I see, changing his property,
>   Turns to the sourest and most deadly hate.
>
> (*Richard the Second. Act* 3. *Scene* 2.)

> I do not care: I'll give thrice so much land
> To any well-deserving friend;
> But in the way of bargain, mark you me,
> I'll cavil on the ninth part of a hair.
>
> (*Henry the Fourth. Part One. Act* 3. *Scene* 1. *Hotspur speaking.*)

> Yet the first bringer of unwelcome news
> Hath but a losing office, and his tongue
> Sounds ever after as a sullen bell
> Remembered knolling a departed friend.
>
> (*Henry the Fourth. Part Two. Act* 1. *Scene* 1. *Northumberland speaking.*)

> So did he turn, and over Suffolk's neck
> He threw his wounded arm and kissed his lips;
> And so, espoused to death, with blood he sealed
> A testament of noble-ending love.
>
> (*Henry the Fifth. Act* 4. *Scene* 6. *Exeter speaking.*)

>   Not a man in England
> Can advise me like you: be to yourself
> As you would to your friend.
>
> (*Henry the Eighth. Act* 1. *Scene* 1. *Norfolk speaking.*)

> Where you are liberal of your loves and counsels,
> Be sure you be not loose; for those you make friends
> And give your hearts to, when they once perceive
> The least rub in your fortunes, fall away
> Like water from ye, never found again
> But where they mean to sink ye.
>
> (*Henry the Eighth. Act* 2. *Scene* 1. *Buckingham speaking.*)

> They say all lovers swear more performance than they are able and yet
> reserve an ability that they never perform, vowing more than the
> perfection of ten and discharging less than the tenth part of one.
>
> (*Troilus and Cressida. Act* 3. *Scene* 2. *Cressida speaking.*)

Oh, world, thy slippery turns! Friends now fast sworn,
Whose double bosoms seem to wear one heart,
Whose hours, whose bed, whose meal and exercise
Are still together, who twin as 'twere in love
Unseparable, shall within this hour,
On a dissension of a doit, break out
To bitterest enmity.
(*Coriolanus. Act 4. Scene 4. Coriolanus speaking.*)

Love is a smoke, raised with the fume of sighs;
Being purged, a fire sparkling in lovers' eyes;
Being vexed, a sea nourished with lovers' tears.
What is it else? A madness most discreet,
A choking gall and a preserving sweet.
(*Romeo and Juliet. Act 1. Scene 1. Romeo speaking.*)

Speak to my gossip Venus one fair word,
One nick-name for her purblind son and heir,
Young Adam Cupid; he that shot so trim
When King Cophetua loved the beggar-maid!
(*Romeo and Juliet. Act 2. Scene 1. Mercutio speaking.*)

JULIET   By whose direction found'st thou out this place?
ROMEO   By love, that first did prompt me to inquire;
          He lent me counsel and I lent him eyes.
          I am no pilot; yet, wert thou as far
          As that vast shore washed with the farthest sea,
          I would adventure for such merchandise.
(*Romeo and Juliet. Act 2. Scene 2.*)

                    Sweet, good night!
This bud of love, by Summer's ripening breath,
May prove a beauteous flower when next we meet.
Good night, good night! As sweet repose and rest
Come to thy heart as that within my breast!
(*Romeo and Juliet. Act 2. Scene 2. Juliet speaking.*)

My bounty is as boundless as the sea,
My love as deep; the more I give to thee
The more I have, for both are infinite.
(*Romeo and Juliet. Act 2. Scene 2. Juliet speaking.*)

Love goes toward love, as schoolboys from their books;
But love from love, toward school, with heavy looks.
(*Romeo and Juliet. Act 2. Scene 2. Romeo speaking.*)

Oh, I have bought the mansion of a love,
But not possessed it; and, though I am sold,
Not yet enjoyed.   So tedious is this day,
As is the night before some festival
To an impatient child that hath new robes
And may not wear them.
(*Romeo and Juliet.   Act 3.   Scene 2.   Juliet speaking.*)

Nay, my lords, ceremony was but devised at first
To set a gloss on faint deeds, hollow welcomes;
Recanting goodness, sorry ere 'tis shown.
But where there is true friendship, there needs none.
(*Timon of Athens.   Act 1.   Scene 2.   Timon speaking.*)

> Thou hast described
A hot friend cooling: ever note, Lucilius;
When love begins to sicken and decay,
It useth an enforcèd ceremony.
(*Julius Cæsar.   Act 4.   Scene 2.   Brutus speaking.*)

> Brutus hath rived my heart:
A friend should bear his friend's infirmities,
But Brutus makes mine greater than they are.
(*Julius Cæsar.   Act 4.   Scene 3.   Cassius speaking.*)

This is the very ecstasy of love;
Whose violent property fordoes itself,
And leads the will to desperate undertakings
As oft as any passion under heaven
That does afflict our natures.
(*Hamlet.   Act 2.   Scene 1.   Polonius speaking.*)

Since my dear soul was mistress of her choice
And could of men distinguish, her election
Hath sealed thee for herself: for thou hast been
As one, in suffering all, that suffers nothing;
A man that fortune's buffets and rewards
Hast ta'en with equal thanks.   And blessed are those
Whose blood and judgment are so well commingled
That they are not a pipe for fortune's finger
To sound what stop she please.   Give me that man
That is not passion's slave, and I will wear him
In my heart's core, ay, in my heart of heart,
As I do thee.
(*Hamlet.   Act 3.   Scene 2.   Hamlet speaking.*)

Love's not love
When it is mingled with regards that stand
Aloof from the entire point.
(*King Lear.   Act* 1.   *Scene* 1.   *The King of France speaking.*)

I will a round unvarnished tale deliver
Of my whole course of love; what drugs, what charms,
What conjuration and what mighty magic . . .
For such proceeding I am charged withal . . .
I won his daughter.
(*Othello.   Act* 1.   *Scene* 3.   *Othello speaking.*)

She loved me for the dangers I had passed,
And I loved her that she did pity them:
This only is the witchcraft I have used.
(*Othello.   Act* 1.   *Scene* 3.   *Othello speaking.*)

Excellent wretch!   Perdition catch my soul,
But I do love thee!   And when I love thee not,
Chaos is come again.
(*Othello.   Act* 3.   *Scene* 3.   *Othello speaking.*)

I had rather be a toad
And live upon the vapour of a dungeon,
Than keep a corner in the thing I love
For others' uses.
(*Othello.   Act* 3.   *Scene* 3.   *Othello speaking.*)

Thou dost conspire against thy friend, Iago,
If thou but think'st him wronged and makest his ear
A stranger to thy thoughts.
(*Othello.   Act* 3.   *Scene* 3.   *Othello speaking.*)

CLEOPATRA   If it be love indeed, tell me how much.
ANTONY   There's beggary in the love that can be reckoned.
(*Antony and Cleopatra.   Act* 1.   *Scene* 1.)

Love is not love
Which alters when it alteration finds,
Or bends with the remover to remove.
Oh, no!   It is an ever-fixèd mark
That looks on tempests and is never shaken.
It is the star to every wandering bark,
Whose worth's unknown although his height be taken.
Love's not Time's fool, though rosy lips and cheeks
Within his bending sickle's compass come;
Love alters not with his brief hours and weeks,
But bears it out even to the edge of doom.
(*Sonnet* 116.)

HOUSEHOLD ITEMS

SPEED   Item; she can spin.
LAUNCE   Then may I set the world on wheels, when she can spin for
         her living.
(*The Two Gentlemen of Verona. Act 3. Scene 1.*)

There's his chamber, his house, his castle, his standing-bed and truckle-bed:
     'tis painted about with the story of the Prodigal, fresh and new.
(*The Merry Wives of Windsor. Act 4. Scene 5. Host speaking, referring
to Falstaff.*)

We, Hermia, like two artificial gods,
Have with our neelds created both one flower,
Both on one sampler, sitting on one cushion.
(*A Midsummer-Night's Dream. Act 3. Scene 2. Helena speaking.*)
Neelds: needles.

. . . as wine comes out of a narrow-mouthed bottle, either too much at
     once or none at all.
(*As You Like It. Act 3. Scene 2. Rosalind speaking.*)

                  I see no more in you
Than without candle may go dark to bed.
(*As You Like It. Act 3. Scene 5. Rosalind speaking.*)

'Tis not her glass, but you that flatters her.
(*As You Like It. Act 3. Scene 5. Rosalind speaking.*)

Make the doors upon a woman's wit and it will out at the casement; shut
     that, and 'twill out at the key-hole; stop that, 'twill fly with the smoke
     out at the chimney.
(*As You Like It. Act 4. Scene 1. Rosalind speaking.*)

First, as you know, my house within the city
Is richly furnished with plate and gold;
Basins and ewers to lave her dainty hands;
My hangings all of Tyrian tapestry;
In ivory coffers I have stuffed my crowns;
In cypress chests my arras counterpoints,
Costly apparel, tents, and canopies,
Fine linen, Turkey cushions bossed with pearl,

Valance of Venice gold in needlework,
Pewter and brass and all things that belong
To house or house-keeping.
(*The Taming of the Shrew. Act 2. Scene 1. Gremio speaking.*)
Arras counterpoints: tapestry counterpanes.
Tents and canopies: bed hangings.

Where's the cook? Is supper ready, the house trimmed, rushes strewed, cobwebs swept; the serving-men in their new fustian, their white stockings, and every officer his wedding-garment on? Be the jacks fair within, the jills fair without, the carpets laid and everything in order?
(*The Taming of the Shrew. Act 4. Scene 1. Grumio speaking.*)
Jacks: leather drinking-vessels. Also men-servants.
Jills: metal drinking-vessels. Also maid-servants. A play upon words.

And be it moon or sun or what you please:
An if you please to call it a rush-candle,
Henceforth I vow it shall be so for me.
(*The Taming of the Shrew. Act 4. Scene 5. Katharina speaking.*)

PRINCE HENRY   Go, hide thee behind the arras: the rest walk up above.
                Now, my masters, for a true face and good conscience.
FALSTAFF   Both which I have had; but their date is out, and therefore
                I'll hide me.
(*Henry the Fourth. Part One. Act 2. Scene 4.*)
Arras: tapestry hangings for the walls.

                        Oh, he's as tedious
As a tired horse, a railing wife;
Worse than a smoky house. I had rather live
With cheese and garlic in a windmill, far,
Than feed on cates and have *him* talk to me
In any Summer-house in Christendom.
(*Henry the Fourth. Part One. Act 3. Scene 1. Hotspur speaking.*)
Cates: dainties.

MISTRESS QUICKLY By this heavenly ground I tread on, I must be fain to
                pawn both my plate and the tapestry of my
                dining-chambers.
FALSTAFF   Glasses, glasses is the only drinking; and for thy walls,
                a pretty slight drollery, or the story of the Prodigal,
                or the German hunting in water-work, is worth
                a thousand of these bed-hangings and these
                fly-bitten tapestries.
(*Henry the Fourth. Part Two. Act 2. Scene 1.*)
Water-work: water-colour painting.

Away with the joint-stools, remove the court-cupboard, look to the plate.
   Good thou, save me a piece of marchpane.
(*Romeo and Juliet. Act* 1. *Scene* 5. *First Servingman speaking.*)
Joint-stools: folding chairs.
Court-cupboard: a side-board, used for plate.
Marchpane: almond paste.   (Marzipan?)

I do remember an apothecary,
And hereabouts he dwells, which late I noted
In tattered weeds, with overwhelming brows,
Culling of simples.   Meagre were his looks;
Sharp misery had worn him to the bones.
And in his needy shop a tortoise hung,
An alligator stuffed, and other skins
Of ill-shaped fishes.   And about his shelves
A beggarly account of empty boxes,
Green earthen pots, bladders and musty seeds,
Remnants of packthread and old cakes of roses
Were thinly scattered, to make up a show.
(*Romeo and Juliet. Act* 5. *Scene* 1. *Romeo speaking.*)

The taper burneth in your closet, sir.
Searching the window for a flint, I found
This paper thus sealed up; and I am sure
It did not lie there when I went to bed.
(*Julius Cæsar. Act* 2. *Scene* 1. *Lucius speaking.*)

                        No.   When light-winged toys
Of feathered Cupid seel with wanton dullness
My speculative and offic'd instruments,
That my disports corrupt and taint my business,
Let housewives make a skillet of my helm,
And all indign and base adversities
Make head against my estimation!
(*Othello. Act* 1. *Scene* 3. *Othello speaking.*)
Seel: to blind; a term in falconry.
Skillet: a kettle.
Indign: unworthy.

                    SECTION XVIII

                 LEARNING AND WIT

                    I pray thee, mark me:
I, thus neglecting worldly ends, all dedicated
To closeness and the bettering of my mind. . . .
(*The Tempest. Act* 1. *Scene* 2. *Prospero speaking.*)

K

So, of his gentleness,
Knowing I loved my books, he furnished me
From mine own library with volumes that
I prize above my dukedom.
(*The Tempest. Act 1. Scene 2. Prospero speaking.*)

You taught me language; and my profit on't
Is, I know how to curse.   The red plague rid you
For learning me your language!
(*The Tempest. Act 1. Scene 2. Caliban speaking.*)

Unheedful vows may heedfully be broken;
And he wants wit that wants resolvèd will
To learn his wit to exchange the bad for better.
(*The Two Gentlemen of Verona. Act 2. Scene 6. Proteus speaking.*)

See now how wit may be made a Jack-a-Lent, when 'tis upon ill
employment.
(*The Merry Wives of Windsor. Act 5. Scene 5. Falstaff speaking.*)
Jack-a-Lent: a stuffed figure, thrown at during Lent.

ANTIPHOLUS OF SYRACUSE   Why is Time such a niggard of hair, being, as
it is, so plentiful an excrement?
DROMIO OF SYRACUSE   Because it is a blessing that he bestows on beasts;
and what he hath scanted men in hair, he
hath given them in wit.
(*The Comedy of Errors. Act 2. Scene 2.*)

LEONATO   You must not, sir, mistake my niece.   There is a kind of merry
war betwixt Signior Benedick and her: they never meet
but there's a skirmish of wit between them.
BEATRICE   Alas, he gets nothing by that!   In our last conflict four of his
five wits went halting off, and now is the whole man
governed with one: so that if he have wit enough to keep
himself warm, let him bear it for a difference between
himself and his horse; for it is all the wealth that he hath
left, to be known a reasonable creature.
(*Much Ado About Nothing. Act 1. Scene 1.*)

BENEDICK   Thy wit is as quick as the greyhound's mouth: it catches.
MARGARET   And yours as blunt as the fencer's foils, which hit but hurt not.
(*Much Ado About Nothing. Act 5. Scene 2.*)

BEROWNE   What is the end of study?   Let me know.
THE KING   Why, that to know which else we should not know.
BEROWNE   Things hid and barred, you mean, from common sense?
THE KING   Ay, that is study's god-like recompense.
(*Love's Labour's Lost. Act 1. Scene 1.*)

BEROWNE   Study is like the heaven's glorious sun
That will not be deep-searched with saucy looks;
Small have continual plodders ever won,
Save base authority from others' books.
These earthly godfathers of heaven's lights,
That give a name to every fixèd star,
Have no more profit of their shining nights
Than those that walk and wot not what they are.
Too much to know is to know nought but fame;
And every godfather can give a name.

THE KING   How well he's read, to reason against reading!

(*Love's Labour's Lost. Act* I. *Scene* I.)

Assist me some extemporal god of rhyme, for I am sure I shall turn sonneter.
    Devise, wit; write, pen; for I am for whole volumes in folio.

(*Love's Labour's Lost. Act* I. *Scene* 2. *Don Armado speaking.*)

His eye begets occasion for his wit;
For every object that the one doth catch,
The other turns to a mirth-moving jest,
Which his fair tongue, conceit's expositor,
Delivers in such apt and gracious words
That aged ears play truant at his tales
And younger hearings are quite ravishèd;
So sweet and voluble is his discourse.

(*Love's Labour's Lost. Act* 2. *Scene* I. *Rosaline speaking.*)

HOLOFERNES   Oh, thou monster Ignorance! How deformed dost thou look!

NATHANIEL   Sir, he hath never fed of the dainties that are bred of a book.
He hath not ate paper, as it were; he hath not drunk ink;
his intellect is not replenished. He is only an animal;
only sensible in the duller parts.

(*Love's Labour's Lost. Act* 4. *Scene* 2.)

Learning is but an adjunct to ourself,
And where we are our learning likewise is.
Then when ourselves we see in ladies' eyes,
Do we not likewise see our learning there?

. . . .

From women's eyes this doctrine I derive:
They sparkle still the right Promethean fire.
They are the books, the arts, the academes
That show, contain and nourish all the world;
Else none at all in aught proves excellent.

(*Love's Labour's Lost. Act* 4. *Scene* 3. *Berowne speaking.*)

He draweth out the thread of his verbosity finer than the staple of his
    argument.
(*Love's Labour's Lost. Act 5. Scene 1. Holofernes speaking.*)

MOTH   They have been at a great feast of languages and stolen the scraps.
COSTARD Oh, they have lived long on the alms-basket of words!
(*Love's Labour's Lost. Act 5. Scene 1.*)

This fellow pecks up wit as pigeons pease,
And utters it again when God doth please.
He is wit's peddlar, and retails his wares
At wakes and wassails, meetings, markets, fairs;
And we that sell by gross, the Lord doth know,
Have not the grace to grace it with such show.
(*Love's Labour's Lost. Act 5. Scene 2. Berowne speaking.*)

PRINCESS None are so surely caught, when they are catched,
          As wit turned fool: folly, in wisdom hatched,
          Hath wisdom's warrant and the help of school,
          And wit's own grace to grace a learnèd fool.
ROSALINE The blood of youth burns not with such excess
          As gravity's revolt to wantonness.
MARIA   Folly in fools bears not so strong a note
          As foolery in the wise, when wit doth dote:
          Since all the power thereof it doth apply
          To prove, by wit, worth in simplicity.
(*Love's Labour's Lost. Act 5. Scene 2.*)

How every fool can play upon the word! I think the best grace of wit will
    shortly turn into silence; and discourse grow commendable in none
    only but parrots.
(*The Merchant of Venice. Act 3. Scene 5. Lorenzo speaking.*)

TOUCHSTONE The more pity, that fools may not speak wisely what wise
            men do foolishly.
CELIA   By my troth, thou sayest true; for since the little wit that
            fools have was silenced, the little foolery that wise
            men have makes a great show.
(*As You Like It. Act 1. Scene 2.*)

LE BEAU   How shall I answer you?
ROSALIND   As wit and fortune will.
TOUCHSTONE Or as the destinies decree.
CELIA   Well said: that was laid on with a trowel.
(*As You Like It. Act 1. Scene 2.*)

ROSALIND   Thou speakest wiser than thou art ware of.
TOUCHSTONE   Nay, I shall ne'er be ware of mine own wit till I break my
                    shins against it.
(*As You Like It. Act 2. Scene 4.*)

                         And in his brain
Which is as dry as the remainder biscuit
After a voyage, he hath strange places crammed
With observation, the which he vents
In mangled forms.
(*As You Like It. Act 2. Scene 7. Jaques speaking.*)

You have a nimble wit: I think 'twas made of Atalanta's heels.
(*As You Like It. Act 3. Scene 2. Jaques speaking.*)

TOUCHSTONE (*to Audrey*)   I am here with thee and thy goats, as the most
                         capricious poet, honest Ovid, was among
                         the Goths.
JAQUES (*aside*)   Oh, knowledge ill-inhabited! Worse than
                         Jove in a thatched house!
TOUCHSTONE   When a man's verses cannot be understood, nor
                         a man's good wit seconded with the forward
                         child, Understanding, it strikes a man more
                         dead than a great reckoning in a little room.
                         Truly, I would the gods had made thee
                         poetical.
(*As You Like It. Act 3. Scene 3.*)

Make the doors upon a woman's wit and it will out at the casement; shut
    that and 'twill out at the key-hole; stop that, 'twill fly with the smoke
    out at the chimney.
(*As You Like It. Act 4. Scene 1. Rosalind speaking.*)

It is meat and drink to me to see a clown: by my troth, we that have good
    wits have much to answer for.
(*As You Like It. Act 5. Scene 1. Touchstone speaking.*)

TOUCHSTONE   Art thou wise?
WILLIAM   Ay, sir, I have a pretty wit.
TOUCHSTONE   Why, thou sayest well. I do now remember a saying:
                    'The fool doth think he is wise, but the wise man
                    knows himself to be a fool.'
(*As You Like It. Act 5. Scene 1.*)

He uses his folly like a stalking-horse; and under the presentation of that
    he shoots his wit.
(*As You Like It. Act 5. Scene 4. The Banished Duke speaking.*)
Stalking-horse: either a real or an artificial horse, behind which the shooter
    hid himself from the game.

KATHARINA   Where did you study all this goodly speech?
PETRUCHIO   It is extempore, from my mother-wit.
KATHARINA   A witty mother! Witless else her son.
(*The Taming of the Shrew. Act 2. Scene 1.*)

Methinks sometimes I have no more wit than a Christian or an ordinary
man has; but I am a great eater of beef, and I believe that does harm
to my wit.
(*Twelfth Night. Act 1. Scene 3. Sir Andrew speaking.*)

Wit, an't be thy will, put me into good fooling! Those wits that think
they have thee do very oft prove fools; and I, that am sure I lack thee,
may pass for a wise man: for what says Quinapalus? 'Better a witty
fool than a foolish wit!'
(*Twelfth Night. Act 1. Scene 5. Feste speaking.*)

　　　　　　　Tell her, Emilia,
I'll use that tongue I have. If wit flow from't
As boldness from my bosom, let it not be doubted
I shall do good.
(*The Winter's Tale. Act 2. Scene 2. Paulina speaking.*)

Men of all sorts take a pride to gird at me. The brain of this foolish-
compounded clay, man, is not able to invent anything that tends to
laughter, more than I invent or is invented on me: I am not only witty
in myself, but the cause that wit is in other men.
(*Henry the Fourth. Part Two. Act 1. Scene 2. Falstaff speaking.*)
Gird: to be sarcastic.

Nay, the man hath no wit that cannot, from the rising of the lark to the
lodging of the lamb, vary deserved praise on my palfrey: it is a theme
as fluent as the sea.
(*Henry the Fifth. Act 3. Scene 7. The Dauphin speaking.*)

Large gifts have I bestowed on learnèd clerks,
Because my book preferred me to the king;
And seeing ignorance is the curse of God,
Knowledge the wing wherewith we fly to heaven,
Unless you be possessed with devilish spirits
You cannot but forbear to murder me.
(*Henry the Sixth. Part Two. Act 4. Scene 7. Lord Say speaking.*)

Even so; a great deal of your wit too lies in your sinews, or else there be
liars. Hector shall have a great catch if he knock out either of your
brains: a' were as good crack a fusty nut with no kernel.
(*Troilus and Cressida. Act 2. Scene 1. Thersites speaking.*)

APEMANTUS Canst not read?
PAGE No.
APEMANTUS There will little learning die then, that day thou art hanged.
(*Timon of Athens. Act 2. Scene 2.*)

Therefore, since brevity is the soul of wit
And tediousness the limbs and outward flourishes,
I will be brief.
(*Hamlet. Act 2. Scene 2. Polonius speaking.*)

SECTION XIX

LONDON IN SHAKESPEARE'S PLAYS

Come, I cannot cog and say thou art this and that, like a many of these
  lisping hawthorn-buds that come like women in men's apparel and
  smell like Bucklersbury in simple-time.
(*The Merry Wives of Windsor. Act 3. Scene 3. Falstaff speaking.*)
Cog: cheat, or to wheedle.
Bucklersbury, in the City, was in Shakespeare's day chiefly inhabited by
  druggists.

LONGAVILLE Am I the first that have been perjured so?
BEROWNE   I could put thee in comfort. Not by two that I know.
           Thou makest the triumviry, the corner-cap of society,
           The shape of Love's Tyburn that hangs up simplicity.
(*Love's Labour's Lost. Act 4. Scene 3.*)
'*The shape of Love's Tyburn*': an allusion to the angular-shaped gallows at
  Tyburn. Tyburn was, in Shakespeare's time, close to where Marble
  Arch now stands: a place of execution West of London; and in
  Elizabethan literature the customary expression 'to go West' meant,
  as it does now, to end life.

This way the king will come. This is the way
To Julius Cæsar's ill-erected tower,
To whose flint bosom my condemnèd lord
Is doomed a prisoner by proud Bolingbroke.
(*Richard the Second. Act 5. Scene 1. The Queen speaking.*)
   In Shakespeare's time the Tower of London was commonly supposed
to be of Roman origin. This may have been due to the fact that The Tower
is to London Wall . . . which is Roman in foundation . . . somewhat in
the nature of a padlock on a chain. Stow, however, is sceptical; and
informs us that Roman writers make no mention of any such building as
The Tower having been erected by Julius Cæsar.

. . . and when I am king of England, I shall command all the good lads
in Eastcheap.
(*Henry the Fourth.   Part One.   Act 2.   Scene 4.   Prince Henry speaking.*)

Heart, you swear like a comfit-maker's wife. . . .
And givest such sarcenet surety for thy oaths
As if thou never walk'st further than Finsbury.
(*Henry the Fourth.   Part One.   Act 3.   Scene 1.   Hotspur speaking.*)
Sarcenet: fine silk.

FALSTAFF   How now, lad! Is the wind in that door, i' faith? Must
             we all march?
BARDOLPH   Yea, two and two; Newgate fashion.
(*Henry the Fourth.   Part One.   Act 3.   Scene 3.*)
Newgate fashion: a reference to the prisoners, tied two and two together.

FALSTAFF   Where's Bardolph?
PAGE   ,He's gone into Smithfield to buy your worship a horse.
FALSTAFF   *I* bought *him* in Paul's, and *he'll* buy *me* a horse in Smithfield.
(*Henry the Fourth.   Part Two.   Act 1.   Scene 2.*)
St. Paul's Cathedral was used for many secular purposes, among them the
hiring of servants.

This same starved Justice hath done nothing but prate to me of the wildness
of his youth and the feats he hath done about Turnbull Street; and
every third word a lie, duer paid to the hearer than the Turk's tribute.
I do remember him at Clement's Inn, like a man made after supper of
a cheese-paring: when a' was naked he was for all the world like a
forked radish, with a head fantastically carved upon it with a knife.
(*Henry the Fourth.   Part Two.   Act 3.   Scene 2.   Falstaff, referring to Justice
Shallow.*)
Clement's Inn stood in the parish of St. Clement Danes.   It was attached to
the Inner Temple and was, in 1470, a house of law.   All traces of it
finally disappeared during the Aldwych-Kingsway improvements
between 1900 and 1905.   Turnbull Street was, in Shakespeare's time,
on the banks of the river Fleet.   In modern days it has been known as
Turnmill Street, Clerkenwell.

Would I were in an alehouse in London!   I would give all my fame for
a pot of ale and safety.
(*Henry the Fifth.   Act 3.   Scene 2.   Boy speaking.*)

I am come to survey the Tower this day;
Since Henry's death, I fear there is conveyance.

Where be these warders that they wait not here?
Open the gates! 'Tis Gloucester that calls.
(*Henry the Sixth. Part One. Act 1. Scene 3. Gloucester speaking.*)

PLANTAGENET   Great lords and gentlemen, what means this silence?
                        Dare no man answer in a case of truth?
SUFFOLK   Within the Temple hall we were too loud;
                        The garden here is more convenient.
(*Henry the Sixth. Part One. Act 2. Scene 4.*)

The rebels are in Southwark; fly, my lord!
Jack Cade proclaims himself Lord Mortimer,
Descended from the Duke of Clarence' house;
And calls your Grace usurper openly,
And vows to crown himself in Westminster.
(*Henry the Sixth. Part Two. Act 4. Scene 4. First Messenger speaking.*)

Jack Cade hath gotten London Bridge;
The citizens fly and forsake their houses.
(*Henry the Sixth. Part Two. Act 4. Scene 4. Second Messenger speaking.*)

Now is Mortimer lord of this city.   And here, sitting upon London Stone,
    I charge and command that, of the city's cost, the pissing-conduit run
    nothing but claret wine this first year of our reign.
(*Henry the Sixth. Part Two. Act 4. Scene 6. Jack Cade speaking.*)
    The scene is Cannon Street.   In Shakespeare's day, London Stone was
on the South side of Cannon Street; and Stow tells us: 'It was fixed in the
ground very deep, fastened with a bar of iron, and otherwise so strongly
set that if carts do run against it through negligence, the wheel be broken
and the stone itself unshaken.'

So, sirs.   Now go some and pull down the Savoy; others to the Inns of
    Court.   Down with them all!
(*Henry the Sixth. Part Two. Act 4. Scene 7. Jack Cade speaking. The
scene is Smithfield.*)
The Savoy: the Savoy Palace, which stood beside the Thames not far from
    the present-day Somerset House.   It was left a ruin by the Wat Tyler
    rebels; and the instructions here quoted seem to be the result of some
    confusion on Shakespeare's part.   Henry the Seventh built a chapel
    here about 1504, which still remains to us though it underwent much
    restoration as the result of fire in 1864.   The last remnants of the
    Savoy Palace disappeared when Waterloo Bridge was constructed
    between 1815 and 1817.

Up Fish Street! Down St. Magnus' Corner! Kill and knock down! Throw them into Thames!

(*Henry the Sixth. Part Two. Act 4. Scene 8. Jack Cade speaking.*)

That it would please thee leave these sad designs
To him that hath more cause to be a mourner,
And presently repair to Crosby Place;
Where, after I have solemnly interred
At Chertsey monastery this noble king,
And wet his grave with my repentant tears,
I will with all expedient duty see you.

(*Richard the Third. Act 1. Scene 2. Gloucester, afterwards Richard the Third, speaking.*)

Crosby Place was built by Sir John Crosby in 1466 and was erected on the East side of Bishopsgate. Gloucester was living there in 1483. In 1523 it came into the hands of Sir Thomas More; but it is not known for certain that he dwelt there, though this is probable. In 1908 Crosby Hall was removed and re-erected close to the Chelsea Embankment.

GLOUCESTER Sirs, take up the corse.
GENTLEMEN   Towards Chertsey, noble lord?
GLOUCESTER No, to White-Friars; there attend my coming.

(*Richard the Third. Act 1. Scene 2.*)

In 1241 Sir Richard Grey founded a house of Carmelites between Fleet Street and the Thames. The priory covered all the area between Serjeants' Inn and Whitefriars Street; and its garden stretched down to the river. There was a crypt of the Whitefriars Priory under Britton's Court, Whitefriars Street.

GLOUCESTER My lord of Ely!
ELY   My lord?
GLOUCESTER When I was last in Holborn,
                  I saw good strawberries in your garden there.
                  I do beseech you send for some of them.

(*Richard the Third. Act 3. Scene 4.*)

The garden alluded to was that of the Bishop of Ely's palace in Holborn, which was famous for its strawberries. The palace was erected about the end of the thirteenth century; and the chapel, though considerably restored, still stands, in Ely Place, Holborn.

Go, after, after, cousin Buckingham:
The mayor towards Guildhall hies him in all post.

(*Richard the Third. Act 3. Scene 5. Gloucester speaking.*)

Bid them both
Meet me within this hour at Baynard's castle.
(*Richard the Third. Act 3. Scene 5. Gloucester speaking.*)
Baynard's Castle was so named from a nobleman who came over with
William the Conqueror, and was originally situated in Blackfriars.
At some date after 1278, however, another castle was built on the
banks of the river. This bore the same name; and it was here that
Richard Duke of Gloucester had his headquarters while he was plotting
for the throne.

This is the indictment of the good Lord Hastings,
Which in a set hand fairly is engrossed
That it may be this day read o'er in Paul's.
(*Richard the Third. Act 3. Scene 6. A Scrivener speaking.*)
Paul's: St. Paul's Cathedral, of course. In Shakespeare's time, and for
many years previously, the cathedral was used not only as a place of
worship, but also for various secular purposes.

Not long before your highness sped to France,
The Duke being at the Rose, within the parish
Saint Lawrence Poultney, did of me demand
What was the speech among the Londoners
Concerning the French journey.
(*Henry the Eighth. Act 1. Scene 2. The Surveyor speaking.*)
The Rose: According to Stow 'The Rose, in Suffolk Lane, sometime
belonged to the Duke of Buckingham.' The Merchant Taylors'
School occupied it in Shakespeare's time.

FIRST GENTLEMAN   God save you, sir! Where have you been broiling?
THIRD GENTLEMAN   Among the crowd i' the Abbey, where a finger
                   Could not be wedged in more. I am stifled
                   With the mere rankness of their joy.
(*Henry the Eighth. Act 4. Scene 1.*)

Sir,
You must no more call it York Place. That's past;
For since the Cardinal fell, that title's lost.
'Tis now the King's, and called Whitehall.
(*Henry the Eighth. Act 4. Scene 1. First Gentleman speaking.*)

York Place . . . or York House . . . was originally Suffolk Place, standing
between Charing Cross and the Thames. It was in the possession of
the Duke of Suffolk in 1539, but belonged to Wolsey at a later date.
Scene 4, Act 1, of Shakespeare's 'Henry the Eighth' is staged in the
Presence-Chamber in York Place. On Wolsey's fall from power, it
became the king's and was re-named the Palace of Whitehall.

You'll leave your noise anon, ye rascals. Do you take the Court for
Paris Garden? Ye rude slaves, leave your gaping.
(*Henry the Eighth. Act 5. Scene 4. A Porter speaking.*)
Paris Garden was a popular pleasure resort of Shakespeare and his con-
temporaries, and of earlier generations. It was in Bankside. The
name is commemorated in Paris Street, off Stamford Street, Blackfriars.

These are the youths that thunder at a playhouse, and fight for bitten
apples; that no audience, but the Tribulation of Tower Hill, or the
Limbs of Limehouse, their dear brothers, are able to endure.
(*Henry the Eighth. Act 5. Scene 4. A Porter speaking.*)
Tribulation: a name given to Puritans, either to the whole sect or to some
particular congregation. As regards the 'Limbs of Limehouse' one
can only suppose that the term is used in the same sense in which a
refractory child is rebuked as a 'little limb.'

I missed the meteor once and hit that woman, who cried out 'Clubs!'
when I might see from far some forty truncheoners draw to her
succour, which were the hope o' the Strand where she was quartered.
(*Henry the Eighth. Act 5. Scene 4. The Porter's Man speaking.*)

That which hath made them drunk hath made me bold;
What hath quenched them hath given me fire. Hark! Peace!
It was the owl that shrieked, the fatal bellman
Which gives the stern'st good-night.
(*Macbeth. Act 2. Scene 2. Lady Macbeth speaking.*)
'*the fatal bellman*': In 1605 Robert Dowe presented the church of St.
Sepulchre's, Newgate, with fifty pounds; with the instructions that
the bellman of the church should ring his bell, at the midnight
preceding an execution, outside the condemned cell. A few not
particularly encouraging lines were then recited for the benefit of the
unfortunate prisoner. 'Macbeth' was written shortly after this bequest
was made.

Sleep shall neither night nor day
Hang upon his pent-house lid;
He shall live, a man forbid.
(*Macbeth. Act 1. Scene 3. First Witch speaking.*)
Pent-house: in Shakespeare's day, London shops had no glazed windows
but merely shutters; and the narrow sloping roof was called a pent-
house. Here, of course, the reference is to the eye-lid . . . the
'shutter' of the eye.

GOOD WISHES AND THEIR OPPOSITES

JUNO (*singing*)   Honour, riches, marriage-blessing,
     Long continuance and increasing,
     Hourly joys be still upon you!
     Juno sings her blessings on you.
CERES (*singing*) Earth's increase, foison plenty,
     Barns and garners never empty;
     Vines with clustering bunches growing,
     Plants with goodly burthen bowing;
     Spring come to you at the farthest
     In the very end of harvest!
     Scarcity and want shall shun you;
     Ceres' blessing so is on you.
(*The Tempest. Act* 4. *Scene* 1.)
Foison: abundance.

Joy, gentle friends! Joy and fresh days of love
Accompany your hearts!
(*A Midsummer-Night's Dream. Act* 5. *Scene* 1. *Theseus speaking.*)

LORENZO   Fair thoughts and happy hours attend on you!
JESSICA   I wish your ladyship all heart's content.
PORTIA   I thank you for your wish, and am well pleased
     To wish it back on you.
(*The Merchant of Venice. Act* 3. *Scene* 4.)

ROSALIND   The little strength that I have, I would it were with you.
CELIA   And mine, to eke out hers.
ROSALIND   Fare you well. Pray heaven I be deceived in you!
CELIA   Your heart's desires be with you!

     . . . .

ROSALIND   Now Hercules be thy speed, young man!
(*As You Like It. Act* 1. *Scene* 2.)

JAQUES   God buy you: let's meet as little as we can.
ORLANDO   I do desire we may be better strangers.
(*As You Like It. Act* 3. *Scene* 2.)
God buy you: God be with you.

The best wishes that can be forged in your thoughts be servants to you.
(*All's Well That Ends Well. Act* 1. *Scene* 1. *Bertram speaking.*)

157

Each day still better other's happiness;
Until the heavens, envying earth's good hap,
Add an *immortal* title to your crown!
(*Richard the Second. Act* 1. *Scene* 1. *Mowbray speaking.*)

Most mighty liege, and my companion peers,
Take from my mouth the wish of happy years.
(*Richard the Second. Act* 1. *Scene* 3. *Mowbray speaking.*)

Thy ignomy sleep with thee in the grave,
But not remembered in thy epitaph.
(*Henry the Fourth. Part One. Act* 5. *Scene* 4. *Prince Henry speaking.*)
Ignomy: ignominy.

CHIEF JUSTICE Well, God send the prince a better companion!
FALSTAFF   God send the companion a better prince! I cannot rid
               my hands of him.
(*Henry the Fourth. Part Two. Act* 1. *Scene* 2.)

Mischance and sorrow go along with you!
Heart's discontent and sour affliction
Be playfellows to keep you company!
There's two of you; the devil make a third,
And threefold vengeance tend upon your steps!
(*Henry the Sixth. Part Two. Act* 3. *Scene* 2. *Queen Margaret speaking.*)

The common curse of mankind, folly and ignorance, be thine in great
     revenue! Heaven bless thee from a tutor and discipline come not
     near thee! Let thy blood be thy direction till thy death; then, if she
     that lays thee out says thou art a fair corpse I'll be sworn and sworn
     upon't she never shrouded any but lazars. Amen.
(*Troilus and Cressida. Act* 2. *Scene* 3. *Thersites speaking.*)

                    Now the fair goddess, Fortune,
Fall deep in love with thee; and her great charms
Misguide thy opposers' swords! Bold gentleman,
Prosperity be thy page!
(*Coriolanus. Act* 1. *Scene* 5. *Titus Lartius speaking.*)

Are yet two Romans living such as these?
The last of all the Romans, fare thee well!
(*Julius Cæsar. Act* 5. *Scene* 3. *Brutus speaking.*)

Now good digestion wait on appetite,
And health on both!
(*Macbeth. Act* 3. *Scene* 4. *Macbeth speaking.*)

So, gentlemen,
With all my love I do commend me to you;
And what so poor a man as Hamlet is
May do to express his love and friending to you,
God willing, shall not lack.
(*Hamlet. Act 1. Scene 5. Hamlet speaking.*)

Oh, behold!
The riches of the ship is come on shore!
Ye men of Cyprus, let her have your knees.
Hail to thee, lady! And the grace of heaven,
Before, behind thee, and on every hand,
Enwheel thee round!
(*Othello. Act 2. Scene 1. Cassio speaking.*)

The heavens forbid
But that our loves and comforts should increase,
Even as our days do grow!
(*Othello. Act 2. Scene 1. Desdemona speaking.*)

OCTAVIUS CÆSAR   Adieu.   Be happy.
LEPIDUS   Let all the number of the stars give light
                         To thy fair way!
(*Antony and Cleopatra. Act 3. Scene 2.*)

Look what is best, that best I wish in thee.
This wish I have; then ten times happy me!
(*Sonnet 37.*)

SECTION XXI

CATCH PHRASES, EPITHETS, ETC.

What says my bully-rook? Speak scholarly and wisely.
(*The Merry Wives of Windsor. Act 1. Scene 3. Host speaking.*)
Bully-rook: a fine and swaggering cheater.

MISTRESS PAGE   Here comes little Robin.   (*Enter Robin.*)
MISTRESS FORD   How now, my eyas-musket!   What news with you?
(*The Merry Wives of Windsor. Act 3. Scene 3.*)
Eyas-musket: a young sparrow-hawk.

Out of my door, you witch, you rag, you baggage, you polecat, you
    ronyon! Out, out! I'll conjure you, I'll fortune-tell you!
(*The Merry Wives of Windsor. Act 4. Scene 2. Ford speaking.*)
Rag: a beggarly person.
Ronyon: a scurvy wretch.

I will teach the children their behaviours; and I will be like a jack-an-apes also, to burn the knight with my taper.
(*The Merry Wives of Windsor.   Act 4.   Scene 4.   Evans speaking.*)
Jack-an-apes: a monkey; an impertinent fellow.

Bully knight! Bully Sir John! Speak from thy lungs military. Art thou there? It is thine host, thine Ephesian, calls.
(*The Merry Wives of Windsor.   Act 4.   Scene 5.   Host speaking.*)
Ephesian: a boon companion.
Bully: fine.   (Is this the origin of the American expression?)

I have spoke with her, and we have a nayword how to know one another: I come to her in white and cry 'Mum.'   She cries 'Budget.'   And by that we know one another.
(*The Merry Wives of Windsor.   Act 5.   Scene 2.   Slender speaking.*)
Nayword: in this instance, a watchword.

See now how wit may be made a Jack-a-Lent, when 'tis upon ill employment!
(*The Merry Wives of Windsor.   Act 5.   Scene 5.   Falstaff speaking.*)
Jack-a-Lent: a stuffed figure, thrown at during Lent.

A back-friend, a shoulder-clapper, one that countermands
The passages of alleys, creeks and narrow lands.
(*The Comedy of Errors.   Act 4.   Scene 2.   Dromio of Syracuse speaking.*)

They brought one Pinch, a hungry lean-faced villain,
A mere anatomy, a mountebank,
A threadbare juggler, and a fortune-teller,
A needy, hollow-eyed, sharp-looking wretch;
A living-dead man.
(*The Comedy of Errors.   Act 5.   Scene 1.   Antipholus of Ephesus speaking.*)

What the good-year, my lord!   Why are you thus out of measure sad?
(*Much Ado About Nothing.   Act 1.   Scene 3.   Conrade speaking.*)
Good-year: supposed to be a corruption of 'goujere,' a disease.   A mild imprecation.

A very forward March-chick!
(*Much Ado About Nothing.   Act 1.   Scene 3.   Don John speaking.*)
March-chick: denoting precocity . . . a chicken hatched in March.

Therefore I will even take sixpence in earnest of the bear-ward, and lead his apes into hell.
(*Much Ado About Nothing.   Act 2.   Scene 1.   Beatrice speaking.*)
Bear-ward: bear-leader.
'*And lead his apes into hell*': referring to the superstition that old maids had to lead apes in hell.

A good old man, sir; he will be talking. As they say: 'When the age is
in, the wit is out.'
(*Much Ado About Nothing. Act 3. Scene 5. Dogberry speaking.*)

God knows I loved my niece;
And she is dead; slandered to death by villains,
That dare as well answer a man indeed
As I dare take a serpent by the tongue.
Boys, apes, braggarts, Jacks, milksops!
(*Much Ado About Nothing. Act 5. Scene 1. Antonio speaking.*)
Jacks: a term of contempt. See: Jackanapes, Jack-a-Lent.

ARMADO   But oh! But oh . . .!
MOTH   'The hobby-horse is forgot.'
ARMADO   Callest thou my love 'hobby-horse'?
(*Love's Labour's Lost. Act 3. Scene 1.*)
Hobby-horse: an expression referring either to the principal part in the
morris-dance, or to a loose woman.

My sweet ounce of man's flesh! My incony Jew!
(*Love's Labour's Lost. Act 3. Scene 1. Costard speaking.*)
Incony: delicate, pretty.

LYSANDER (*to* HERMIA)   Thy love! Out, tawny Tartar, out!
                         Out loathèd medicine! Hated poison, hence!
                         . . . .
HERMIA (*to* HELENA)   Oh, me! You juggler! You canker-blossom!
HELENA (*to* HERMIA)   . . . you counterfeit, you puppet, you!
HERMIA (*to* HELENA)   . . . thou painted maypole! . . .
LYSANDER (*to* HERMIA)   Get you gone, you dwarf;
                         You minimus, of hindering knot-grass made;
                         You bead, you acorn!
(*A Midsummer-Night's Dream. Act 3. Scene 2. Helena was tall, Hermia
short.*)

I do now remember a saying: 'The fool doth think he is wise, but the wise
man knows himself to be a fool.'
(*As You Like It. Act 5. Scene 1. Touchstone speaking.*)

I' faith, sir, you shall never need to fear.
I wis it is not half way to her heart;
But if it were, doubt not her care should be
To comb your noddle with a three-legged stool,
And paint your face, and use you like a fool.
(*The Taming of the Shrew. Act 1. Scene 1. Katharina speaking.*)
'*To comb your noddle with a three-legged stool*': a popular catch phrase.

Their love is not so great, Hortensio, but we may blow our nails together, and fast it fairly out: our cake's dough on both sides.
(*The Taming of the Shrew. Act* 1. *Scene* 1. *Gremio speaking.*)
'*Our cake's dough*': an expression, commonly in use, denoting disappointment.

Faith, as you say, there's small choice in rotten apples.
(*The Taming of the Shrew. Act* 1. *Scene* 1. *Hortensio speaking.*)

Sweet Bianca! Happy man be his dole! He that runs fastest gets the ring.
(*The Taming of the Shrew. Act* 1. *Scene* 1. *Hortensio speaking.*)
Dole: reward, wages.

Why, give him gold enough and marry him to a puppet or an aglet-baby; or an old trot with ne'er a tooth in her head, though she have as many diseases as two and fifty horses: why, nothing comes amiss, so money comes withal.
(*The Taming of the Shrew. Act* 1. *Scene* 2. *Grumio speaking.*)
Aglet-baby: the tag end of a point or lace, shaped into a small figure.
Trot: a hag. (Is this the origin of the present-day expression 'the old trout'?)

Oh this woodcock, what an ass it is!
(*The Taming of the Shrew. Act* 1. *Scene* 2. *Grumio speaking.*)

For shame, thou hilding of a devilish spirit.
(*The Taming of the Shrew. Act* 2. *Scene* 1. *Baptista speaking.*)
Hilding: menial, base. A term of contempt.

Oh, you are novices; 'tis a world to see,
How tame, when men and women are alone,
A meacock wretch can make the curstest shrew.
(*The Taming of the Shrew. Act* 2. *Scene* 1. *Petruchio speaking.*)
Meacock: timid.

CURTIS   There's fire ready; and therefore, good Grumio, the news?
GRUMIO   Why, 'Jack, boy! Ho, boy!' and as much news as thou wilt.
CURTIS   Come, you are so full of cony-catching.
(*The Taming of the Shrew. Act* 4. *Scene* 1.)
'*Jack, boy*,' etc.: an old 'catch.'
Cony-catching: foolery.

This is a way to kill a wife with kindness.
(*The Taming of the Shrew. Act* 4. *Scene* 1. *Petruchio speaking.*)
'*To kill a wife with kindness*' was a proverbial expression.

Oh, monstrous arrogance! Thou liest, thou thread, thou thimble,
Thou yard, three-quarters, half-yard, quarter, nail!
Thou flea, thou nit, thou Winter-cricket thou!
Braved in mine own house with a skein of thread?
Away, thou rag, thou quantity, thou remnant.
(*The Taming of the Shrew. Act 4. Scene 3. Petruchio, addressing the tailor.*)

Not in my house, Lucentio; for, you know,
Pitchers have ears, and I have many servants.
(*The Taming of the Shrew. Act 4. Scene 4. Baptista speaking.*)

He that is giddy thinks the world turns round.
(*The Taming of the Shrew. Act 5. Scene 2. The Widow speaking.*)

MARIA   I can tell thee where that saying was born, of 'I fear no colours.'
FESTE   Where, good mistress Mary?
MARIA   In the wars; and that may you be bold to say in your foolery.
(*Twelfth Night. Act 1. Scene 5.*)

How now, my hearts! Did you never see the picture of 'we three'?
(*Twelfth Night. Act 2. Scene 3. Feste speaking.*)
The picture of 'we three': a common sign, in which two heads were exhibited, with this inscription beneath it: 'We three loggerheads be.' The spectator was supposed to make the third.

MARIA   For this night, to bed, and dream on the event. Farewell.
SIR TOBY   Good night, Penthesilia.
(*Twelfth Night. Act 2. Scene 3.*)
Penthesilia: the queen of the Amazons.

CONSTANCE (*to* QUEEN ELINOR)
            Thy sins are visited in this poor child;
            The canon of the law is laid on him,
            Being but the second generation
            Removed from thy sin-conceiving womb.
KING JOHN   Bedlam, have done.
(*King John. Act 2. Scene 1.*)
Bedlam: lunatic.

Farewell, thou latter Spring! Farewell, All-Hallow'n Summer!
(*Henry the Fourth. Part One. Act 1. Scene 2. Prince Henry, speaking to Falstaff.*)

PRINCE HENRY   Here comes lean Jack, here comes bare-bone. How
                now, my sweet creature of bombast! How long
                is't ago, Jack, since thou sawest thine own knee?

FALSTAFF   Mine own knee! When I was about thy years, Hal, I
                  was not an eagle's talon in the waist; I could have
                  crept into any alderman's thumb-ring.
(*Henry the Fourth. Part One. Act 2. Scene 4.*)

FALSTAFF (*pretending to be Henry the Fourth*)
                  For God's sake, lords, convey my tristful queen,
                  For tears do stop the flood-gates of her eyes.
MISTRESS QUICKLY Oh, Jesu! He doth it as like one of these harlotry
                  players as ever I see!
FALSTAFF   Peace, good pint-pot! Peace, good tickle-brain!
(*Henry the Fourth. Part One. Act 2. Scene 4.*)

PRINCE HENRY (*pretending to be Henry the Fourth*)
                  There is a devil haunts thee in the likeness of a fat old
                  man; a tun of man is thy companion. Why dost
                  thou converse with that trunk of humours, that
                  bolting-hutch of beastliness, that swolen parcel of
                  dropsies, that huge bombard of sack, that stuffed
                  cloak-bag of guts, that roasted Manningtree ox with
                  the pudding in his belly, that reverend vice, that
                  grey iniquity, that father ruffian, that vanity in
                  years? Wherein is he good, but to taste sack and
                  drink it? Wherein neat and cleanly, but to carve a
                  capon and eat it? Wherein cunning, but in craft?
                  Wherein crafty, but in villany? Wherein villan-
                  ous, but in all things? Wherein worthy, but in
                  nothing?
FALSTAFF (*pretending to be Prince Henry*)
                  I would your Grace would take me with you: whom
                  means your Grace?
PRINCE HENRY   That villanous abominable misleader of youth, Falstaff;
                  that old white-bearded Satan.
(*Henry the Fourth. Part One. Act 2. Scene 4.*)

Away, you scullion! You rampallian! You fustilarian! I'll tickle your
      catastrophe.
(*Henry the Fourth. Part Two. Act 2. Scene 1. Falstaff speaking.*)
Rampallian and fustilarian: terms of low abuse.

FALSTAFF   A rascal bragging slave! The rogue fled from me
                  like quicksilver.

DOLL TEARSHEET   I' faith, and thou followed'st him like a church. Thou whoreson little tidy Bartholomew boar-pig, when wilt thou leave fighting a' days and foining o' nights, and begin to patch up thine old body for heaven?

(*Henry the Fourth. Part Two. Act 2. Scene 4.*)

Bartholomew boar-pig: no doubt a reference to Bartholomew Fair, which was held every Summer from 1123 to 1855.

Foining: a fencing term.

Why, thou globe of sinful continents, what a life dost thou lead!

(*Henry the Fourth. Part Two. Act 2. Scene 4. Prince Henry, addressing Falstaff.*)

Up to the breach, you dogs! Avaunt, you cullions!

(*Henry the Fifth. Act 3. Scene 2. Fluellen speaking.*)

Cullion: a mean fellow.

The king's a bawcock, and a heart of gold;
A lad of life, an imp of fame:
Of parents good, of fist most valiant:
I kiss his dirty shoe, and from my heart-string
I love the lovely bully.

(*Henry the Fifth. Act 4. Scene 1. Pistol speaking.*)

The ancient proverb will be well effected:
'A staff is quickly found to beat a dog.'

(*Henry the Sixth. Part Two. Act 3. Scene 1. Gloucester speaking.*)

Vouchsafe, divine perfection of a woman,
Of these supposèd evils, to give me leave
By circumstance, but to acquit myself.

(*Richard the Third. Act 1. Scene 2. Gloucester speaking.*)

Poor painted queen, vain flourish of my fortune!
Why strew'st thou sugar on that bottled spider,
Whose deadly web ensnareth thee about?

(*Richard the Third. Act 1. Scene 3. Queen Margaret speaking.*)

Bottled: bloated.

A thousand pounds a year for pure respect!
No other obligation! By my life,
That promises more thousands: honour's train
Is longer than his foreskirt.

(*Henry the Eighth. Act 2. Scene 3. Old Lady, speaking to Ann Bullen.*)

Thy ambition,
Thou scarlet sin, robbed this bewailing land
Of noble Buckingham, my father-in-law.
(*Henry the Eighth.   Act 3.   Scene 2.   Surrey, addressing Wolsey.*)

Was it discretion, lords, to let this man,
This good man . . . few of you deserve that title . . .
This honest man, wait like a lousy footboy
At chamber-door?   And one as great as you are?
Why, what a shame was this!
(*Henry the Eighth.   Act 5.   Scene 3.   Henry speaking.*)

And that I would not for a cow, God save her!
(*Henry the Eighth.   Act 5.   Scene 4.   The Porter's Man speaking.*)
A proverbial expression, still used in certain parts of the country.

He that will have a cake out of the wheat must tarry the grinding.
(*Troilus and Cressida.   Act 1.   Scene 1.   Pandarus speaking.*)

What, lamb!   What, lady-bird!
God forbid!   Where's this girl?   What, Juliet!
(*Romeo and Juliet.   Act 1.   Scene 3.   The Nurse speaking.*)

I know what:
You must contrary me!   Marry, 'tis time.
Well said, my hearts!   You are a princox.   Go!
(*Romeo and Juliet.   Act 1.   Scene 5.   Capulet, addressing Tybalt.*)
Princox: a cheeky boy.

I tell you, he that can lay hold of her
Shall have the chinks.
(*Romeo and Juliet.   Act 1.   Scene 5.   The Nurse speaking.*)
Chinks: Tudor slang for money.

Oh, serpent heart, hid with a flowering face!
Did ever dragon keep so fair a cave?
Beautiful tyrant!   Fiend angelical!
Dove-feathered raven!   Wolvish-ravening lamb!
Despisèd substance of divinest show!
(*Romeo and Juliet.   Act 3.   Scene 2.   Juliet speaking.*)

Ancient damnation!   Oh, most wicked fiend!
Is it more sin to wish me thus forsworn,
Or to dispraise my lord with that same tongue
Which she hath praised him with above compare
So many thousand times?   Go, counsellor;
Thou and my bosom henceforth shall be twain.
(*Romeo and Juliet.   Act 3.   Scene 5.   Juliet, referring to the Nurse.*)

JULIET   What must be shall be.
FRIAR LAURENCE   That's a certain text.
(*Romeo and Juliet. Act* 4. *Scene* 1.)

Go, you cot-quean, go!
Get you to bed. Faith, you'll be sick to-morrow
For this night's watching.
(*Romeo and Juliet. Act* 4. *Scene* 4. *The Nurse, speaking to Capulet.*)
Cot-quean: a man who interferes with, and tries to direct, women's
    household affairs.

FIRST WITCH   I come, Graymalkin.
THREE WITCHES   Paddock calls. Anon!
                Fair is foul, and foul is fair.
                Hover through the fog and filthy air.
(*Macbeth. Act* 1. *Scene* 1.)
Graymalkin: a grey cat . . . the familiar spirit of the First Witch. 'Malkin'
    is a diminutive of Mary.
Paddock: a toad; another 'familiar.'

Honey, you shall be well desired in Cyprus;
I have found great love amongst them. Oh, my sweet,
I prattle out of fashion, and I dote
In mine own comforts.
(*Othello. Act* 2. *Scene* 1. *Othello, to Desdemona.*)

SECTION XXII

YOUTH AND OLD AGE

Cease to persuade, my loving Proteus:
Home-keeping youth have ever homely wits.
Were't not affection chains thy tender days
To the sweet glances of thy honoured love,
I rather would entreat thy company
To see the wonders of the world abroad
Than, living dully sluggardized at home,
Wear out thy youth with shapeless idleness.
(*The Two Gentlemen of Verona. Act* 1. *Scene* 1. *Valentine speaking.*)

Bodykins, Master Page, though I now be old and of the peace, if I see a
    sword out my finger itches to make one. Though we are justices, and
    doctors, and churchmen, Master Page, we have some salt of our
    youth in us; we are the sons of women, Master Page.
(*The Merry Wives of Windsor. Act* 2. *Scene* 3. *Justice Shallow speaking.*)

LEONATO   You may light on a husband that hath no beard.
BEATRICE   What should I do with him? Dress him in my apparel and make him my waiting-gentlewoman? He that hath a beard is more than a youth; and he that hath no beard is less than a man. And he that is more than a youth is not for me; and he that is less than a man, I am not for him. Therefore I will even take sixpence in earnest of the bear-ward, and lead his apes into hell.

(*Much Ado About Nothing.   Act 2.   Scene 1.*)

Apes into hell': a reference to the superstition that old maids had to lead apes in hell.

Bear-ward: bear-leader.

A good old man, sir. He will be talking. As they say: 'When the age is in, the wit is out.'

(*Much Ado About Nothing.   Act 3.   Scene 5.   Dogberry, referring to Verges.*)

Beauty doth varnish age, as if new-born;
And gives the crutch the cradle's infancy.

(*Love's Labour's Lost.   Act 4.   Scene 3.   Berowne speaking.*)

He hears merry tales and smiles not: I fear he will prove the weeping philosopher when he grows old, being so full of unmannerly sadness in his youth.

(*The Merchant of Venice.   Act 1.   Scene 2.   Portia speaking.*)

LAUNCELOT   Talk not of Master Launcelot, father; for the young gentleman, according to Fates and Destinies and such odd sayings, the Sisters Three and such branches of learning, is indeed deceased, or, as you would say in plain terms, gone to heaven.
OLD GOBBO   Marry, God forbid! The boy was the very staff of my age, my very prop.

(*The Merchant of Venice.   Act 2.   Scene 2.*)

Had you been as wise as bold,
Young in limbs, in judgment old,
Your answer had not been inscrolled:
Fare you well; your suit is cold.

(*The Merchant of Venice.   Act 2.   Scene 7.   Morocco, reading from a scroll.*)

I beseech you, let his lack of years be no impediment to let him lack a reverend estimation; for I never knew so young a body with so old a head.

(*The Merchant of Venice.   Act 4.   Scene 1.   A Clerk, reading from a letter.*)

Let me be your servant.
Though I look old, yet I am strong and lusty;
For in my youth I never did apply
Hot and rebellious liquors in my blood,
Nor did not with unbashful forehead woo
The means of weakness and debility.
Therefore my age is as a lusty Winter:
Frosty, but kindly.
(*As You Like It.   Act 2.   Scene 3.   Adam speaking.*)

No, Corin, being old thou canst not guess;
Though in thy youth thou wast as true a lover
As ever sighed upon a midnight pillow.
(*As You Like It.   Act 2.   Scene 4.   Silvius speaking.*)

There is an old poor man,
Who after me hath many a weary step
Limped in pure love.   Till he be first sufficed,
Oppressed with two weak evils, age and hunger,
I will not touch a bit.
(*As You Like It.   Act 2.   Scene 7.   Orlando speaking.*)

All the world's a stage,
And all the men and women merely players:
They have their exits and their entrances;
And one man in his time plays many parts,
His acts being seven ages.   At first the infant,
Mewling and puking in the nurse's arms.
Then the whining school-boy, with his satchel
And shining morning face, creeping like snail
Unwillingly to school.   And then the lover,
Sighing like furnace, with a woeful ballad
Made to his mistress' eyebrow.

. . . .
The sixth age shifts
Into the lean and slippered pantaloon,
With spectacles on nose and pouch on side,
His youthful hose, well saved, a world too wide
For his shrunk shank; and his big manly voice,
Turning again toward childish treble, pipes
And whistles in his sound.   Last scene of all
That ends this strange eventful history
Is second childishness and mere oblivion:
Sans teeth, sans eyes, sans taste, sans everything.
(*As You Like It.   Act 2.   Scene 7.   Jaques speaking.*)

What is love? 'Tis not hereafter.
Present mirth hath present laughter;
What's to come is still unsure.
In delay there lies no plenty,
Then come kiss me, sweet and twenty,
Youth's a stuff will not endure.
(*Twelfth Night. Act 2. Scene 3. Feste singing.*)

When that I was and a little tiny boy,
With hey, ho, the wind and the rain,
A foolish thing was but a toy,
For the rain it raineth every day.
(*Twelfth Night. Act 5. Scene 1. Feste singing.*)

We were, fair queen,
Two lads that thought there was no more behind;
But such a day to-morrow as to-day,
And to be boy eternal.
(*The Winter's Tale. Act 1. Scene 2. Polixenes speaking.*)

The king is come; deal mildly with his youth,
For young hot colts being raged do rage the more.
(*Richard the Second. Act 2. Scene 1. Duke of York speaking.*)

FALSTAFF   I would your Grace would take me with you: whom
                means your Grace?
PRINCE HENRY   That villanous abominable misleader of youth, Falstaff;
                that old white-bearded Satan.
(*Henry the Fourth. Part One. Act 2. Scene 4.*)

For though the camomile, the more it is trodden on the faster it grows,
    yet youth, the more it is wasted the sooner it wears.
(*Henry the Fourth. Part One. Act 2. Scene 4. Falstaff speaking.*)

Your lordship, though not clean past your youth, hath yet some smack
    of age in you, some relish of the saltness of time; and I most humbly
    beseech your lordship to have a reverend care of your health.
(*Henry the Fourth. Part Two. Act 1. Scene 2. Falstaff speaking.*)

FALSTAFF   You that are old consider not the capacities of us that
                are young. You measure the heat of our livers with
                the bitterness of your galls; and we that are in the
                vaward of our youth, I must confess, are wags too.

CHIEF JUSTICE   Do you set down your name in the scroll of youth, that are
written down old with all the characters of age?
Have you not a moist eye, a dry hand, a yellow cheek,
a white beard, a decreasing leg, an increasing belly?
Is not your voice broken, your wind short, your chin
double, your wit single, and every part about you
blasted with antiquity? And will you yet call yourself
young? Fie, fie, fie, Sir John!

FALSTAFF   My lord, I was born about three of the clock in the
afternoon, with a white beard and something a round
belly. For my voice, I have lost it with hollaing and
singing of anthems. To approve my youth further,
I will not. The truth is I am only old in judgment
and understanding; and he that will caper with me
for a thousand marks, let him lend me the money and
have at him.

(*Henry the Fourth. Part Two. Act* 1. *Scene* 2.)

He was indeed the glass
Wherein the noble youth did dress themselves.
(*Henry the Fourth. Part Two. Act* 2. *Scene* 3. *Lady Percy, referring to
Hotspur.*)

Lord! Lord! How subject we old men are to this vice of lying!
(*Henry the Fourth. Part Two. Act* 3. *Scene* 2. *Falstaff speaking.*)

As young as I am, I have observed these three swashers. I am boy to them
all three; but all they three, though they would serve me, could not
be man to me. For, indeed, three such antiques do not amount to
a man.
(*Henry the Fifth. Act* 3. *Scene* 2. *The Boy speaking.*)

So wise so young, they say do never live long.
(*Richard the Third. Act* 3. *Scene* 1. *Gloucester speaking.*)

Nay, sit, nay, sit, good cousin Capulet;
For you and I are past our dancing days.
How long is't now since last yourself and I
Were in a mask?
(*Romeo and Juliet. Act* 1. *Scene* 5. *Capulet speaking.*)

Care keeps his watch in every old man's eye,
And where care lodges, sleep will never lie;
But where unbruised youth, with unstuffed brain,
Doth couch his limbs, there golden sleep doth reign.
(*Romeo and Juliet. Act* 2. *Scene* 3. *Friar Laurence speaking.*)

I have lived long enough: my way of life
Is fall'n into the sear, the yellow leaf;
And that which should accompany old age,
As honour, love, obedience, troops of friends,
I must not look to have.
(*Macbeth. Act 5. Scene 3. Macbeth speaking.*)

The chariest maid is prodigal enough
If she unmask her beauty to the moon:
Virtue itself 'scapes not calumnious strokes:
The canker galls the infants of the Spring
Too oft before their buttons be disclosed,
And in the morn and liquid dew of youth
Contagious blastments are most imminent.
(*Hamlet. Act 1. Scene 3. Laertes speaking.*)

HAMLET   Hark you, Guildenstern; and you, too: at each ear a
hearer.   That great baby you see there is not yet out
of his swaddling clouts.
ROSENCRANTZ Happily he's the second time come to them; for they say
an old man is twice a child.
(*Hamlet. Act 2. Scene 2.*)

LAERTES   What part is that, my lord?
THE KING   A very riband in the cap of youth,
Yet needful too; for youth no less becomes
The light and careless livery that it wears
Than settled age his sables and his weeds,
Importing health and graveness.
(*Hamlet. Act 4. Scene 7.*)
Weeds: robes.

LEAR   How old art thou?
KENT   Not so young, sir, to love a woman for singing; nor so old to
dote on her for any thing.   I have years on my back,
forty-eight.
(*King Lear. Act 1. Scene 4.*)

Haply, for I am black
And have not those soft parts of conversation
That chamberers have, or for I am declined
Into the vale of years . . . yet that's not much . . .
She's gone.   I am abused; and my relief
Must be to loathe her.
(*Othello. Act 3. Scene 3. Othello speaking.*)
Chamberers: men of effeminate character.

To him again: tell him he wears the rose
Of youth upon him, from which the world should note
Something particular.
(*Antony and Cleopatra. Act 3. Scene 13 . . . Scene 11 in some editions . . .*
Antony speaking.)

By Jupiter, an angel! Or, if not,
An earthly paragon! Behold divineness
No elder than a boy.
(*Cymbeline. Act 3. Scene 6. Belarius speaking.*)

When forty Winters shall besiege thy brow
And dig deep trenches in thy beauty's field,
Thy youth's proud livery, so gazed on now,
Will be a tattered weed of small worth held.
Then being asked where all thy beauty lies,
Where all the treasure of thy lusty days,
To say, within thine own deep-sunken eyes,
Were an ill-eating shame and thriftless praise.
(*Sonnet 2.*)
Ill-eating: all-eating, in *The Oxford Shakespeare.*

That time of year thou mayest in me behold
When yellow leaves, or none, or few, do hang
Upon those boughs which shake against the cold,
Bare ruined choirs, where late the sweet birds sang.
(*Sonnet 73.*)

Some say thy fault is youth, some wantonness;
Some say thy grace is youth and gentle sport.
Both grace and faults are loved of more and less.
(*Sonnet 96.*)

Section XXIII

FOOD AND DRINK

ALONSO   Prithee, peace!
SEBASTIAN   He receives comfort like cold porridge.
(*The Tempest. Act 2. Scene 1.*)

I drink the air before me, and return
Or ere your pulse twice beat.
(*The Tempest. Act 5. Scene 1. Ariel speaking.*)

Ay, but hearken, sir: though the chameleon, Love, can feed on the air,
   I am one that am nourished by my victuals and would fain have meat.
(*The Two Gentlemen of Verona. Act 2. Scene 1. Speed speaking.*)

SPEED   Launce! By mine honesty, welcome to Milan!
LAUNCE   Forswear not thyself, sweet youth, for I am not welcome.
               I reckon this always: that a man is never undone till he be
               hanged; nor never welcome to a place till some certain
               shot be paid and the hostess say 'Welcome.'
SPEED   Come on, you madcap; I'll to the alehouse with you presently.
(*The Two Gentlemen of Verona. Act 2. Scene 5.*)

I bruised my shin the other day with playing at sword and dagger with a
   master of fence: three veneys for a dish of stewed prunes.
(*The Merry Wives of Windsor. Act 1. Scene 1. Slender speaking.*)
Veney: a bout at fencing.

You love sack, and so do I. Would you desire better sympathy?
(*The Merry Wives of Windsor. Act 2. Scene 1. Mistress Page, reading
   a letter.*)

The capon burns, the pig falls from the spit.
The clock hath strucken twelve upon the bell;
My mistress made it one upon my cheek:
She is so hot because the meat is cold;
The meat is cold because you come not home.
(*The Comedy of Errors. Act 1. Scene 2. Dromio of Ephesus speaking.*)

Thou sayest his meat was sauced with thy upbraidings:
Unquiet meals make ill digestions.
(*The Comedy of Errors. Act 5. Scene 1. The Abbess speaking.*)

Therefore, for fear of the worst, I pray thee set a deep glass of Rhenish
   wine on the contrary casket; for if the devil be within and that
   temptation without, I know he will choose it. I will do anything,
   Nerissa, ere I will be married to a sponge.
(*The Merchant of Venice. Act 1. Scene 2. Portia speaking.*)

SHYLOCK   May I speak with Antonio?
BASSANIO If it please you to dine with us.
SHYLOCK   Yes, to smell pork; to eat of the habitation which your prophet
               the Nazarite conjured the devil into!
(*The Merchant of Venice. Act 1. Scene 3.*)

ROSALIND   Where learned you that oath, fool?
TOUCHSTONE Of a certain knight that swore by his honour they were
                  good pancakes, and swore by his honour the mustard
                  was naught.
(*As You Like It. Act 1. Scene 2.*)

As dry as the remainder biscuit
After a voyage.
(*As You Like It. Act 2. Scene 7. Jaques speaking.*)

Truly, thou art damned; like an ill-roasted egg, all on one side.
(*As You Like It. Act 3. Scene 2. Touchstone speaking.*)

He calls for wine: 'A health!' quoth he; as if
He had been aboard, carousing to his mates
After a storm: quaffed off the muscadel,
And threw the sops all in the sexton's face.
(*The Taming of the Shrew. Act 3. Scene 2. Gremio, describing the wedding
of Katharina and Petruchio.*)

PETRUCHIO	What's this? Mutton?
FIRST SERVANT	Ay.
PETRUCHIO	Who brought it?
PETER	I.
PETRUCHIO	'Tis burnt; and so is all the meat.
	What dogs are these! Where is the rascal cook?
	How durst you, villains, bring it from the dresser
	And serve it thus to me that love it not?
	There, take it to you, trenchers, cups and all! (*Throws
	the meat about the stage.*)

(*The Taming of the Shrew. Act 4. Scene 1.*)

GRUMIO	What say you to a neat's foot?
KATHARINA	'Tis passing good: I prithee, let me have it.
GRUMIO	I fear it is too choleric a meat.
	How say you to a fat tripe, finely broiled?
KATHARINA	I like it well: good Grumio, fetch it me.
GRUMIO	I cannot tell; I fear 'tis choleric.
	What say you to a piece of beef and mustard?
KATHARINA	A dish that I do love to feed upon.
GRUMIO	Ay, but the mustard is too hot a little.
KATHARINA	Why then, the beef, and let the mustard rest.
GRUMIO	Nay then, I will not: you shall have the mustard,
	Or else you get no beef of Grumio.
KATHARINA	Then both, or one, or anything thou wilt.
GRUMIO	Why then, the mustard without the beef.
KATHARINA	Go, get thee gone, thou false deluding slave,
	That feed'st me with the very name of meat! (*Beats him.*)

(*The Taming of the Shrew. Act 4. Scene 3.*)

I knew a wench married in an afternoon, as she went to the garden for
parsley to stuff a rabbit.
(*The Taming of the Shrew. Act 4. Scene 4. Biondello speaking.*)

SIR ANDREW	Fair lady, do you think you have fools in hand?
MARIA	Sir, I have not you by the hand.
SIR ANDREW	Marry, but you shall have; and here's my hand.
MARIA	Now, sir, 'thought is free': I pray you, bring your hand to the buttery-bar and let it drink.

(*Twelfth Night.   Act* I.   *Scene* 3.)

Buttery-bar: the buttery was where food and drink were kept; the bar was where they were served.

| FALSTAFF | Now, Hal, what time of day is it, lad? |
| PRINCE HENRY | Thou art so fat-witted with drinking of old sack,. and unbuttoning of thee after supper, and sleeping upon benches after noon, that thou hast forgotton to demand that truly which thou wouldst truly know. What a devil hast thou to do with the time of the day? Unless hours were cups of sack, and minutes capons, and clocks the tongues of bawds, and dials the signs of leaping-houses, and the blessed sun himself a fair hot wench in flame-coloured taffeta, I see no reason why thou should'st be so superfluous to demand the time of the day. |

(*Henry the Fourth.   Part One.   Act* I.   *Scene* 2.)

What says Monsieur Remorse? What says Sir John Sack-and-Sugar? Jack, how agrees the devil and thee about thy soul that thou soldest him on Good Friday last, for a cup of Madeira and a cold capon's leg?

(*Henry the Fourth.   Part One.   Act* I.   *Scene* 2.   *Poins speaking.*)

Go, hang thyself in thine own heir-apparent garters! If I be taken, I'll peach for this. An I have not ballads made on you all, and sung to filthy tunes, let a cup of sack be my poison.

(*Henry the Fourth.   Part One.   Act* 2.   *Scene* 2.   *Falstaff, addressing Prince Henry.*)

Peach: to turn King's Evidence.

If sack and sugar be a fault, God help the wicked!

(*Henry the Fourth.   Part One.   Act* 2.   *Scene* 4.   *Falstaff speaking.*)

He hath eaten me out of house and home: he hath put all my substance into that fat belly of his. But I will have some of it out again, or I will ride thee o' nights like the mare.

(*Henry the Fourth.   Part Two.   Act* 2.   *Scene* 1.   *Mistress Quickly speaking, with reference to Falstaff.*)

Mare: the nightmare.

If I had a thousand sons, the first human principle I would teach them
should be to forswear thin potations and to addict themselves to sack.
(*Henry the Fourth. Part Two. Act 4. Scene 3. Falstaff speaking.*)

There's a dish of leather-coats for you.
(*Henry the Fourth. Part Two. Act 5. Scene 3. Davey speaking.*)
Leather-coats: a special sort of apple.

Would I were in an alehouse in London! I would give all my fame for
a pot of ale, and safety.
(*Henry the Fifth. Act 3. Scene 2. Boy speaking.*)

. . . the wretched slave,
Who with a body filled and vacant mind
Gets him to rest, crammed with distressful bread.
(*Henry the Fifth. Act 4. Scene 1. The King speaking.*)

CHARLES OF FRANCE At pleasure here we lie near Orleans;
Otherwhiles the famished English, like pale ghosts,
Faintly besiege us one hour in a month.
ALENCON They want their porridge and their fat bull-beeves:
Either they must be dieted like mules
And have their provender tied to their mouths,
Or piteous they will look, like drownèd mice.
(*Henry the Sixth. Part One. Act 1. Scene 2.*)

MENENIUS You'll sup with me?
VOLUMNIA Anger's my meat; I sup upon myself,
And so shall starve with feeding.
(*Coriolanus. Act 4. Scene 2.*)

Here's that which is too weak to be a sinner:
Honest water, which ne'er left man i' the mire.
(*Timon of Athens. Act 1. Scene 2. Apemantus speaking.*)

CASSIUS Will you sup with me to-night, Casca?
CASCA No, I am promised forth.
CASSIUS Will you dine with me to-morrow?
CASCA Ay, if I be alive, and your mind hold, and your dinner be worth
the eating.
(*Julius Cæsar. Act 1. Scene 2.*)

HAMLET But what is your affair in Elsinore?
We'll teach you to drink deep ere you depart.
HORATIO My lord, I came to see your father's funeral.

HAMLET   I pray thee, do not mock me, fellow student;
           I think it was to see my mother's wedding.
HORATIO   Indeed, my lord, it followed hard upon.
HAMLET   Thrift, thrift, Horatio! The funeral baked-meats
           Did coldly furnish forth the marriage tables.
(*Hamlet. Act* 1. *Scene* 2.)

The king doth wake to-night and takes his rouse,
Keeps wassail, and the swaggering up-spring reels;
And as he drains his draughts of Rhenish down,
The kettle-drum and trumpet thus bray out
The triumph of his pledge.
(*Hamlet. Act* 1. *Scene* 4. *Hamlet speaking.*)
Up-spring: the culminating dance at a German merry-making.

Oh, thou invisible spirit of wine! If thou hast no name to be known by,
     let us call thee devil!
(*Othello. Act* 2. *Scene* 3. *Cassio speaking.*)

Come, come! Good wine is a good familiar creature, if it be well used.
     Exclaim no more against it.
(*Othello. Act* 2. *Scene* 3. *Iago speaking.*)

Come, let's all take hands,
Till that the conquering wine hath steeped our sense
In soft and delicate Lethe.
(*Antony and Cleopatra. Act* 2. *Scene* 7. *Antony speaking.*)

                    Come,
Let's have one other gaudy night. Call to me
All my sad captains. Fill our bowls once more.
Let's mock the midnight bell.
(*Antony and Cleopatra. Act* 3. *Scene* 13. *Antony speaking. The Oxford
Shakespeare: Scene* 11.)

Die, quoth-a? Now, gods forbid! I have a gown here: come, put it
     on; keep thee warm. Now, afore me, a handsome fellow! Come,
     thou shalt go home, and we'll have flesh for holidays, fish for fasting-
     days, and moreover puddings and flap-jacks. And thou shalt be
     welcome.
(*Pericles. Act* 2. *Scene* 1. *First Fisherman speaking.*)
Flap-jacks: pancakes.

So are you to my thoughts as food to life,
Or as sweet-seasoned showers are to the ground.
(*Sonnet* 75.)

SLEEP AND DREAMS

And then, in dreaming,
The clouds methought would open and show riches
Ready to drop upon me; that when I waked
I cried to dream again.
(*The Tempest. Act 3. Scene 2. Caliban speaking.*)

You do look, my son, in a moved sort,
As if you were dismayed: be cheerful, sir.
Our revels now are ended. These our actors,
As I foretold you, were all spirits, and
Are melted into air, into thin air;
And, like the baseless fabric of this vision,
The cloud-capped towers, the gorgeous palaces,
The solemn temples, the great globe itself,
Yea, all which it inherit, shall dissolve,
And, like this insubstantial pageant faded,
Leave not a rack behind. We are such stuff
As dreams are made on; and our little life
Is rounded with a sleep.
(*The Tempest. Act 4. Scene 1. Prospero speaking.*)

Thy best of rest is sleep,
And that thou oft provok'st; yet grossly fear'st
Thy death, which is no more.

. . . .

Thou hast nor youth nor age,
But, as it were, an after-dinner's sleep,
Dreaming on both.
(*Measure For Measure. Act 3. Scene 1. The Duke speaking.*)

HERMIA   Oh, hell! To choose love by another's eyes!
LYSANDER Or, if there were a sympathy in choice,
        War, death, or sickness did lay siege to it,
        Making it momentary as a sound,
        Swift as a shadow, short as any dream. . . .
(*A Midsummer-Night's Dream. Act 1. Scene 1.*)

LYSANDER Here is my bed; sleep give thee all his rest!
HERMIA   With half that wish the wisher's eyes be pressed!
(*A Midsummer-Night's Dream. Act 2. Scene 2.*)

There is no following her in this fierce vein;
Here, therefore, for a while I will remain.
So sorrow's heaviness doth heavier grow
For debt that bankrupt sleep doth sorrow owe . . .
(*A Midsummer-Night's Dream.   Act* 3.   *Scene* 2.   *Demetrius speaking.*)

And sleep, that sometimes shuts up sorrow's eye,
Steal me awhile from mine own company.
(*A Midsummer-Night's Dream.   Act* 3.   *Scene* 2.   *Helena speaking.*)

But, I pray you, let none of your people stir me: I have an exposition of
    sleep come upon me.
(*A Midsummer-Night's Dream.   Act* 4.   *Scene* 1.   *Bottom speaking.*)

When my cue comes, call me and I will answer. . . .   I have had a dream,
    past the wit of man to say what dream it was.   Man is but an ass if
    he go about to expound this dream.
(*A Midsummer-Night's Dream.   Act* 4.   *Scene* 1.   *Bottom speaking.*)

What relish is in this?   How runs the stream?
Or I am mad, or else this is a dream.
Let fancy still my sense in Lethe steep;
If it be thus to dream, still let me sleep!
(*Twelfth Night.   Act* 4.   *Scene* 1.   *Sebastian speaking.*)
Lethe: one of the rivers of the nether world, a draught of whose waters
    was supposed to induce oblivion.

How many thousand of my poorest subjects
Are at this hour asleep!   Oh, sleep!   Oh, gentle sleep!
Nature's soft nurse!   How have I frighted thee,
That thou no more wilt weigh my eyelids down
And steep my senses in forgetfulness?
(*Henry the Fourth.   Part Two.   Act* 3.   *Scene* 1.   *The King speaking.*)

Oh, I have passed a miserable night,
So full of ugly sights, of ghastly dreams,
That, as I am a Christian faithful man,
I would not spend another such a night
Though 'twere to buy a world of happy days;
So full of dismal terror was the time!
(*Richard the Third.   Act* 1.   *Scene* 4.   *Clarence speaking.*)

ROMEO   Peace, peace, Mercutio, peace!
              Thou talk'st of nothing.
MERCUTIO   True, I talk of dreams;
              Which are the children of an idle brain,
              Begot of nothing but vain fantasy,
              Which is as thin of substance as the air
              And more inconstant than the wind, who woos
              Even now the frozen bosom of the North
              And, being angered, puffs away from thence,
              Turning his face to the dew-dropping South.
(*Romeo and Juliet. Act* 1. *Scene* 4.)

Sleep dwell upon thine eyes, peace in thy breast!
Would I were sleep and peace, so sweet to rest!
(*Romeo and Juliet. Act* 2. *Scene* 2. *Romeo speaking.*)

Between the acting of a dreadful thing
And the first motion, all the interim is
Like a phantasma, or a hideous dream.
(*Julius Cæsar. Act* 2. *Scene* 1. *Brutus speaking.*)

Methought I heard a voice cry 'Sleep no more!
Macbeth does murder sleep' . . . the innocent sleep,
Sleep that knits up the ravelled sleave of care,
The death of each day's life, sore labour's bath,
Balm of hurt minds, great nature's second course,
Chief nourisher in life's feast. . . .
(*Macbeth. Act* 2. *Scene* 2. *Macbeth speaking.*)

Banquo and Donalbain! Malcolm! Awake!
Shake off this downy sleep, death's counterfeit,
And look on death itself! Up, up, and see
The great doom's image.
(*Macbeth. Act* 2. *Scene* 3. *Macduff speaking.*)

                        Duncan is in his grave;
After life's fitful fever he sleeps well.
(*Macbeth. Act* 3. *Scene* 2. *Macbeth speaking.*)

You lack the season of all natures: sleep.
(*Macbeth. Act* 3. *Scene* 4. *Lady Macbeth speaking.*)

HAMLET   Oh, God! I could be bounded in a nut-shell and count
              myself a king of infinite space, were it not that I have
              bad dreams.
GUILDENSTERN Which dreams, indeed, are ambition; for the very substance
              of the ambitious is merely the shadow of a dream.
(*Hamlet. Act 2. Scene 2.*)

                    To die: to sleep;
No more; and by a sleep to say we end
The heart-ache and the thousand natural shocks
That flesh is heir to, 'tis a consummation
Devoutly to be wished. To die, to sleep.
To sleep: perchance to dream! Ay, there's the rub,
For in that sleep of death what dreams may come,
When we have shuffled off this mortal coil,
Must give us pause.
(*Hamlet. Act 3. Scene 1. Hamlet speaking.*)

                    Not poppy, nor mandragora,
Nor all the drowsy syrups of the world
Shall ever medicine thee to that sweet sleep
Which thou owedst yesterday.
(*Othello. Act 3. Scene 3. Iago speaking.*)

DOLABELLA   Assuredly you know me.
CLEOPATRA   No matter, sir, what I have heard or known.
             You laugh when boys or women tell their dreams;
             Is't not your trick?
DOLABELLA   I understand not, madam.
CLEOPATRA   I dreamed there was an Emperor Antony:
             Oh, such another sleep, that I might see
             But such another man!
(*Antony and Cleopatra. Act 5. Scene 2.*)

SECTION XXV

PITY

                 Oh, the cry did knock
Against my very heart! Poor souls, they perished!
Had I been any god of power, I would
Have sunk the sea within the earth or ere
It should the good ship so have swallowed and
The fraughting souls within her.
(*The Tempest. Act 1. Scene 2. Miranda speaking.*)

DUKE   What, is Antonio here?
ANTONIO   Ready, so please your Grace.
DUKE   I am sorry for thee: thou art come to answer
            A stony adversary, an inhuman wretch
            Uncapable of pity, void and empty
            From any dram of mercy.
The Merchant of Venice. Act 4. Scene 1.)

VIOLA   If I did love you in my master's flame,
            With such a suffering, such a deadly life,
            In your denial I would find no sense;
            I would not understand it.
OLIVIA   Why, what would *you*?
VIOLA   Make me a willow cabin at your gate,
            And call upon my soul within the house;
            Write loyal cantons of contemnèd love
            And sing them loud, even in the dead of night;
            Halloo your name to the reverberate hills,
            And make the babbling gossip of the air
            Cry out 'Olivia!' Oh, you should not rest
            Between the elements of air and earth
            But you should pity me!
(Twelfth Night. Act 1. Scene 5.)

VIOLA   I pity you.
OLIVIA   That's a degree to love.
VIOLA   No, not a grize; for 'tis a vulgar proof
            That very oft we pity enemies.
(Twelfth Night. Act 3. Scene 1.)
Grize: a degree, a short distance or a step.

                    Good my lords,
I am not prone to weeping, as our sex
Commonly are; the want of which vain dew
Perchance shall dry your pities.
(The Winter's Tale. Act 2. Scene 1. Hermione speaking.)

Though some of you with Pilate wash your hands,
Showing an outward pity; yet you Pilates
Have here delivered me to my sour cross,
And water cannot wash away your sin.
(Richard the Second. Act 4. Scene 1. Richard speaking.)

For he is gracious, if he be observed:
He hath a tear for pity and a hand
Open as day for melting charity.
*(Henry the Fourth. Part Two. Act 4. Scene 4. The King, referring to
    Prince Henry.)*

Oh, how this discord doth afflict my soul!
Can you, my lord of Winchester, behold
My sighs and tears and will not once relent?
Who should be pitiful if you be not?
Or who should study to prefer a peace
If holy churchmen take delight in broils?
(*Henry the Sixth. Part One. Act* 3. *Scene* 1. *The King speaking.*)

My gracious liege, this too much lenity
And harmful pity must be laid aside.
To whom do lions cast their gentle looks?
Not to the beast that would usurp their den.
Whose hand is that the forest bear doth lick?
Not his that spoils her young before her face.
Who 'scapes the lurking serpent's mortal sting?
Not he that sets his foot upon her back.
The smallest worm will turn, being trodden on;
And doves will peck in safeguard of their brood.
(*Henry the Sixth. Part Three. Act* 2. *Scene* 2. *Clifford speaking.*)

Oh, pity, pity!   Gentle heaven, pity!
The red rose and the white are on his face,
The fatal colours of our striving houses.
(*Henry the Sixth. Part Three. Act* 2. *Scene* 5. *The King speaking.*)

Stay yet, look back with me unto the Tower.
Pity, you ancient stones, those tender babes
Whom envy hath immured within your walls!
Rough cradle for such little pretty ones!
Rude ragged nurse, old sullen playfellow
For tender princes, use my babies well!
So foolish sorrow bids your stones farewell.
(*Richard the Third. Act* 4. *Scene* 1. *Queen Elizabeth speaking.*)

Oh, my lord!
Press not a falling man too far; 'tis virtue:
His faults lie open to the laws; let them,
Not you, correct him.   My heart weeps to see him
So little of his great self.
(*Henry the Eighth. Act* 3. *Scene* 2. *The Lord Chamberlain, speaking of Wolsey.*)

I tell you he does sit in gold, his eye
Red as 'twould burn Rome, and his injury
The gaoler to his pity.
(*Coriolanus. Act* 5. *Scene* 1. *Cominius, referring to Coriolanus.*)

Is there no pity sitting in the clouds,
That sees into the bottom of my grief?
(*Romeo and Juliet.   Act* 3.   *Scene* 5.   *Juliet speaking*.)

                    Besides, this Duncan
Hath borne his faculties so meek, hath been
So clear in his great office, that his virtues
Will plead like angels trumpet-tongued against
The deep damnation of his taking-off;
And pity, like a naked new-born babe,
Striding the blast, or heaven's cherubin horsed
Upon the sightless couriers of the air,
Shall blow the horrid deed in every eye,
That tears shall drown the wind.
(*Macbeth.   Act* 1.   *Scene* 7.   *Macbeth speaking*.)

GHOST   My hour is almost come
            When I to sulphurous and tormenting flames
            Must render up myself.
HAMLET   Alas, poor ghost!
GHOST   Pity me not, but lend thy serious hearing
            To what I shall unfold.
HAMLET   Speak; I am bound to hear.
(*Hamlet.   Act* 1.   *Scene* 5.)

GLOUCESTER Now, good sir, what are you?
EDGAR   A most poor man, made tame to fortune's blows;
            Who, by the art of known and feeling sorrows,
            Am pregnant to good pity.
(*King Lear.   Act* 4.   *Scene* 6.)

                    Upon this hint I spake:
She loved me for the dangers I had passed,
And I loved her that she did pity them.
This only is the witchcraft I have used.
Here comes the lady; let her witness it.
(*Othello.   Act* 1.   *Scene* 3.   *Othello speaking*.)

                    Good faith,
I tremble still with fear; but if there be
Yet left in heaven as small a drop of pity
As a wren's eye, feared gods, a part of it!
(*Cymbeline.   Act* 4.   *Scene* 2.   *Imogen speaking*.)

Thou that art now the world's fresh ornament
And only herald to the gaudy Spring,
Within thine own bud buriest thy content
And, tender churl, mak'st waste in niggarding.
Pity the world, or else this glutton be:
To eat the world's due, by the grave and thee.
(*Sonnet* 1.)

Section XXVI

OF KINGS AND KINGSHIP

How long a time lies in one little word!
Four lagging Winters and four wanton Springs
End in a word: such is the breath of kings.
(*Richard the Second. Act* 1. *Scene* 3. *Bolingbroke speaking.*)

AUMERLE   How brooks your grace the air,
            After your late tossing on the breaking seas?
RICHARD   Needs must I like it well: I weep for joy
            To stand upon my kingdom once again.
            Dear earth, I do salute thee with my hand,
            Though rebels wound thee with their horses' hoofs.
(*Richard the Second. Act* 3. *Scene* 2.)

Not all the water in the rough rude sea
Can wash the balm from an anointed king;
The breath of worldly men cannot depose
The deputy elected by the Lord.
(*Richard the Second. Act* 3. *Scene* 2. *Richard speaking.*)
The Oxford Shakespeare has: 'Can wash the balm from an anointed king.'
    The Everyman Edition has: 'Can wash the balm off from an anointed
    king.'

I had forgot myself: am I not king?
Awake, thou coward majesty! Thou sleepest.
Is not the king's name twenty thousand names?
Arm, arm, my name! A puny subject strikes
At thy great glory.
(*Richard the Second. Act* 3. *Scene* 2. *Richard speaking.*)

For God's sake, let us sit upon the ground
And tell sad stories of the death of kings:
How some have been deposed, some slain in war,
Some haunted by the ghosts they have deposed,
Some poisoned by their wives, some sleeping killed;
All murdered.   For within the hollow crown
That rounds the mortal temples of a king,
Keeps Death his court; and there the antic sits,
Scoffing his state and grinning at his pomp,
Allowing him a breath, a little scene,
To monarchize, be feared and kill with looks,
Infusing him with self and vain conceit,
As if this flesh which walls about our life
Were brass impregnable.   And, humoured thus,
Comes at the last and with a little pin
Bores through his castle wall . . . and farewell, king!
(*Richard the Second.   Act 3.   Scene 2.   Richard speaking.*)

What must the king do now?   Must he submit?
The king shall do it.   Must he be deposed?
The king shall be contented.   Must he lose
The name of king?   O' God's name, let it go!
I'll give my jewels for a set of beads,
My gorgeous palace for a hermitage,
My gay apparel for an almsman's gown,
My figured goblets for a dish of wood,
My sceptre for a palmer's walking-staff,
My subjects for a pair of carvèd saints,
And my large kingdom for a little grave. . . .
(*Richard the Second.   Act 3.   Scene 3.   Richard speaking.*)

Down, down I come; like glistering Phæthon,
Wanting the manage of unruly jades.
In the base court?   Base court, where kings grow base
To come at traitors' calls and do them grace.
In the base court?   Come down?   Down, court!   Down king!
For night-owls shriek where mounting larks should sing.
(*Richard the Second.   Act 3.   Scene 3.   Richard speaking.*)

BOLINGBROKE   I thought you had been willing to resign.
RICHARD   My crown, I am; but still my griefs are mine.
               You may my glories and my state depose,
               But not my griefs; still am I king of those.
(*Richard the Second.   Act 4.   Scene 1.*)

Oh, that I were a mockery king of snow,
Standing before the sun of Bolingbroke
To melt myself away in water-drops!
(*Richard the Second. Act 4. Scene 1. Richard speaking.*)

Thus play I in one person many people,
And none contented: sometimes am I king;
Then treasons make me wish myself a beggar,
And so I am. Then crushing penury
Persuades me I was better when a king.
Then am I kinged again; and by and by
Think that I am unkinged by Bolingbroke
And straight am nothing.
Richard the Second. Act 5. Scene 5. Richard speaking.)

Canst thou, oh, partial sleep, give thy repose
To the wet sea-boy in an hour so rude;
And in the calmest and most stillest night,
With all appliances and means to boot,
Deny it to a king? Then happy low, lie down!
Uneasy lies the head that wears a crown.
(*Henry the Fourth. Part Two. Act 3. Scene 1. The King speaking.*)

Every subject's duty is the king's; but every subject's soul is his own.
(*Henry the Fifth. Act 4. Scene 1. The King speaking.*)

Upon the king! Let us our lives, our souls,
Our debts, our careful wives,
Our children and our sins lay on the king!
We must bear all. Oh, hard condition,
Twin-born with greatness, subject to the breath
Of every fool, whose sense no more can feel
But his own wringing! What infinite heart's-ease
Must kings neglect, that private men enjoy!
And what have kings that privates have not too,
Save ceremony, save general ceremony?

        . . . .
         No, thou proud dream
That play'st so subtly with a king's repose;
I am a king that find thee, and I know
'Tis not the balm, the sceptre and the ball,
The sword, the mace, the crown imperial,
The intertissued robe of gold and pearl,
The farcèd title running 'fore the king,
The throne he sits on, nor the tide of pomp
That beats upon the high shore of this world,

No, not all these, thrice-gorgeous ceremony,
Not all these, laid in bed majestical,
Can sleep so soundly as the wretched slave
Who, with a body filled and vacant mind,
Gets him to rest, crammed with distressful bread. . . .
(*Henry the Fifth. Act 4. Scene 1. The King speaking.*)

My crown is in my heart, not on my head;
Not decked with diamonds and Indian stones,
Nor to be seen: my crown is called 'Content';
A crown it is that seldom kings enjoy.
(*Henry the Sixth. Part Three. Act 3. Scene 1. The King speaking.*)

Peace, impudent and shameless Warwick, peace!
Proud setter-up and puller-down of kings.
(*Henry the Sixth. Part Three. Act 3. Scene 3. Queen Margaret speaking.*)

True hope is swift and flies with swallow's wings;
Kings it makes gods, and meaner creatures kings.
(*Richard the Third. Act 5. Scene 2. Richmond speaking.*)

Oh, how wretched
Is that poor man that hangs on princes' favours!
There is, betwixt that smile we would aspire to,
That sweet aspect of princes, and their ruin,
More pangs and fears than wars or women have:
And when he falls, he falls like Lucifer,
Never to hope again.
(*Henry the Eighth. Act 3. Scene 2. Wolsey speaking.*)

Oh, Cromwell, Cromwell!
Had I but served my God with half the zeal
I served my king, He would not in mine age
Have left me naked to mine enemies.
(*Henry the Eighth. Act 3. Scene 2. Wolsey speaking.*)

When beggars die, there are no comets seen;
The heavens themselves blaze forth the death of princes.
(*Julius Cæsar. Act 2. Scene 2. Calpurnia speaking.*)

That it should come to this!
But two months dead; nay, not so much, not two!
So excellent a king; that was, to this,
Hyperion to a satyr. So loving to my mother
That he might not beteem the winds of heaven
Visit her face too roughly.
(*Hamlet. Act 1. Scene 2. Hamlet speaking.*)

HAMLET   A murderer and a villain;
A slave that is not twentieth part the tithe
Of your precedent lord; a vice of kings;
A cutpurse of the empire and the rule,
That from a shelf the precious diadem stole
And put it in his pocket!
THE QUEEN   No more!
HAMLET   A king of shreds and patches. . . .
(*Hamlet. Act 3. Scene 4.*)

There's such divinity doth hedge a king
That treason can but peep to what it would,
Acts little of his will.
(*Hamlet. Act 4. Scene 5. The King speaking.*)

GLOUCESTER The trick of that voice I do well remember.
             Is't not the king?
LEAR   Ay, every inch a king;
             When I do stare, see how the subject quakes.
(*King Lear. Act 4. Scene 6.*)

SECTION XXVII

JUSTICE AND THE LAW

We must not make a scarecrow of the law,
Setting it up to fear the birds of prey;
And let it keep one shape, till custom make it
Their perch and not their terror.
(*Measure For Measure. Act 2. Scene 1. Angelo speaking.*)

                    I not deny
The jury, passing on the prisoner's life,
May in the sworn twelve have a thief or two
Guiltier than him they try.   What's open made to justice,
That justice seizes: what know the laws
That thieves do pass on thieves?
(*Measure For Measure. Act 2. Scene 1. Angelo speaking.*)

                 How would you be
If He, which is the top of judgment, should
But judge you as you are?   Oh, think on that;
And mercy then will breathe within your lips
Like man new made.
(*Measure For Measure. Act 2. Scene 2. Isabella speaking.*)

So may the outward shows be least themselves:
The world is still deceived with ornament.
In law, what plea so tainted and corrupt
But being seasoned with a gracious voice
Obscures the show of evil?
(*The Merchant of Venice. Act 3. Scene 2. Bassanio speaking.*)

The Duke cannot deny the course of law:
For the commodity that strangers have
With us in Venice, if it be denied,
'Twill much impeach the justice of his state;
Since that the trade and profit of the city
Consisteth of all nations.
(*The Merchant of Venice. Act 3. Scene 3. Antonio speaking.*)

But mercy is above this sceptred sway;
It is enthronèd in the *hearts* of kings.
It is an attribute to God Himself;
And earthly power doth then show likest God's
When mercy seasons justice. Therefore, Jew,
Though justice be thy plea, consider this:
That in the course of justice none of us
Should see salvation.
(*The Merchant of Venice. Act 4. Scene 1. Portia speaking.*)

My deeds upon my head! I crave the law,
The penalty and forfeit of my bond.
(*The Merchant of Venice. Act 4. Scene 1. Shylock speaking.*)

It doth appear you are a worthy judge.
You know the law; your exposition
Hath been most sound. I charge you by the law,
Whereof you are a well-deserving pillar,
Proceed to judgment.
(*The Merchant of Venice. Act 4. Scene 1.*)

A Daniel come to judgment! Yea, a Daniel!
Oh, wise young judge, how I do honour thee!
(*The Merchant of Venice. Act 4. Scene 1. Shylock speaking.*)

And then the justice,
In fair round belly with good capon lined,
With eyes severe and beard of formal cut,
Full of wise saws and modern instances;
And so he plays his part.
(*As You Like It. Act 2. Scene 7. Jaques speaking.*)

I knew when seven justices could not take up a quarrel; but when the parties were met themselves, one of them thought but of an 'If'; as, '*If* you said *so*, then *I* said *so*.' And they shook hands and swore brothers. Your If is the only peace-maker; much virtue in If.
(*As You Like It.   Act 5.   Scene 4.   Touchstone speaking.*)

And do as adversaries do in law:
Strive mightily, but eat and drink as friends.
(*The Taming of the Shrew.   Act 1.   Scene 2.   Tranio speaking.*)

FABIAN   I will prove it legitimate, sir, upon the oaths of judgment and
              reason.
SIR TOBY   And they have been grand-jurymen since before Noah was a
              sailor.
(*Twelfth Night.   Act 3.   Scene 2.*)

Still you keep o' the windy side of the law: good.
(*Twelfth Night.   Act 3.   Scene 4.   Fabian speaking.*)

PANDULPH   There's law and warrant, lady, for my curse.
CONSTANCE   And for mine, too: when law can do no right,
                Let it be lawful that law bar no wrong.
                Law cannot give my child his kingdom here,
                For he that holds his kingdom holds the law;
                Therefore, since law itself is perfect wrong,
                How can the law forbid my tongue to curse?
(*King John.   Act 3.   Scene 1.*)

But, I prithee, sweet wag, shall there be gallows standing in England when thou art king, and resolution thus fobbed, as it is, with the rusty curb of old father antic, the law? Do not thou, when thou art king, hang a thief.
(*Henry the Fourth.   Part One.   Act 1.   Scene 2.   Falstaff speaking.*)

But in these nice sharp quillets of the law,
Good faith, I am no wiser than a daw.
(*Henry the Sixth.   Part One.   Act 2.   Scene 4.   Warwick speaking.*)

What stronger breastplate than a heart untainted!
Thrice is he armed that hath his quarrel just;
And he but naked, though locked up in steel,
Whose conscience with injustice is corrupted.
(*Henry the Sixth.   Part Two.   Act 3.   Scene 2.   The King speaking.*)

All good people,
You that thus far have come to pity me,
Hear what I say and then go home and lose me.
I have this day received a traitor's judgment,
And by that name must die.   Yet heaven bear witness,
And if I have a conscience let it sink me
Even as the axe falls, if I be not faithful!
The law I bear no malice for my death;
It has done upon the premises but justice.
But those that sought it I could wish more Christians.
(*Henry the Eighth.   Act 2.   Scene 1.   Buckingham speaking.*)

Sir, I desire you do me right and justice,
And to bestow your pity on me; for
I am a most poor woman, and a stranger
Born out of your dominions, having here
No judge indifferent, nor no more assurance
Of equal friendship and proceeding.
(*Henry the Eighth.   Act 2.   Scene 4.   Queen Katharine speaking.*)

Section XXVIII

TRUTHS AND TRUISMS

There's nothing ill can dwell in such a temple:
If the ill spirit have so fair a house,
Good things will strive to dwell with't.
(*The Tempest.   Act 1.   Scene 2.   Miranda speaking.*)

TRINCULO   Oh, forgive me my sins!
STEPHANO   He that dies pays all debts.
(*The Tempest.   Act 3.   Scene 2.*)

Look thou be true.   Do not give dalliance
Too much the rein: the strongest oaths are straw
To the fire i' the blood.
(*The Tempest.   Act 4.   Scene 1.   Prospero speaking.*)

That man that hath a tongue, I say, is no man,
If with his tongue he cannot win a woman.
(*The Two Gentlemen of Verona.   Act 3.   Scene 1.   Valentine speaking.*)

How use doth breed a habit in a man!
(*The Two Gentlemen of Verona.   Act 5.   Scene 4.   Valentine speaking.*)

Oh, heaven!   Were man
But constant, he were perfect.
(*The Two Gentlemen of Verona.   Act 5.   Scene 4.   Proteus speaking.*)

. . . for they say, if money go before, all ways do lie open.
(*The Merry Wives of Windsor.   Act 2.   Scene 2.   Ford speaking.*)

Oh, what a world of vile ill-favoured faults
Looks handsome in three hundred pounds a year!
(*The Merry Wives of Windsor.   Act 3.   Scene 4.   Anne Page speaking.*)

Spirits are not finely touched
But to fine issues; nor Nature never lends
The smallest scruple of her excellence,
But, like a thrifty goddess, she determines
Herself the glory of a creditor:
Both thanks and use.
(*Measure For Measure.   Act 1.   Scene 1.   The Duke speaking.*)

Well, heaven forgive him!   And forgive us all!
Some rise by sin, and some by virtue fall.
(*Measure For Measure.   Act 2.   Scene 1.   Escalus speaking.*)

Oh, it is excellent
To have a giant's strength; but it is tyrannous
To use it like a giant.
(*Measure For Measure.   Act 2.   Scene 2.   Isabella speaking.*)

The miserable have no other medicine
But only hope.
(*Measure For Measure.   Act 3.   Scene 1.   Claudio speaking.*)

Every true man's apparel fits your thief.
(*Measure For Measure.   Act 4.   Scene 2.   Abhorson speaking.*)

A wretched soul, bruised with adversity,
We bid be quiet when we hear it cry;
But were we burdened with like weight of pain,
As much, or more, we should ourselves complain.
(*The Comedy of Errors.   Act 2.   Scene 1.   Adriana speaking.*)

Small cheer and great welcome makes a merry feast.
(*The Comedy of Errors.   Act 3.   Scene 1.   Balthazar speaking.*)

Silence is the perfectest herald of joy: I were but little happy, if I could
say how much.
(*Much Ado About Nothing.   Act 2.   Scene 1.   Claudio speaking.*)

Well, everyone can master a grief but he that has it.
(*Much Ado About Nothing.   Act 3.   Scene 2.   Benedick speaking.*)

All this I see; and I see that the fashion wears out more apparel than the
     man.
(*Much Ado About Nothing.   Act 3.   Scene 3.   Conrade speaking.*)

Oh, what authority and show of truth
Can cunning sin cover itself withal!
(*Much Ado About Nothing.   Act 4.   Scene 1.   Claudio speaking.*)

              For it so falls out
That what we have we prize not to the worth
Whiles we enjoy it; but being lacked and lost,
Why, then we rack the value, then we find
The virtue that possession would not show us
Whiles it was ours.
(*Much Ado About Nothing.   Act 4.   Scene 1.   Friar Francis speaking.*)

But there is no such man: for, brother, men
Can counsel and speak comfort to that grief
Which they themselves not feel; but, tasting it,
Their counsel turns to passion, which before
Would give preceptial medicine to rage,
Fetter strong madness in a silken thread,
Charm ache with air and agony with words.
No, no; 'tis all men's office to speak patience
To those that wring under the load of sorrow,
But no man's virtue nor sufficiency
To be so moral when he shall endure
The like himself.   Therefore give me no counsel:
My griefs cry louder than advertisement.
(*Much Ado About Nothing.   Act 5.   Scene 1.   Leonato speaking.*)

A jest's prosperity lies in the ear
Of him that hears it, never in the tongue
Of him that makes it.
(*Love's Labour's Lost.   Act 5.   Scene 2.   Rosaline speaking.*)

Look: when I vow, I weep; and vows so born,
In their nativity all truth appears.
(*A Midsummer-Night's Dream.   Act 3.   Scene 2.   Lysander speaking.*)

              I will hear that play;
For never anything can be amiss
When simpleness and duty tender it.

·   ·   ·   ·   ·   ·   ·   ·   ·

Love, therefore, and tongue-tied simplicity
In least speak most, to my capacity.
(*A Midsummer-Night's Dream.   Act 5.   Scene 1.   Theseus speaking.*)

You would be, sweet madam, if your miseries were in the same abundance
    as your good fortunes are: and yet, for aught I see, they are as sick
    that surfeit with too much as they that starve with nothing.   It is no
    mean happiness, therefore, to be seated in the mean.
(*The Merchant of Venice.   Act 1.   Scene 2.   Nerissa speaking.*)

If to do were as easy as to know what were good to do, chapels had been
    churches and poor men's cottages princes' palaces.   It is a good divine
    that follows his own instructions: I can easier teach twenty what were
    good to be done, than be one of the twenty to follow mine own
    teaching.
(*The Merchant of Venice.   Act 1.   Scene 2.   Portia speaking.*)

The brain may devise laws for the blood; but a hot temper leaps o'er a
    cold decree: such a hare is madness, the youth, to skip o'er the meshes
    of good counsel, the cripple.
(*The Merchant of Venice.   Act 1.   Scene 2.   Portia speaking.*)

It is a wise father that knows his own child. . . . Truth will come to
    light; murder cannot be hid long.
(*The Merchant of Venice.   Act 2.   Scene 2.   Launcelot speaking.*)

All that glisters is not gold;
Often have you heard that told.
(*The Merchant of Venice.   Act 2.   Scene 7.   Morocco, reading from a scroll.*)

There is no vice so simple, but assumes
Some mark of virtue on his outward parts.
(*The Merchant of Venice.   Act 3.   Scene 2.   Bassanio speaking.*)

The quality of mercy is not strained;
It droppeth as the gentle rain from heaven
Upon the place beneath.   It is twice bless'd:
It blesseth him that gives and him that takes.
'Tis mightiest in the mightiest.   It becomes
The thronèd monarch better than his crown. . . .
(*The Merchant of Venice.   Act 4.   Scene 1.   Portia speaking.*)

He is well paid that is well satisfied;
And I, delivering you, am satisfied,
And therein do account myself well paid.
(*The Merchant of Venice.   Act 4.   Scene 1.   Portia speaking.*)

That light we see is burning in my hall.
How far that little candle throws his beams!
So shines a good deed in a naughty world.
(*The Merchant of Venice. Act 5. Scene 1. Portia speaking.*)

Beauty provoketh thieves sooner than gold.
(*As You Like It. Act 1. Scene 3. Rosalind speaking.*)

JAQUES   Oh, noble fool!
              A worthy fool! Motley's the only wear.
DUKE   What fool is this?
JAQUES   Oh, worthy fool! One that hath been a courtier,
              And says, if ladies be but young and fair
              They have the gift to know it.
(*As You Like It. Act 2. Scene 7.*)

Faith, as you say, there's small choice in rotten apples.
(*The Taming of the Shrew. Act 1. Scene 1. Hortensio speaking.*)

A woman moved is like a fountain troubled,
Muddy, ill-seeming, thick, bereft of beauty;
And while it is so, none so dry or thirsty
Will deign to sip or touch one drop of it.
(*The Taming of the Shrew. Act 5. Scene 2. Katharina speaking.*)

Our remedies oft in ourselves do lie,
Which we ascribe to heaven: the fated sky
Gives us free scope; only doth backward pull
Our slow designs when we ourselves are dull.
(*All's Well That Ends Well. Act 1. Scene 1. Helena speaking.*)

. . . and he must needs go that the devil drives.
(*All's Well That Ends Well. Act 1. Scene 3. The Clown speaking.*)

A young man married is a man that's marred.
(*All's Well That Ends Well. Act 2. Scene 3. Parolles speaking.*)

The web of our life is of a mingled yarn, good and ill together: our virtues
        would be proud, if our faults whipped them not; and our crimes
        would despair, if they were not cherished by our virtues.
(*All's Well That Ends Well. Act 4. Scene 3. First Lord speaking.*)

                          Praising what is lost
Makes the remembrance dear.
(*All's Well That Ends Well. Act 5. Scene 3. The King speaking.*)

All yet seems well; and if it end so meet,
The bitter past, more welcome is the sweet.
(*All's Well That Ends Well.   Act 5.   Scene 3.   The King speaking.*)

Some are born great, some achieve greatness, and some have greatness
   thrust upon 'em.
(*Twelfth Night.   Act 2.   Scene 5.   Malvolio, reading from a letter.*)

A merry heart goes all the day,
Your sad tires in a mile-a.
(*The Winter's Tale.   Act 4.   Scene 3, The Temple Shakespeare and Everyman
   Edition.   Act 4.   Scene 2, The Oxford Shakespeare Song.*)

But this is worshipful society,
And fits the mounting spirit like myself;
For he is but a bastard to the time
That doth not smack of observation.
(*King John.   Act 1.   Scene 1.   The Bastard speaking.*)

No, no; when Fortune means to men most good
She looks upon them with a threatening eye.
(*King John.   Act 3.   Scene 4.   Cardinal Pandulph speaking.*)

And oftentimes excusing of a fault
Doth make the fault the worse by the excuse;
As patches set upon a little breach
Discredit more in hiding of the fault
Than did the fault before it was so patched.
(*King John.   Act 4.   Scene 2.   Pembroke speaking.*)

How oft the sight of means to do ill deeds
Makes ill deeds done!
(*King John.   Act 4.   Scene 2.   The King speaking.*)

As gentle and as jocund as to jest
Go I to fight: truth hath a quiet breast.
(*Richard the Second.   Act 1.   Scene 3.   Mowbray speaking.*)

Where words are scarce they are seldom spent in vain;
For they breathe truth that breathe their words in pain.
          .   .   .   .
He tires betimes that spurs too fast betimes.
(*Richard the Second.   Act 2.   Scene 1.   John of Gaunt speaking.*)

The ripest fruit first falls, and so doth he;
His time is spent, our pilgrimage must be.
(*Richard the Second.   Act 2.   Scene 1.   Richard speaking.*)

Well you deserve: they well deserve to have,
That know the strong'st and surest way to get.
(*Richard the Second. Act 3. Scene 3. Richard speaking.*)

If all the year were playing holidays,
To sport would be as tedious as to work.
(*Henry the Fourth. Part One. Act 1. Scene 2. Prince Henry speaking.*)

That, being daily swallowed by men's eyes,
They surfeited with honey and began
To loathe the taste of sweetness, whereof a little
More than a little is by much too much.
(*Henry the Fourth. Part One. Act 3. Scene 2. The King speaking.*)

A habitation giddy and unsure
Hath he that buildeth on the vulgar heart.
. . . .
Past and to come seem best; things present, worst.
(*Henry the Fourth. Part Two. Act 1. Scene 3. The Archbishop of York
speaking.*)

Self-love, my liege, is not so vile a sin
As self-neglecting.
(*Henry the Fifth. Act 2. Scene 4. The Dauphin speaking.*)

There is some soul of goodness in things evil,
Would men observingly distil it out.
(*Henry the Fifth. Act 4. Scene 1. The King speaking.*)

And I have heard it said, unbidden guests
Are often welcomest when they are gone.
(*Henry the Sixth. Part One. Act 2. Scene 2. Bedford speaking.*)

Defer no time, delays have dangerous ends.
(*Henry the Sixth. Part One. Act 3. Scene 2. Alençon speaking (The
Oxford Shakespeare). Reignier speaking (The Everyman Edition).*)

Smooth runs the water where the brook is deep.
(*Henry the Sixth. Part Two. Act 3. Scene 1. Suffolk speaking.*)

Suspicion always haunts the guilty mind:
The thief doth fear each bush an officer.
(*Henry the Sixth. Part Three. Act 5. Scene 6. Gloucester speaking.*)

Oh, momentary grace of mortal men,
Which we more hunt for than the grace of God!
Who builds his hopes in air of your fair looks
Lives like a drunken sailor on a mast,
Ready, with every nod, to tumble down
Into the fatal bowels of the deep.
(*Richard the Third. Act 3. Scene 4. Hastings speaking.*)

TROILUS   You have bereft me of all words, lady.
PANDARUS   Words pay no debts.   Give her deeds.
(*Troilus and Cressida. Act 3. Scene 2.*)

Wilt thou draw near the nature of the gods?
Draw near them then in being merciful:
Sweet mercy is nobility's true badge.
(*Titus Andronicus. Act 1. Scene 1. Tamora speaking.*)

What, man! More water glideth by the mill
Than wots the miller of.
(*Titus Andronicus. Act 2. Scene 1. Demetrius speaking.*)

That shows thee a weak slave; for the weakest goes to the wall.
(*Romeo and Juliet. Act 1. Scene 1. Gregory speaking.*)

Tut, man, one fire burns out another's burning;
One pain is lessened by another's anguish;
Turn giddy, and be holp by backward turning;
One desperate grief cures with another's languish.
(*Romeo and Juliet. Act 1. Scene 2. Benvolio speaking.*)

He jests at scars that never felt a wound.
(*Romeo and Juliet. Act 2. Scene 2. Romeo speaking.*)

Good night, good night! Parting is such sweet sorrow
That I shall say good night till it be morrow.
(*Romeo and Juliet. Act 2. Scene 2. Juliet speaking.*)

Mercy but murders, pardoning those that kill.
(*Romeo and Juliet. Act 3. Scene 1. Escalus speaking.*)

But 'tis a common proof
That lowliness is young ambition's ladder,
Whereto the climber-upward turns his face;
But when he once attains the upmost round
He then unto the ladder turns his back,
Looks in the clouds, scorning the base degrees
By which he did ascend.
(*Julius Cæsar. Act 2. Scene 1. Brutus speaking.*)

The labour we delight in physics pain.
(*Macbeth. Act 2. Scene 3. Macbeth speaking.*)

Nought's had, all's spent,
When our desire is got without content:
'Tis safer to be that which we destroy
Than by destruction dwell in doubtful joy.
(*Macbeth. Act 3. Scene 2. Lady Macbeth speaking.*)

Better be with the dead
Whom we, to gain our peace, have sent to peace,
Than on the torture of the mind to lie
In restless ecstasy.
(*Macbeth. Act 3. Scene 2. Macbeth speaking.*)

Things bad begun make strong themselves by ill.
(*Macbeth. Act 3. Scene 2. Macbeth speaking.*)

My royal lord,
You do not give the cheer: the feast is sold
That is not often vouched, while 'tis a-making,
'Tis given with welcome.   To feed were best at home;
From thence, the sauce to meat is ceremony.
Meeting were bare without it.
(*Macbeth. Act 3. Scene 4. Lady Macbeth speaking.*)

The night is long that never finds the day.
(*Macbeth. Act 4. Scene 3. Malcolm speaking.*)

Thou know'st 'tis common: all that lives must die,
Passing through nature to eternity.
(*Hamlet. Act 1. Scene 2. The Queen speaking.*)

Foul deeds will rise,
Though all the earth o'erwhelm them, to men's eyes.
(*Hamlet. Act 1. Scene 2. Hamlet speaking.*)

Rosencrantz   We think not so, my lord.
Hamlet   Why, then 'tis none to you; for there is nothing either
               good or bad, but thinking makes it so.
(*Hamlet. Act 2. Scene 2.*)

HAMLET   No, not I:
          I never gave you aught.
OPHELIA   My honoured lord, you know right well you did;
          And with them words of so sweet breath composed
          As made the things more rich.   Their perfume lost,
          Take these again; for to the noble mind
          Rich gifts wax poor when givers prove unkind.
          There, my lord.
(*Hamlet.   Act 3.   Scene 1.*)

My words fly up, my thoughts remain below;
Words without thoughts never to heaven go.
(*Hamlet.   Act 3.   Scene 3.   The King speaking.*)

Lord, we know what we are, but know not what we may be!
(*Hamlet.   Act 4.   Scene 5.   Ophelia speaking.*)

Turn all her mother's pains and benefits
To laughter and contempt; that she may feel
How sharper than a serpent's tooth it is
To have a thankless child!
(*King Lear.   Act 1.   Scene 4.   Lear speaking.*)

The gods are just, and of our pleasant vices
Make instruments to plague us.
(*King Lear.   Act 5.   Scene 3.   Edgar speaking.*)

We cannot all be masters, nor all masters
Cannot be truly followed.
(*Othello.   Act 1.   Scene 1.   Iago speaking.*)

                    Trifles light as air
Are to the jealous confirmations strong
As proofs of holy writ.
(*Othello.   Act 3.   Scene 3.   Iago speaking.*)

SECTION XXIX

SOLDIERS AND WARFARE

There's not a soldier of us all, that, in the thanksgiving before meat, doth
    relish the petition well that prays for peace.
(*Measure For Measure.   Act 1.   Scene 2.   First Gentleman speaking.*)

That in the captain's but a choleric word
Which in the soldier is flat blasphemy.
(*Measure For Measure.   Act 2.   Scene 2.   Isabella speaking.*)

LEONATO   How many gentlemen have you lost in this action?
MESSENGER   But few of any sort, and none of name.
LEONATO   A victory is twice itself when the achiever brings home full
           numbers.
(*Much Ado About Nothing. Act 1. Scene 1.*)

He was wont to speak plain and to the purpose, like an honest man and a
    soldier; and now is he turned orthography: his words are a very
    fantastical banquet, just so many strange dishes.
(*Much Ado About Nothing. Act 2. Scene 3. Benedick speaking.*)

Then a soldier,

Full of strange oaths and bearded like the pard,
Jealous in honour, sudden and quick in quarrel,
Seeking the bubble reputation
Even in the cannon's mouth.
(*As You Like It. Act 2. Scene 7. Jaques speaking.*)
Pard: leopard.

His present gift

Shall furnish me to those Italian fields
Where noble fellows strike.   War is no strife
To the dark house and the detested wife.
(*All's Well That Ends Well. Act 2. Scene 3. Bertram speaking.*)

This very day,

Great Mars, I put myself into thy file.
Make me but like my thoughts and I shall prove
A lover of thy drum, hater of love.
(*All's Well That Ends Well. Act 3. Scene 3. Bertram speaking.*)

The peace of heaven is theirs that lift their swords
In such a just and charitable war.
(*King John. Act 2. Scene 1. The Duke of Austria speaking.*)

No more the thirsty entrance of this soil
Shall daub her lips with her own children's blood;
No more shall trenching war channel her fields,
Nor bruise her flowerets with the armèd hoofs
Of hostile paces.
(*Henry the Fourth. Part One. Act 1. Scene 1. The King speaking.*)

Oh, let the hours be short,

Till fields and blows and groans applaud our sport!
(*Henry the Fourth. Part One. Act 1. Scene 3. Hotspur speaking.*)

CHIEF JUSTICE   I hear you are going with Lord John of Lancaster against the Archbishop and the Earl of Northumberland.

FALSTAFF   Yea; I thank your pretty sweet wit for it.   But look you pray, all you that kiss my Lady Peace at home, that our armies join not in a hot day; for, by the Lord, I take but two shirts out with me, and I mean not to sweat extraordinarily. If it be a hot day, and I brandish anything but my bottle, I would I might never spit white again.

(*Henry the Fourth.   Part Two.   Act* I.   *Scene* 2.)

Once more unto the breach, dear friends, once more;
Or close the wall up with our English dead!
In peace there's nothing so becomes a man
As modest stillness and humility.
But when the blast of war blows in our ears,
Then imitate the action of the tiger;
Stiffen the sinews, summon up the blood,
Disguise fair nature with hard-favoured rage.
Then lend the eye a terrible aspect;
Let it pry through the portage of the head
Like the brass cannon.   Let the brow o'erwhelm it
As fearfully as doth a gallèd rock
O'erhang and jutty his confounded base
Swilled with the wild and wasteful ocean.
Now set the teeth and stretch the nostril wide.
Hold hard the breath, and bend up every spirit
To his full height!   On, on, you noblest English!
(*Henry the Fifth.   Act* 3.   *Scene* I.   *The King speaking.*)

Now entertain conjecture of a time
When creeping murmur and the poring dark
Fills the wide vessel of the universe.
From camp to camp, through the foul womb of night,
The hum of either army stilly sounds,
That the fixed sentinels almost receive
The secret whispers of each other's watch.
(*Henry the Fifth.   Act* 4.   *Chorus speaking.*)

                    Oh, war, thou son of hell,
Whom angry heavens do make their minister,
Throw in the frozen bosoms of our part
Hot coals of vengeance!   Let no soldier fly:
He that is truly dedicate to war
Hath no self-love.
(*Henry the Sixth.   Part Two.   Act* 5.   *Scene* 2.   *Young Clifford speaking.*)

Their weapons like to lightning came and went;
Our soldiers' . . . like the night-owl's lazy flight,
Or like a lazy thresher with a flail . . .
Fell gently down, as if they struck their friends.
(*Henry the Sixth. Part Three. Act 2. Scene 1. Warwick speaking.*)

Let me have war, say I. It exceeds peace as far as day does night. It's
spritely, waking, audible, and full of vent. Peace is a very apoplexy,
lethargy; mulled, deaf, sleepy, insensible; a getter of more bastard
children than war's a destroyer of men.
(*Coriolanus. Act 4. Scene 5. First Servingman speaking.*)

AUFIDIUS   Do they still fly to the Roman?
LIEUTENANT I do not know what witchcraft's in him, but
           Your soldiers use him as the grace 'fore meat,
           Their talk at table and their thanks at end;
           And you are darkened in this action, sir,
           Even by your own.
(*Coriolanus. Act 4. Scene 7.*)

Sometime she driveth o'er a soldier's neck,
And then dreams he of cutting foreign throats,
Of breaches, ambuscadoes, Spanish blades,
Of healths five fathom deep; and then, anon,
Drums in his ear; at which he starts and wakes,
And being thus frighted swears a prayer or two
And sleeps again.
(*Romeo and Juliet. Act 1. Scene 4. Mercutio speaking.*)

Fie, my lord, fie! A soldier, and afeard? What need we fear who knows
it, when none can call our power to account? Yet who would have
thought the old man to have had so much blood in him?
(*Macbeth. Act 5. Scene 1. Lady Macbeth speaking.*)

SIWARD   Had he his hurts before?
ROSS   Ay, on the front.
SIWARD   Why, then, God's soldier be he!
         Had I as many sons as I have hairs,
         I would not wish them to a fairer death.
         And so his knell is knolled.
(*Macbeth. Act 5. Scene 8. Scene 7. The Oxford Shakespeare.*)

One Michael Cassio, a Florentine,
A fellow almost damned in a fair wife,
That never set a squadron in the field
Nor the division of a battle knows
More than a spinster; unless the bookish theoric,
Wherein the togèd consuls can propose
As masterly as he: mere prattle without practice
Is all his soldiership.
(*Othello.   Act* 1.   *Scene* 1.   *Iago speaking.*)
Toged: robed.

Hold your hands,
Both you of my inclining and the rest.
Were it my cue to fight, I should have known it
Without a prompter.
(*Othello.   Act* 1.   *Scene* 2.   *Othello speaking.*)

Rude am I in my speech,
And little blest with the soft phrase of peace;
For since these arms of mine had seven years' pith,
Till now some nine moons wasted, they have used
Their dearest action in the tented field.
And little of this great world can I speak,
More than pertains to feats of broil and battle.
(*Othello.   Act* 1.   *Scene* 3.   *Othello speaking.*)

The tyrant, custom, most grave senators,
Hath made the flinty and steel couch of war
My thrice-driven bed of down.
(*Othello.   Act* 1.   *Scene* 3.   *Othello speaking.*)

Oh, now for ever
Farewell the tranquil mind!   Farewell content!
Farewell the plumèd troop and the big wars
That make ambition virtue!   Oh, farewell,
Farewell the neighing steed and the shrill trump,
The spirit-stirring drum, the ear-piercing fife,
The royal banner and all quality,
Pride, pomp and circumstance of glorious war!
(*Othello.   Act* 3.   *Scene* 3.   *Othello speaking.*)

His captain's heart,
Which in the scuffles of great fights hath burst
The buckles on his breast, reneges all temper,
And is become the bellows and the fan
To cool a gipsy's lust.
(*Antony and Cleopatra.   Act* 1.   *Scene* 1.   *Philo, speaking of Antony.*)
Reneges: denies.

Nay, pray you, seek no colour for your going,
But bid farewell and go. When you sued staying,
Then was the time for words. No going then.
Eternity was in our lips and eyès,
Bliss in our brows bent; none our parts so poor
But was a race of heaven. They are so still;
Or thou, the greatest soldier of the world,
Art turned the greatest liar.
(*Antony and Cleopatra. Act* 1. *Scene* 3. *Cleopatra speaking.*)

The Jove of power make me . . . most weak, most weak! . . .
Your reconciler. Wars 'twixt you twain would be
As if the world should cleave, and that slain men
Should solder up the rift.
(*Antony and Cleopatra. Act* 3. *Scene* 4. *Octavia speaking.*)

I would they'd fight i' the fire or i' the air;
We'd fight there, too.
Antony and Cleopatra. Act 4. *Scene* 10. *Antony speaking.*)

The hearts
That spanieled me at heels, to whom I gave
Their wishes, do discandy, melt their sweets
On blossoming Cæsar; and this pine is barked,
That overtopped them all. Betrayed I am.
Oh, this false soul of Egypt! This grave charm,
Whose eyes becked forth my wars, and called them home,
Whose bosom was my crownet, my chief end,
Like a right gipsy, hath, at fast and loose,
Beguiled me to the very heart of loss.
(*Antony and Cleopatra. Act* 4. *Scene* 12. *Antony speaking. Scene* 10,
The Oxford Shakespeare.)

Unarm, Eros; the long day's task is done
And we must sleep. . . .
. . . Off, pluck off:
The seven-fold shield of Ajax cannot keep
The battery from my heart. Oh, cleave, my sides!
Heart, once be stronger than thy continent,
Crack thy frail case! Apace, Eros! Apace!
No more a soldier. Bruisèd pieces, go;
You have been nobly borne.
(*Antony and Cleopatra. Act* 4. *Scene* 14. *Antony speaking. Scene* 12,
The Oxford Shakespeare.)

I had rather not be so noble as I am.   They dare not fight with me because of the queen, my mother.   Every Jack-slave hath his bellyful of fighting, and I must go up and down like a cock that nobody can match !

(*Cymbeline.   Act 2.   Scene 1.   Cloten speaking.*)

Cymbeline loved me;
And when a soldier was the theme, my name
Was not far off.   Then was I as a tree
Whose boughs did bend with fruit; but, in one night,
A storm or robbery, call it what you will,
Shook down my mellow hangings, nay, my leaves,
And left me bare to weather.

(*Cymbeline.   Act 3.   Scene 3.   Belarius speaking.*)

Not marble, nor the gilded monuments
Of princes, shall outlive this powerful rhyme;
But you shall shine more bright in these contents
Than unswept stone, besmeared with sluttish time.
When wasteful war shall statues overturn,
And broils root out the work of masonry,
Nor Mars his sword nor war's quick fire shall burn
The living record of your memory.

(*Sonnet 55.*)

Section XXX

GOOD   ADVICE

Hope is a lover's staff; walk hence with that,
And manage it against despairing thoughts.

(*The Two Gentlemen of Verona.   Act 3.   Scene 1.   Proteus speaking.*)

Sigh no more, ladies, sigh no more,
Men were deceivers ever;
One foot in sea and one on shore,
To one thing constant never.
Then sigh not so, but let them go
And be you blithe and bonny;
Converting all your sounds of woe
Into hey nonny, nonny.

(*Much Ado About Nothing.   Act 2.   Scene 3.   Balthazar singing.*)

You look not well, Signior Antonio.
You have too much respect upon the world:
They lose it that do buy it with much care.
(*The Merchant of Venice. Act* 1. *Scene* 1. *Gratiano speaking.*)

But fish not with this melancholy bait
For this fool gudgeon, this opinion.
(*The Merchant of Venice. Act* 1. *Scene* 1. *Gratiano speaking.*)

Come, shepherd, let us make an honourable retreat; though not with bag
and baggage, yet with scrip and scrippage.
(*As You Like It. Act* 3. *Scene* 2. *Touchstone speaking.*)

Nay, you were better speak first; and when you were gravelled for lack
of matter, you might take occasion to kiss. Very good orators, when
they are out they will spit; and for lovers lacking . . . God warn
us! . . . matter, the cleanliest shift is to kiss.
(*As You Like It. Act* 4. *Scene* 1. *Rosalind speaking.*)

No profit grows where is no pleasure ta'en:
In brief, sir, study what you most affect.
(*The Taming of the Shrew. Act* 1. *Scene* 1. *Tranio speaking.*)

Love all, trust a few,
Do wrong to none. Be able for thine enemy
Rather in power than use; and keep thy friend
Under thy own life's key. Be checked for silence,
But never taxed for speech.
(*All's Well That Ends Well. Act* 1. *Scene* 1. *The Countess of Rousillon
speaking.*)

What, man! Defy the devil: consider, he's an enemy to mankind.
(*Twelfth Night. Act* 3. *Scene* 4. *Sir Toby speaking.*)

What, man! 'Tis not for gravity to play at cherry-pit with Satan. Hang
him, foul collier!
(*Twelfth Night. Act* 3. *Scene* 4. *Sir Toby speaking.*)
Cherry-pit: a childish game consisting of pitching cherry-stones into a
small hole.

What's gone and what's past help
Should be past grief.
(*The Winter's Tale. Act* 3. *Scene* 2. *Paulina speaking.*)

Therefore, to be possessed with double pomp,
To guard a title that was rich before,
To gild refinèd gold, to paint the lily,
To throw a perfume on the violet,
To smooth the ice, or add another hue
Unto the rainbow, or with taper-light
To seek the beauteous eye of heaven to garnish,
Is wasteful and ridiculous excess.
(*King John. Act 4. Scene 2. Salisbury speaking.*)

BOLINGBROKE   Must I not serve a long apprenticehood
                To foreign passages, and in the end,
                Having my freedom, boast of nothing else
                But that I was a journeyman to grief?
GAUNT   All places that the eye of heaven visits
                Are to a wise man ports and happy havens.
                Teach thy necessity to reason thus:
                There is no virtue like necessity.
(*Richard the Second. Act 1. Scene 3.*)

Oh, while you live, tell truth and shame the devil!
(*Henry the Fourth. Part One. Act 3. Scene 1. Hotspur speaking.*)

           Yield not thy neck
To fortune's yoke, but let thy dauntless mind
Still ride in triumph over all mischance.
(*Henry the Sixth. Part Three. Act 3. Scene 3. Lewis of France speaking.*)

           Be advised:
Heat not a furnace for your foe so hot
That it do singe yourself. We may outrun,
By violent swiftness, that which we run at,
And lose by over-running.
(*Henry the Eighth. Act 1. Scene 1. Norfolk speaking.*)

Cromwell, I charge thee, fling away ambition.
By that sin fell the angels; how can man, then,
The image of his Maker, hope to win by it?
Love thyself last; cherish those hearts that hate thee;
Corruption wins not more than honesty.
Still in thy right hand carry gentle peace
To silence envious tongues. Be just, and fear not.
Let all the ends thou aim'st at be thy country's,
Thy God's, and truth's; then if thou fall'st, oh, Cromwell,
Thou fall'st a blessed martyr!
(*Henry the Eighth. Act 3. Scene 2. Wolsey speaking.*)

Take the instant way;
For honour travels in a strait so narrow,
Where one but goes abreast. Keep then the path,
For emulation hath a thousand sons
That one by one pursue. If you give way,
Or hedge aside from the direct forthright,
Like to an entered tide they all rush by
And leave you hindmost.
(*Troilus and Cressida. Act* 3. *Scene* 3. *Ulysses speaking.*)

Therefore love moderately. Long love doth so.
Too swift arrives as tardy as too slow.
(*Romeo and Juliet. Act* 2. *Scene* 6. *Friar Laurence speaking.*)

Things without all remedy
Should be without regard: what's done is done.
(*Macbeth. Act* 3. *Scene* 2. *Lady Macbeth speaking.*)

Give sorrow words: the grief that does not speak
Whispers the o'erfraught heart, and bids it break.
(*Macbeth. Act* 4. *Scene* 3. *Malcolm speaking.*)

Let's make us medicines of our great revenge,
To cure this deadly grief.
(*Macbeth. Act* 4. *Scene* 3. *Malcolm speaking.*)

But to persever
In obstinate condolement is a course
Of impious stubbornness; 'tis unmanly grief.
It shows a will most incorrect to heaven,
A heart unfortified, a mind impatient,
An understanding simple and unschooled.
(*Hamlet. Act* 1. *Scene* 2. *The King speaking.*)

Be wary, then; best safety lies in fear.
Youth to itself rebels, though none else near.
(*Hamlet. Act* 1. *Scene* 3. *Laertes speaking.*)

There; my blessing with thee!
And these few precepts in thy memory
Look thou character. Give thy thoughts no tongue
Nor any unproportioned thought his act.
Be thou familiar, but by no means vulgar.
Those friends thou hast, and their adoption tried,
Grapple them to thy soul with hoops of steel,
But do not dull thy palm with entertainment
Of each new-hatched unfledged comrade. Beware
Of entrance to a quarrel; but being in,
Bear't, that the opposed may beware of thee.

Give every man thy ear, but few thy voice.
Take each man's censure, but reserve thy judgment.
Costly thy habit as thy purse can buy,
But not expressed in fancy; rich, not gaudy,
For the apparel oft proclaims the man.

. . . .

Neither a borrower nor a lender be:
For loan oft loses both itself and friend,
And borrowing dulls the edge of husbandry.
This above all: to thine own self be true,
And it must follow, as the night the day,
Thou canst not then be false to any man.
(*Hamlet. Act 1. Scene 3. Polonius speaking.*)

Be not too tame neither, but let your own discretion be your tutor. Suit
    the action to the word, the word to the action; with this special
    observance, that you o'erstep not the modesty of nature: for anything
    so overdone is from the purpose of playing, whose end, both at the
    first and now, was and is, to hold as 'twere the mirror up to nature;
    to show virtue her own feature, scorn her own image, and the very
    age and body of the time his form and pressure.
(*Hamlet. Act 3. Scene 2. Hamlet's advice to the players.*)

Assume a virtue, if you have it not.
That monster, custom, who all sense doth eat,
Of habits devil, is angel yet in this:
That to the use of actions fair and good
He likewise gives a frock or livery
That aptly is put on.
(*Hamlet. Act 3. Scene 4. Hamlet speaking.*)

HORATIO   If your mind dislike anything, obey it. I will forestal their
    repair hither and say you are not fit.
HAMLET   Not a whit. We defy augury. There is special providence
    in the fall of a sparrow. If it be now, 'tis not to come;
    if it be not to come, it will be now; if it be not now, yet
    it will come: the readiness is all; since no man has aught
    of what he leaves, what is't to leave betimes? Let be.
(*Hamlet. Act 5. Scene 2.*)

Oh, beware, my lord, of jealousy;
It is the green-eyed monster, which doth mock
The meat it feeds on.
(*Othello. Act 3. Scene 3. Iago speaking.*)

Section XXXI

GAMES, SPORTS, OLD CUSTOMS, ETC.

GONZALO   You are gentlemen of brave mettle: you would lift the moon
out of her sphere, if she would continue in it five weeks
without changing.

SEBASTIAN   We would so; and then go a bat-fowling.

(*The Tempest. Act 2. Scene 1.*)

Bat-fowling: a term used for catching birds by night.

. . . for, at Pentecost,
When all our pageants of delight were played,
Our youth got me to play the woman's part.

(*The Two Gentlemen of Verona. Act 4. Scene 4. Julia speaking.*)

I never prospered since I forswore myself at Primero. Well, if my wind
were but long enough to say my prayers, I would repent.

(*The Merry Wives of Windsor. Act 4. Scene 5. Falstaff speaking.*)

Primero: a game of cards.

Since I plucked geese, played truant and whipped top, I knew not what
it was to be beaten till lately.

(*The Merry Wives of Windsor. Act 5. Scene 1. Falstaff speaking.*)

Am I so round with you as you with me,
That like a football you do spurn me thus?
You spurn me hence, and *he* will spurn me hither:
If I last in this service, you must case me in leather.

(*The Comedy of Errors. Act 2. Scene 1. Dromio of Ephesus speaking.*)

He set up his bills here in Messina and challenged Cupid at the flight; and
my uncle's fool, reading the challenge, subscribed for Cupid and
challenged him at the bird-bolt.

(*Much Ado About Nothing. Act 1. Scene 1. Beatrice speaking.*)

Bird-bolt: a short arrow with a broad flat end, used to kill birds without
piercing.

Oh, me! With what strict patience have I sat
To see a king transformèd to a gnat;
To see great Hercules whipping a gig,
And profound Solomon to tune a jig,
And Nestor play at push-pin with the boys,
And critic Timon laugh at idle toys!

(*Love's Labour's Lost. Act 4. Scene 3. Berowne speaking.*)

Gig: a top.

Push-pin: a childish game.

213

Thou art easier swallowed than a flap-dragon.
(*Love's Labour's Lost. Act 5. Scene 1. Costard speaking.*)
Flap-dragon: a small object, lighted and put afloat in a glass of liquor, to
   be swallowed burning.

I'll make one in a dance, or so; or I will play the tabor to the Worthies,
   and let them dance the 'Hay.'
(*Love's Labour's Lost. Act 5. Scene 1. Dull speaking.*)
The Hay: a circular dance.   Also an exclamation used by a fencer when he
   hits his adversary.

The nine-men's morris is filled up with mud;
And the quaint mazes in the wanton green,
For lack of tread are undistinguishable.
(*A Midsummer-Night's Dream. Act 2. Scene 1. Titania speaking.*)
Nine-men's morris: a game played with stones, on figures cut in the turf.

To-morrow, sir, I wrestle for my credit; and he that escapes me without
   some broken limb shall acquit him well.
(*As You Like It. Act 1. Scene 1. Charles speaking.*)

My better parts
Are all thrown down, and that which here stands up
Is but a quintain, a mere lifeless block.
(*As You Like It. Act 1. Scene 2. Orlando speaking.*)
Quintain: a figure set up for tilting at.

Come, shall we go and kill us venison?
(*As You Like It. Act 2. Scene 1. The Banished Duke speaking.*)

Love is merely a madness; and, I tell you, deserves as well a dark house
   and a whip as madmen do.
(*As You Like It. Act 3. Scene 2. Rosalind speaking.*)

The common executioner,
Whose heart the accustomed sight of death makes hard,
Falls not the axe upon the humbled neck
But first begs pardon.
(*As You Like It. Act 3. Scene 5. Silvius speaking.*)

He uses his folly like a stalking-horse, and under the presentation of that
   he shoots his wit.
(*As You Like It. Act 5. Scene 4. The Banished Duke speaking.*)

Or wilt thou ride?   Thy horses shall be trapped,
Their harness studded all with gold and pearl.
Dost thou love hawking?   Thou hast hawks will soar
Above the morning lark.   Or wilt thou hunt?
Thy hounds shall make the welkin answer them
And fetch shrill echoes from the hollow earth.
(*The Taming of the Shrew.   Induction.   Scene 2.   A Lord speaking.*)
The welkin: the firmament.

Well, was it fit for a servant to use his master so, being perhaps, for aught
    I see, two-and-thirty, a pip out?
(*The Taming of the Shrew.   Act 1.   Scene 2.   Grumio speaking.*)
Two-and-thirty, a pip out: a popular phrase meaning intoxicated, derived
    from an old game called Bone-ace, or One-and-Thirty.
A pip: a mark on a card.

She is your treasure, she must have a husband;
I must dance bare-foot on her wedding day
And for your love to her lead apes in hell.
(*The Taming of the Shrew.   Act 2.   Scene 1.   Katharina speaking.*)
Dance bare-foot: according to an old custom, the elder unmarried sisters
    danced without shoes at the youngest daughter's wedding.
Lead apes in hell: the old belief that spinsters led apes in hell!

Oh, sir, Lucentio slipped me like his greyhound,
Which runs himself and catches for his master.
(*The Taming of the Shrew.   Act 5.   Scene 2.   Tranio speaking.*)

SIR TOBY	Come thy ways, Signior Fabian.
FABIAN	Nay, I'll come. If I lose a scruple of this sport, let me be boiled to death with melancholy.
SIR TOBY	Wouldst thou not be glad to have the niggardly, rascally sheep-biter come by some notable shame?
FABIAN	I would exult, man: you know, he brought me out o' favour with my lady about a bear-baiting here.

(*Twelfth Night.   Act 2.   Scene 5.*)
Bear-baiting was a favourite sport in Shakespeare's time.
Sheep-biter: a thief.

MALVOLIO	Having been three months married to her, sitting in my state . . .
SIR TOBY	Oh, for a stone-bow, to hit him in the eye!

(*Twelfth Night.   Act 2.   Scene 5.*)
Stone-bow: a cross-bow from which stones and bullets were fired.

Shall I play my freedom at tray-trip, and become thy bond-slave?
(*Twelfth Night.   Act 2.   Scene 5.   Sir Toby speaking.*)
Tray-trip: a game that resembled backgammon.

CLOWN   What manner of fellow was he that robbed you?
AUTOLYCUS   A fellow, sir, that I have known to go about with troll-my-
             dames.

(*The Winter's Tale. Act 4. Scene 3. Scene 2, The Oxford Shakespeare.*)
Troll-my-dames: Trou-madame; a French game.

QUEEN   What sport shall we devise, here in this garden,
             To drive away the heavy thought of care?
FIRST LADY   Madam, we'll play at bowls.
QUEEN   'Twill make me think the world is full of rubs,
             And that my fortune runs against the bias.

(*Richard the Second. Act 3. Scene 4.*)

THE KING   What treasure, uncle?
EXETER   Tennis-balls, my liege.
THE KING   We are glad the Dauphin is so pleasant with us:
             His present and your pains we thank you for.
             When we have matched our rackets to these balls,
             We will in France, by God's grace, play a set
             Shall strike his father's crown into the hazard.

(*Henry the Fifth. Act 1. Scene 2.*)

I see you stand like greyhounds in the slips,
Straining upon the start.
(*Henry the Fifth. Act 3. Scene 1. The King speaking.*)

LORD RAMBURES   That island of England breeds very valiant creatures:
                their mastiffs are of unmatchable courage.
ORLEANS   Foolish curs, that run winking into the mouth of a
                Russian bear and have their heads crushed like
                rotten apples!

(*Henry the Fifth. Act 3. Scene 7.*)
into the mouth, etc.*:* a reference to the sport of bear-baiting.

Proud of their numbers and secure in soul,
The confident and over-lusty French
Do the low-rated English play at dice.
(*Henry the Fifth. Act 4. Chorus speaking.*)

If I could win a lady at leap-frog, or by vaulting into my saddle with my
    armour on my back, under the correction of bragging be it spoken,
    I should quickly leap into a wife. Or if I might buffet for my love, or
    bound my horse for her favours, I could lay on like a butcher and sit
    like a jack-an-apes, never off.
(*Henry the Fifth. Act 5. Scene 2. The King speaking.*)

I have ventured,
Like little wanton boys that swim on bladders,
This many Summers in a sea of glory;
But far beyond my depth.
(*Henry the Eighth. Act 3. Scene 2. Wolsey speaking.*)

. . . those that tame wild horses
Pace 'em not in their hands to make 'em gentle,
But stop their mouths with stubborn bits and spur 'em
Till they obey the manage.
(*Henry the Eighth. Act 5. Scene 3. Gardiner speaking.*)

I have been
The book of his good acts, whence men have read
His fame unparallel'd, haply amplified;
For I have ever glorified my friends,
Of whom he's chief, with all the size that verity
Would without lapsing suffer. Nay, sometimes,
Like to a bowl upon a subtle ground,
I have tumbled past the throw, and in his praise
Have almost stamped the leasing.
(*Coriolanus. Act 5. Scene 2. Menenius speaking.*)
Stamped: given currency to.
Leasing: lies.

BENVOLIO Why, Romeo, art thou mad?
ROMEO Not mad, but bound more than a madman is:
        Shut up in prison, kept without food,
        Whipped and tormented.
(*Romeo and Juliet. Act 1. Scene 2.*)

Hist! Romeo, hist! Oh, for a falconer's voice
To lure this tassel-gentle back again!
(*Romeo and Juliet. Act 2. Scene 2. Juliet speaking.*)
Tassel-gentle: a male hawk.

Come, I'll go see this Italian. What I have lost to-day at bowls I'll win
    to-night of him.
(*Cymbeline. Act 2. Scene 1. Cloten speaking.*)

SECOND FISHERMAN What a drunken knave was the sea,
                To cast thee in our way!
PERICLES A man whom both the waters and the wind,
                In that vast tennis-court, have made the ball
                For them to play upon, entreats you pity him.
(*Pericles. Act 2. Scene 1.*)

Section XXXII

THE SUPERNATURAL

GLENDOWER   I can call spirits from the vasty deep.
HOTSPUR   Why, so can I; or so can any man.
            But will they come when you do call for them?
(*Henry the Fourth.   Part One.   Act 3.   Scene 1.*)

KATHARINE   Spirits of peace, where are ye?   Are ye all gone,
            And leave me here in wretchedness behind ye?
GRIFFITH   Madam, we are here.
KATHARINE   It is not you I call for.
            Saw ye none enter since I slept?
(*Henry the Eighth.   Act 4.   Scene 2.*)

MERCUTIO   Oh, then, I see Queen Mab hath been with you.
BENVOLIO   Queen Mab!   What's she?   (*Oxford Shakespeare.*)
MERCUTIO   She is the fairies' midwife, and she comes
            In shape no bigger than an agate-stone
            On the fore-finger of an alderman,
            Drawn with a team of little atomies
            Athwart men's noses as they lie asleep.
(*Romeo and Juliet.   Act 1.   Scene 4.*)
Atomies: little creatures as small as atoms.

And Cæsar's spirit, ranging for revenge,
With Ate by his side come hot from hell,
Shall in these confines with a monarch's voice
Cry 'Havoc!' and let slip the dogs of war;
That this foul deed shall smell above the earth
With carrion men, groaning for burial.
(*Julius Cæsar.   Act 3.   Scene 1.   Antony speaking.*)

BRUTUS   Let me see, let me see; is not the leaf turned down
            Where I left reading?   Here it is, I think.
                        (*Enter the ghost of Cæsar.*)
            How ill this taper burns!   Ha!   Who comes here?
            I think it is the weakness of mine eyes
            That shapes this monstrous apparition.
            It comes upon me.   Art thou any thing?
            Art thou some god, some angel, or some devil,
            That makest my blood cold and my hair to stare?
            Speak to me, what thou art.

GHOST Thy evil spirit, Brutus.
BRUTUS   Why comest thou?
GHOST To tell thee thou shalt see me at Philippi.
BRUTUS Well; then I shall see thee again?
GHOST Ay, at Philippi.
BRUTUS Why, I will see thee at Philippi then.
(*Julius Cæsar.   Act 4.   Scene 3.*)

MACBETH   Say from whence
 You owe this strange intelligence?   Or why
 Upon this blasted heath you stop our way
 With such prophetic greeting?   Speak, I charge you.
         (*The Witches vanish.*)
BANQUO The earth hath bubbles as the water has,
 And these are of them.   Whither are they vanished?
MACBETH Into the air; and what seemed corporal melted
 As breath into the wind.
(*Macbeth.   Act 1.   Scene 3.*)
Owe: own.

This supernatural soliciting
Cannot be ill; cannot be good.   If ill,
Why hath it given me earnest of success,
Commencing in a truth?   I *am* Thane of Cawdor.
If good, why do I yield to that suggestion
Whose horrid image doth unfix my hair
And make my seated heart knock at my ribs,
Against the use of nature?
(*Macbeth.   Act 1.   Scene 3.   Macbeth, speaking aside.*)

A mote it is to trouble the mind's eye.
In the most high and palmy state of Rome,
A little ere the mightiest Julius fell,
The graves stood tenantless, and the sheeted dead
Did squeak and gibber in the Roman streets.

   . . . .
     (*Re-enter Ghost.*)
But soft, behold!   Lo, where it comes again!
I'll cross it, though it blast me.   Stay, illusion!
(*Hamlet.   Act 1.   Scene 1.   Horatio speaking.*)

MARCELLUS 'Tis gone.
 We do it wrong, being so majestical,
 To offer it the show of violence;
 For it is as the air, invulnerable,
 And our vain blows malicious mockery.

BERNARDO   It was about to speak, when the cock crew.
HORATIO   And then it started like a guilty thing
            Upon a fearful summons.   I have heard,
            The cock, that is the trumpet to the morn,
            Doth with his lofty and shrill-sounding throat
            Awake the god of day; and at his warning,
            Whether in sea or fire, in earth or air,
            The extravagant and erring spirit hies
            To his confine.   And of the truth herein
            This present object made probation.
MARCELLUS   It faded on the crowing of the cock.
            Some say that ever 'gainst that season comes
            Wherein our Saviour's birth is celebrated,
            The bird of dawning singeth all night long;
            And then, they say, no spirit dare stir abroad,
            The nights are wholesome, then no planets strike,
            No fairy takes, nor witch hath power to charm;
            So hallowed and so gracious is the time.
(*Hamlet.   Act* I.   *Scene* I.)

HAMLET   If it assume my noble father's person,
            I'll speak to it though hell itself should gape
            And bid me hold my peace.   I pray you all,
            If you have hitherto concealed this sight,
            Let it be tenable in your silence still;
            And whatsoever else shall hap to-night,.
            Give it an understanding but no tongue.
            I will requite your loves.   So fare you well.
            Upon the platform, 'twixt eleven and twelve
            I'll visit you.
ALL   Our duty to your honour.
HAMLET   Your loves, as mine to you.   Farewell.
                                   (*Exeunt all but Hamlet.*)
            My father's spirit in arms!   All is not well.
            I doubt some foul play.   Would the night were come!
            Till then sit still, my soul: foul deeds will rise,
            Though all the earth o'erwhelm them, to men's eyes.
(*Hamlet.   Act* I.   *Scene* 2.)

Angels and ministers of grace defend us!
Be thou a spirit of health, or goblin damned,
Bring with thee airs from heaven or blasts from hell,
Be thy intents wicked or charitable,
Thou com'st in such a questionable shape
That I will speak to thee.
(*Hamlet.   Act* I.   *Scene* 4.   *Hamlet speaking.*)

'Tis now the very witching time of night,
When churchyards yawn and hell itself breathes out
Contagion to this world.
(*Hamlet. Act 3. Scene 2. Hamlet speaking.*)

Section XXXIII

CLASSICAL ALLUSIONS

Ye elves of hills, brooks, standing lakes and groves;
And ye that on the sands with printless foot
Do chase the ebbing Neptune, and do fly him
When he comes back.
(*The Tempest. Act 5. Scene 1. Prospero speaking.*)

To the dread rattling thunder
Have I given fire, and rifted Jove's stout oak
With his own bolt.
(*The Tempest. Act 5. Scene 1. Prospero speaking.*)

PROTEUS   For I will be thy beadsman, Valentine.
VALENTINE And on a love-book pray for my success?
PROTEUS   Upon some book I love I'll pray for thee.
VALENTINE That's on some shallow story of deep love:
           How young Leander crossed the Hellespont.
PROTEUS   That's a deep story of a deeper love;
           For he was more than over shoes in love.
(*The Two Gentlemen of Verona. Act 1. Scene 1.*)

Why, Phæthon, for thou art Merops' son,
Wilt thou aspire to guide the heavenly car,
And with thy daring folly burn the world?
Wilt thou reach stars because they shine on thee?
(*The Two Gentlemen of Verona. Act 3. Scene 1. The Duke speaking.*)

For Orpheus' lute was strung with poets' sinews,
Whose golden touch could soften steel and stones;
Make tigers tame and huge leviathans
Forsake unsounded deeps to dance on sands.
(*The Two Gentlemen of Verona. Act 3. Scene 2. Proteus speaking.*)

But what says she to me? Be brief, my good she-Mercury.
(*The Merry Wives of Windsor. Act 2. Scene 2. Falstaff speaking.*)

. . . divulge Page himself for a secure and wilful Actæon; and to these
violent proceedings all my neighbours shall cry aim.
(*The Merry Wives of Windsor. Act 3. Scene 2. Ford speaking.*)

Remember, Jove, thou wast a bull for thy Europa; love set on thy horns.
   Oh, powerful love, that in some respects makes a beast a man! In
   some other, a man a beast! You were also, Jupiter, a swan for the
   love of Leda. Oh, omnipotent love! How near the god drew to
   the complexion of a goose.
(*The Merry Wives of Windsor. Act 5. Scene 5. Falstaff speaking.*)

Why, now is Cupid a child of conscience: he makes restitution.
(*The Merry Wives of Windsor. Act 5. Scene 5. Falstaff speaking.*)

Could great men thunder
As Jove himself does, Jove would ne'er be quiet.
For every pelting, petty officer
Would use his heaven for thunder.   Nothing but thunder.
(*Measure For Measure. Act 2. Scene 2. Isabella speaking.*)

Why, what an intricate impeach is this!
I think you all have drunk of Circe's cup.
(*The Comedy of Errors. Act 5. Scene 1. The Duke speaking.*)

DON PEDRO   My visor is Philemon's roof; within the house is Jove.
HERO   Why, then, your visor should be thatched.
(*Much Ado About Nothing. Act 2. Scene 1.*)
Philemon's roof: an allusion to the story of the peasant Philemon and his
   wife, Baucis, who received Jupiter into their thatched cottage.

If we can do this, Cupid is no longer an archer: his glory shall be ours,
   for we are the only love-gods.
(*Much Ado About Nothing. Act 2. Scene 1. Don Pedro speaking.*)

She would have made Hercules have turned spit; yea, and have cleft his
   club to make the fire too.   Come, talk not of her: you shall find her
   the infernal Ate in good apparel.
(*Much Ado About Nothing. Act 2. Scene 1. Benedick, speaking of Beatrice.*)
Ate: in Greek mythology the personification of criminal folly or
   infatuation.   The daughter of Zeus.

Out on thee! Seeming! I will write against it:
You seem to me as Dian in her orb,
As chaste as is the bud ere it be blown.
But you are more intemperate in your blood
Than Venus.
(*Much Ado About Nothing. Act 4. Scene 1. Claudio speaking.*)

And look, the gentle day,
Before the wheels of Phœbus, round about
Dapples the drowsy East with spots of grey.
(*Much Ado About Nothing. Act 5. Scene 3. Don Pedro speaking.*)
Phœbus: a common epithet of Apollo, in this instance regarded as the
   sun-god.

And, among three, to love the worst of all:
A wightly wanton with a velvet brow,
With two pitch balls stuck in her face for eyes.
Ay, and by heaven, one that will do the deed
Though Argus were her eunuch and her guard!
(*Love's Labour's Lost. Act 3. Scene 1. Berowne speaking.*)
Wightly: nimble.
Argus: In Greek mythology, Argus, with his countless eyes, originally
   denoted the starry heavens.

Thou for whom e'en Jove would swear
Juno but an Ethiop were;
And deny himself for Jove,
Turning mortal for thy love.
(*Love's Labour's Lost. Act 4. Scene 3. Dumaine speaking.*)
Turning mortal for thy love: a reference to the story of Europa and the Bull,
   referred to in a previous quotation in this Section. Juno was Jove's
   wife.

For valour, is not Love a Hercules,
Still climbing trees in the Hesperides?
Subtle as Sphinx; as sweet and musical
As bright Apollo's lute, strung with his hair.
(*Love's Labour's Lost. Act 4. Scene 3. Berowne speaking.*)
Still climbing trees, etc.: this refers to one of the Twelve Labours of Hercules:
   that of procuring the apples from the garden of the Hesperides.

ARMADO   Pardon, sir: error. He is not quantity enough for that
                     Worthy's thumb. He is not so big as the end of his club.
HOLOFERNES Shall I have audience? He shall present Hercules in minority:
                     his enter and exit shall be strangling a snake.
(*Love's Labour Lost. Act 5. Scene 1.*
'*Strangling a snake*': the story of Hercules reports that, even in his cradle,
   he was strong enough to strangle serpents which had been sent to kill
   him.

The words of Mercury are harsh after the songs of Apollo.
You, that way; we, this way.
(*Love's Labour's Lost. Act 5. Scene 2. Armado speaking.*)

My good Lysander!
I swear to thee by Cupid's strongest bow;
By his best arrow with the golden head;
By the simplicity of Venus' doves;
By that which knitteth souls and prospers loves;
And by that fire which burned the Carthage queen
When the false Troyan under sail was seen;
By all the vows that ever men have broke . . .
In number more than ever women spoke . . .
In that same place thou hast appointed me,
To-morrow truly will I meet with thee.
(*A Midsummer-Night's Dream. Act* 1. *Scene* 1. *Hermia speaking.*)

To-morrow night, when Phœbe doth behold
Her silver visage in the watery glass,
Decking with liquid pearl the bladed grass. . . .
(*A Midsummer-Night's Dream. Act* 1. *Scene* 1. *Lysander speaking.*)

Love looks not with the eyes, but with the mind;
And therefore is winged Cupid painted blind.
(*A Midsummer-Night's Dream. Act* 1. *Scene* 1. *Helena speaking.*)

Run when you will, the story shall be changed;
Apollo flies, and Daphne holds the chase.
(*A Midsummer-Night's Dream. Act* 2. *Scene* 1. *Helena speaking.*)

Now, by two-headed Janus,
Nature hath framed strange fellows in her time:
Some that will evermore peep through their eyes
And laugh like parrots at a bag-piper;
And other of such vinegar aspect.
That they'll not show their teeth in way of smile
Though Nestor swear the jest be laughable.
(*The Merchant of Venice. Act* 1. *Scene* 1. *Salarino speaking.*)

Nor is the wide world ignorant of her worth,
For the four winds blow in from every coast
Renownèd suitors; and her sunny locks
Hang on her temples like a golden fleece,
Which makes her seat of Belmont Colchos' strand
And many Jasons come in quest of her.
(*The Merchant of Venice. Act* 1. *Scene* 1. *Bassanio speaking.*)

If I live to be as old as Sybilla, I will die as chaste as Diana unless I be
obtained by the manner of my father's will.
(*The Merchant of Venice. Act* 1. *Scene* 2. *Portia speaking.*)

If Hercules and Lichas play at dice,
Which is the better man, the greater throw
May turn by fortune from the weaker hand.
So is Alcides beaten by his page.
And so may I, blind fortune leading me,
Miss that which one unworthier may attain,
And die with grieving.
(*The Merchant of Venice. Act 2. Scene 1. Morocco speaking.*)

Oh, ten times faster Venus' pigeons fly
To seal love's bonds new-made, than they are wont
To keep obligèd faith unforfeited.
(*The Merchant of Venice. Act 2. Scene 6. Salarino speaking.*)

Now he goes,
With no less presence but with much more love
Than young Alcides, when he did redeem
The virgin tribute paid by howling Troy
To the sea-monster. I stand for sacrifice;
The rest aloof are the Dardanian wives,
With blearèd visages, come forth to view
The issue of the exploit. Go, Hercules!
Live thou, I live. With much, much more dismay
I view the fight than thou that mak'st the fray.
(*The Merchant of Venice. Act 3. Scene 2. Portia speaking.*)

Therefore, thou gaudy gold,
Hard food for Midas, I will none of thee.
(*The Merchant of Venice. Act 3. Scene 2. Bassanio speaking.*)

Truly then, I fear you are damned both by father and mother: thus when
I shun Scylla, your father, I fall into Charybdis, your mother. Well,
you are gone both ways.
(*The Merchant of Venice. Act 3. Scene 5. Launcelot Gobbo speaking.*)

LORENZO   The moon shines bright. In such a night as this
When the sweet wind did gently kiss the trees
And they did make no noise, in such a night
Troilus, methinks, mounted the Troyan walls
And sighed his soul toward the Grecian tents
Where Cressid lay that night.
JESSICA   In such a night
Did Thisbe fearfully o'ertrip the dew;
And saw the lion's shadow ere himself,
And ran dismayed away.

LORENZO   In such a night
          Stood Dido with a willow in her hand
          Upon the wild sea-banks, and waft her love
          To come again to Carthage.
JESSICA   In such a night
          Medea gathered the enchanted herbs
          That did renew old Æson.
(*The Merchant of Venice. Act 5. Scene 1.*)

Come, ho, and wake Diana with a hymn!
With sweetest touches pierce your mistress' ear
And draw her home with music.
(*The Merchant of Venice. Act 5. Scene 1. Lorenzo speaking.*)

Peace, ho! The moon sleeps with Endymion
And would not be awaked.
(*The Merchant of Venice. Act 5. Scene 1. Portia speaking.*)

CELIA   Let us sit and mock the good housewife Fortune from her
             wheel, that her gifts may henceforth be bestowed equally.
ROSALIND   I would we could do so; for her benefits are mightily
             misplaced; and the bountiful blind woman doth most
             mistake in her gifts to women.
CELIA   'Tis true. For those that she makes fair she scarce makes
             honest; and those that she makes honest she makes very
             ill-favouredly.
(*As You Like It. Act 1. Scene 2.*)

Now Hercules be thy speed, young man!
(*As You Like It. Act 1. Scene 2. Rosalind speaking.*)

                         . . . like Juno's swans
Still we went coupled and inseparable.
(*As You Like It. Act 1. Scene 3. Celia speaking.*)

I'll have no worse a name than Jove's own page;
And therefore look you call me Ganymede.
(*As You Like It. Act 1. Scene 3. Rosalind speaking.*)

Oh, Jupiter, how weary are my spirits!
(*As You Like It. Act 2. Scene 4. Rosalind speaking.*)

Jove, Jove! This shepherd's passion
Is much upon my fashion.
(*As You Like It. Act 2. Scene 4. Rosalind speaking.*)

Helen's cheek, but not her heart,
Cleopatra's majesty,
Atalanta's better part,
Sad Lucretia's modesty.
(*As You Like It. Act 3. Scene 2. Celia, reading.*)

I was never so be-rhymed since Pythagoras' time, that I was an Irish rat; which I can hardly remember.
(*As You Like It. Act 3. Scene 2. Rosalind speaking.*)
'*Since Pythagoras' time*': this refers to that philosopher's doctrine of the transmigration of souls.

You must borrow me Gargantua's mouth first.
(*As You Like It. Act 3. Scene 2. Celia speaking.*)
Gargantua: 'the large throated' giant of Rabelais, who swallowed five pilgrims, with their staves, in a salad.

You have a nimble wit: I think 'twas made of Atalanta's heels.
(*As You Like It. Act 3. Scene 2. Jaques speaking.*)
Atalanta: probably another name for Artemis. She was a renowned and swift-footed huntress. She offered to marry anyone who could outrun her; and any competitor who lost the race was to be killed. Hippomenes, who had been given three of the apples of the Hesperides by Aphrodite, dropped these apples when running against Atalanta; and when she stooped to pick them up, he won the race.

I am here with thee and thy goats, as the most capricious poet, honest Ovid, was among the Goths.
(*As You Like It. Act 3. Scene 3. Touchstone speaking.*)

He hath bought a pair of cast lips of Diana: a nun of Winter's sisterhood kisses not more religiously; the very ice of chastity is in them.
(*As You Like It. Act 3. Scene 4. Celia speaking.*)

The poor world is almost six thousand years old, and in all this time there was not any man died in his own person, videlicet, in a love-cause. Troilus had his brains dashed out with a Grecian club; yet he did what he could to die before, and he is one of the patterns of love. Leander, he would have lived many a fair year, though Hero had turned nun, if it had not been for a hot midsummer night; for, good youth, he went but forth to wash him in the Hellespont and being taken with the cramp was drowned. And the foolish chroniclers of that age found it was 'Hero of Sestos.' But these are all lies: men have died from time to time, and worms have eaten them, but not for love.
(*As You Like It. Act 4. Scene 1. Rosalind speaking.*)

Hark, Tranio! Thou may'st hear Minerva speak.
(*The Taming of the Shrew. Act 1. Scene 1. Lucentio speaking.*)
Minerva: the goddess of wisdom.

Oh, yes, I saw sweet beauty in her face,
Such as the daughter of Agenor had,
That made great Jove to humble him to her hand,
When with his knees he kissed the Cretan strand.
(*The Taming of the Shrew. Act 1. Scene 1. Lucentio speaking.*)
'*The daughter of Agenor*': Europa, for whose sake Jupiter took the shape of
   a bull.

Fair Leda's daughter had a thousand wooers;
Then well one more may fair Bianca have.
And so she shall: Lucentio shall make one,
Though Paris come in hope to speed alone.
(*The Taming of the Shrew. Act 1. Scene 2. Tranio speaking.*)
Leda's daughter: Helen.

For patience she will prove a second Grissel,
And Roman Lucrece for her chastity.
(*The Taming of the Shrew. Act 2. Scene 1. Petruchio speaking.*)
Grissel: Griselda, the patient heroine of Chaucer's Clerk's Tale.

Now, Dian, from thy altar do I fly,
And to imperial Love, that god most high,
Do my sighs stream.
(*All's Well That Ends Well. Act 2. Scene 3. Helena speaking.*)

                    I saw your brother,
Most provident in peril, bind himself,
Courage and hope both teaching him the practice,
To a strong mast that lived upon the sea;
Where, like Arion on the dolphin's back,
I saw him hold acquaintance with the waves
So long as I could see.
(*Twelfth Night. Act 1. Scene 2. Sea Captain speaking.*)

Now Mercury endue thee with leasing, for thou speakest well of fools!
(*Twelfth Night. Act 1. Scene 5. Feste speaking.*)
Leasing: lying.

MARIA   If you will see it, follow me.
SIR TOBY To the gates of Tartar, thou most excellent devil of wit!
(*Twelfth Night. Act 2. Scene 5.*)

Tartar: Tartarus. In the Iliad the word denotes an underground prison,
   as far below Hades as earth is below heaven, where those who rebelled
   against Zeus were confined. In later commentaries Tartarus is regarded
   as synonymous with hell.

FESTE   Now Jove, in his next commodity of hair, send thee a beard!
VIOLA   By my troth, I'll tell thee, I am almost sick for one. (*Aside*)
         Though I would not have it grow on *my* chin!
(*Twelfth Night. Act 3. Scene 1.*)

What relish is in this? How runs the stream?
Or I am mad, or else this is a dream.
Let fancy still my sense in Lethe steep;
If it be thus to dream, still let me sleep!
(*Twelfth Night. Act 4. Scene 1. Sebastian speaking.*)
Lethe: 'Oblivion,' in Greek mythology.

                    Apprehend
Nothing but jollity. The gods themselves,
Humbling their deities to love, have taken
The shapes of beasts upon them: Jupiter
Became a bull, and bellowed; the green Neptune
A ram, and bleated; and the fire-robed god,
Golden Apollo, a poor humble swain,
As I seem now.
(*The Winter's Tale. Act 4. Scene 4. Florizel speaking. Scene 3, The Oxford
    Shakespeare.*)

                    Oh, Proserpina,
For the flowers now that frighted thou let'st fall
From Dis's wagon! Daffodils
That come before the swallow dares, and take
The winds of March with beauty; violets dim,
But sweeter than the lids of Juno's eyes
Or Cytherea's breath; pale primroses
That die unmarried, ere they can behold
Bright Phœbus in his strength; a malady
Most incident to maids.
(*The Winter's Tale. Act 4. Scene 4. Perdita speaking. Scene 3, The Oxford
    Shakespeare.*)
Dis's wagon: Pluto's chariot.
Cytherea: Venus.

With him along is come the mother-queen:
An Ate, stirring him to blood and strife.
(*King John. Act 2. Scene 1. Chatillon, referring to Elinor of Acquitaine.*)
Ate: in Greek mythology, the daughter of Zeus. She represented the
    personification of criminal folly.

BLANCH   Oh, well did he become that lion's robe
                That did disrobe the lion of that robe!
THE BASTARD   It lies as sightly on the back of him
                As great Alcides' shows upon an ass.

(*King John. Act 2. Scene 1.*)
'*great Alcides' shows upon an ass*': this alludes to the skin of the Nemean lion
    won by Hercules.

Indeed, you come near me now, Hal; for we that take purses go by the
    moon and the seven stars, and not by Phœbus, he, 'that wandering
    knight so fair.'

(*Henry the Fourth. Part One. Act 1. Scene 2. Falstaff speaking.*)
Phœbus: a frequently employed epithet for Apollo, here referred to as the
    sun-god.

Marry, then, sweet wag, when thou art king let not us that are squires of
    the night's body be called thieves of the day's beauty: let us be Diana's
    foresters, gentlemen of the shade, minions of the moon.

(*Henry the Fourth. Part One. Act 1. Scene 2. Falstaff speaking.*)

I saw young Harry, with his beaver on,
His cushes on his thighs, gallantly armed,
Rise from the ground like feathered Mercury
And vaulted with such ease into his seat,
As if an angel dropped down from the clouds
To turn and wind a fiery Pegasus
And witch the world with noble horsemanship.

(*Henry the Fourth. Part One. Act 4. Scene 1. Vernon speaking.*)
Cushes: armour for the thighs.
Pegasus: the winged horse, sprung from the blood of Medusa.

Thou tremblest, and the whiteness in thy cheek
Is apter than thy tongue to tell thy errand.
Even such a man, so faint, so spiritless,
So dull, so dead in look, so woe-begone,
Drew Priam's curtain in the dead of night
And would have told him half his Troy was burned.

(*Henry the Fourth. Part Two. Act 1. Scene 1. Northumberland speaking.*)

Ah, rogue! I'faith, I love thee. Thou art as valorous as Hector of Troy,
    worth five of Agamemnon, and ten times better than the Nine
    Worthies. Ah, villain!

(*Henry the Fourth. Part Two. Act 2. Scene 4. Doll Tearsheet, speaking
    to Falstaff.*)

FALSTAFF Kiss me, Doll.
PRINCE HENRY (*aside to Poins*)
      Saturn and Venus this year in conjunction! What says the
         almanack to that?
(*Henry the Fourth. Part Two. Act 2. Scene 4.*)

Oh, Phœbus! Hadst thou never given consent
That Phæthon should check thy fiery steeds,
Thy burning car never had scorched the earth.
(*Henry the Sixth. Part Three. Act 2. Scene 6. Clifford speaking.*)
Phæthon: the son of Phœbus and Clymene, who, being at his own request
    permitted to guide the chariot of the sun, nearly set the world on fire,
    but was prevented by Jupiter, who killed him with a thunderbolt.

Orpheus, with his lute, made trees
And the mountain tops that freeze
Bow themselves, when he did sing.
(*Henry the Eighth. Act 3. Scene 1. Song.*)

He hath the joints of everything, but everything so out of joint that he is
    a gouty Briareus, many hands and no use; or purblind Argus, all eyes
    and no sight.
(*Troilus and Cressida. Act 1. Scene 2. Alexander, referring to Ajax.*)
Briareus: in Greek mythology, one of the three hundred-armed, fifty-
    headed Hecatoncheires, the sons of Ouranos and Gaia (heaven and
    earth).
Argus: in Greek mythology, Argus, with his countless eyes, denoted the
    starry heavens.

But let the ruffian Boreas once enrage
The gentle Thetis, and anon behold
The strong-ribbed bark through liquid mountains cut,
Bounding between the two moist elements
Like Perseus' horse.
(*Troilus and Cressida. Act 1. Scene 3. Nestor speaking.*)
Boreas: the North wind.
Thetis: in Greek mythology, the daughter of Nereus, wife of Peleus, and
    mother of Achilles. The chief of the fifty Nereids, she dwelt in the
    depths of the sea with her father and sisters. Thetis is used by Latin
    poets simply for the sea.
Perseus' horse: this probably refers to Pegasus.

And when he speaks

'Tis like a chime a-mending; with terms unsquared,
Which, from the tongue of roaring Typhon dropped,
Would seem hyperboles.
(*Troilus and Cressida. Act 1. Scene 3. Ulysses speaking.*)
Typhon: in Greek mythology, a personification of volcanic forces.

That's done . . . as near as the extremest ends
Of parallels, like as Vulcan and his wife. . . .
Yet good Achilles still cries 'Excellent!
'Tis Nestor right.   Now play him me, Patroclus,
Arming to answer in a night alarm.'
(*Troilus and Cressida.   Act 1.   Scene 3.   Ulysses speaking.*)

But he that disciplined thy arms to fight,
Let Mars divide eternity in twain
And give him half; and, for thy vigour,
Bull-bearing Milo his addition yield
To sinewy Ajax.
(*Troilus and Cressida.   Act 2.   Scene 3.   Ulysses, addressing Ajax.*)

No, Pandarus: I stalk about her door,
Like a strange soul upon the Stygian banks
Staying for waftage.   Oh, be thou my Charon,
And give me swift transportation to those fields
Where I may wallow in the lily-beds
Proposed for the deserver!   Oh, gentle Pandarus!
From Cupid's shoulder pluck his painted wings
And fly with me to Cressid.
(*Troilus and Cressida.   Act 3.   Scene 2.   Troilus speaking.*)
Charon: in Greek mythology, the son of Erebus and Nyx (night).   It was
    his duty to ferry over the Styx those souls of the deceased who had
    received rites of burial.

What music will be in him when Hector has knocked out his brains, I
    know not; but I am sure, none, unless the fiddler Apollo get his sinews
    to make catlings on.
(*Troilus and Cressida.   Act 3.   Scene 3.   Thersites, speaking of Ajax.*)
Catlings: strings, for musical instruments, made from cat-gut.

You would be another Penelope; yet, they say, all the yarn she spun in
    Ulysses' absence did but fill Ithaca full of moths.
(*Coriolanus.   Act 1.   Scene 3.   Valeria, addressing Virgilia.*)

His nature is too noble for the world:
He would not flatter Neptune for his trident,
Or Jove for's power to thunder.
(*Coriolanus.   Act 3.   Scene 1.   Menenius speaking.*)

COMINIUS   He will shake
          Your Rome about your ears.
MENENIUS   As Hercules
          Did shake down mellow fruit.   You have made
          Fair work!

(*Coriolanus.*   Act 4.   Scene 6.)

                  My mother bows,
As if Olympus to a molehill should
In supplication nod.

(*Coriolanus.*   Act 5.   Scene 3.   *Coriolanus speaking.*)

But all so soon as the all-cheering sun
Should in the farthest East begin to draw
The shady curtains from Aurora's bed,
Away from light steals home my heavy son
And private in his chamber pens himself.

(*Romeo and Juliet.*   Act 1.   Scene 1.   *Montague speaking.*)

Aurora: goddess of the dawn.

Speak to my gossip Venus one fair word,
One nick-name for her purblind son and heir,
Young Adam Cupid; he that shot so trim
When King Cophetua loved the beggar-maid!

(*Romeo and Juliet.*   Act 2.   Scene 1.   *Mercutio speaking.*)

The grey-eyed morn smiles on the frowning night,
Chequering the Eastern clouds with streaks of light;
And flecked darkness like a drunkard reels
(From forth day's path and Titan's fiery wheels.

Romeo and Juli et.   Act 2.   Scene 3.   *Friar Laurence speaking.*)

Immoderately she weeps for Tybalt's death,
And therefore have I little talked of love;
For Venus smiles not in a house of tears.

(*Romeo and Juliet.*   Act 4.   Scene 1.   *Paris speaking.*)

I, as Æneas our great ancestor
Did from the flames of Troy upon his shoulder
The old Anchises bear, so from the waves of Tiber
Did I the tired Cæsar.

(*Julius Cæsar.*   Act 1.   Scene 2.   *Cassius speaking.*)

Why, man, he doth bestride the narrow world
Like a Colossus, and we petty men
Walk under his huge legs and peep about
To find ourselves dishonourable graves.
(*Julius Cæsar. Act 1. Scene 2. Cassius speaking.*)
Colossus: a gigantic statue, reputed to have been placed astride the entrance
  to Rhodes Harbour.

Till that Bellona's bridegroom, lapped in proof,
Confronted him with self-comparisons,
Point against point rebellious, arm 'gainst arm,
Curbing his lavish spirit.
(*Macbeth. Act 1. Scene 2. Ross, referring to Macbeth.*)
Bellona: in Roman mythology, the goddess of war.
Lapped in proof: wrapped in armour (proved or tested armour).

Ere the bat hath flown
His cloistered flight; ere to black Hecate's summons
The shard-borne beetle with his drowsy hums
Hath wrung night's yawning peel, there shall be done
A deed of dreadful note.
(*Macbeth. Act 3. Scene 2. Macbeth speaking.*)
Hecate: in Greek mythology, the goddess of magic arts.
Shard-borne: propelled by scaly wings.

A little month, or ere those shoes were old
With which she followed my poor father's body,
Like Niobe, all tears . . . why she, even she! . . .
Oh, God!   A beast that wants discourse of reason
Would have mourned longer . . . married with my uncle,
My father's brother, but no more like my father
Than I to Hercules.
(*Hamlet. Act 1. Scene 2. Hamlet speaking.*)
Niobe: a heroine of Greek fable, who, as she wept for the loss of her seven
  children was turned into stone, and her tears into a fountain.

And never did the Cyclops' hammers fall
On Mars's armour, forged for proof eterne,
With less remorse than Pyrrhus' bleeding sword
Now falls on Priam.
(*Hamlet. Act 2. Scene 2. First Player speaking.*)
Cyclops: in Greek mythology, a race of one-eyed giants.
Pyrrhus: there was a son of Achilles named Pyrrhus; but Priam was slain, in
  the sack of Troy, by Neoptolemus, another of Achilles' sons.

Oh, what a rogue and peasant slave am I!
Is it not monstrous that this player here,
But in a fiction, in a dream of passion,
Could force his soul so to his own conceit
That from her working all his visage wanned:
Tears in his eyes, distraction in's aspect,
A broken voice, and all his function suiting
With forms to his conceit?   And all for nothing!
For Hecuba!
What's Hecuba to him, or he to Hecuba
That he should weep for her?
(*Hamlet.   Act 2.   Scene 2.   Hamlet speaking.*)
Hecuba: the wife of Priam.   When Troy was captured and her husband
   slain, she was made prisoner by the Greeks.

Full thirty times hath Phœbus' cart gone round
Neptune's salt wash and Tellus' orbèd ground;
And thirty dozen moons with borrowed sheen
About the world have times twelve thirties been,
Since love our hearts and Hymen did our hands
Unite commutual in most sacred bands.
(*Hamlet.   Act 3.   Scene 2.   Player King speaking.*)
Phœbus: the sun-god.
Hymen: the god of marriage.

Look here, upon *this* picture, and on *this*,
The counterfeit presentment of two brothers.
See what a grace was seated on this brow:
Hyperion's curls, the front of Jove himself,
An eye like Mars, to threaten and command;
A station like the herald Mercury
New-lighted on a heaven-kissing hill;
A combination and a form indeed,
Where every god did seem to set his seal
To give the world assurance of a man.
(*Hamlet.   Act 3.   Scene 4.   Hamlet speaking.*)
Hyperion: in Greek mythology, one of the Titans.
Mars: the god of war.
A station: an attitude assumed while standing.
Mercury: the messenger of the gods; also the god of merchandise and trade.

I will ask him for my place again; he shall tell me I am a drunkard!   Had
   I as many mouths as Hydra, such an answer would stop them all.
(*Othello.   Act 2.   Scene 3.   Cassio speaking.*)
Hydra: the fabulous, many-headed monster.

Come, thou monarch of the vine,
Plumpy Bacchus, with pink eyne!
In thy fats our cares be drowned,
With thy grapes our hairs be crowned.
Cup us, till the world go round.
(*Antony and Cleopatra. Act 2. Scene 7. Song.*)
Bacchus: the god of wine.

These drums! These trumpets! Flutes! What!
Let Neptune hear we bid a loud farewell
To these great fellows. Sound and be hanged!
Sound!
(*Antony and Cleopatra. Act 2. Scene 7. Menas speaking.*)
Neptune: originally an Italian god of fresh water. Not later than 399 B.C.,
    however, he became identified with Poseidon and was henceforth
    known as a sea-god.

Stay for me!
Where souls do couch on flowers, we'll hand in hand,
And with our sprightly port make the ghosts gaze.
Dido and Æneas shall want troops,
And all the haunt be ours.
(*Antony and Cleopatra. Act 4. Scene 14. Antony speaking. Scene 12,
    The Oxford Shakespeare.*)
Port: deportment.
Dido: queen of Carthage, which city she is reputed to have founded.
    According to Virgil, she was a contemporary of Æneas, with whom
    she fell in love after his landing in Africa; and he attributes her suicide
    to her abandonment by him at the command of Jupiter.
Æneas: son of Anchises and Aphrodite.

But his neat cookery! He cut our roots
In characters,
And sauced our broths as Juno had been sick
And he her dieter.
(*Cymbeline. Act 4. Scene 2. Guiderius speaking.*)
Juno: Jupiter's queen.

Pray you, fetch him hither.
Thersites' body is as good as Ajax'
When neither are alive.
(*Cymbeline. Act 4. Scene 2. Guiderius speaking.*)

He, true knight,
No lesser of her honour confident
Than I did truly find her, stakes this ring.

And would so, had it been a carbuncle
Of Phœbus' wheel.   And might so safely, had it
Been all the worth of's car.
(*Cymbeline.   Act 5.   Scene 5.   Iachimo speaking*.)
'*Of Phœbus' wheel*': a reference to the sun-god's chariot.

Section XXXIV

COMMANDS

FALSTAFF   Go, bear thou this letter to Mistress Page; and thou this to
            Mistress Ford: we will thrive, lads, we will thrive.

PISTOL   Shall I Sir Pandarus of Troy become,
            And by my side wear steel?   Then, Lucifer take all!

NYM   I will run no base humour.   Here, take the humour-letter;
            I will keep the haviour of reputation.

FALSTAFF (*to Robin*)
            Hold, sirrah!   Bear *you* these letters tightly;
            Sail like my pinnace to these golden shores.

(*The Merry Wives of Windsor.   Act 1.   Scene 3*.)

Run, run, Orlando!   Carve on every tree
The fair, the chaste and unexpressive she.
(*As You Like It.   Act 3.   Scene 2.   Orlando speaking*.)

ROSALIND   Answer me in one word.

CELIA   You must borrow me Gargantua's mouth first: 'tis a word
            too great for any mouth of this age's size.

(*As You Like It.   Act 3.   Scene 2*.)

Gargantua's mouth: Gargantua was 'the large-throated giant' of whom
      Rabelais wrote; who was supposed to have swallowed five pilgrims,
      with their staves, in a salad.

But mistress, know yourself.   Down on your knees
And thank heaven, fasting, for a good man's love.
For I must tell you friendly in your ear,
Sell when you can: you are not for all markets.
Cry the man mercy; love him; take his offer;
Foul is most foul, being foul to be a scoffer.
(*As You Like It.   Act 3.   Scene 5.   Rosalind speaking*.)

Let there be gall enough in thy ink; though thou write with a goose-pen,
      no matter.   About it!
(*Twelfth Night.   Act 3.   Scene 2.   Sir Toby speaking*.)

Nay, but make haste; the better foot before.
Oh, let me have no subject enemies,
When adverse foreigners affright my towns
With dreadful pomp of stout invasion!
Be Mercury, set feathers to thy heels
And fly like thought from them to me again.
(*King John. Act 4. Scene 2. The King speaking.*)

Swear me, Kate, like a lady as thou art,
A good mouth-filling oath; and leave 'in sooth'
And such protest of pepper-gingerbread
To velvet-guards and Sunday-citizens.
(*Henry the Fourth. Part One. Act 3. Scene 1. Hotspur speaking.*)
Velvet-guards: those wearing velvet linings.

Dishonour not your mothers; now attest
That those whom you called fathers did beget you.
Be copy now to men of grosser blood
And teach them how to war. And you, good yeomen,
Whose limbs were made in England, show us here
The mettle of your pasture.
. . . .
Follow your spirit, and upon this charge
Cry 'God for Harry, England and Saint George!'
(*Henry the Fifth. Act 3. Scene 1. The King speaking.*)

Off with his head! Now, by Saint Paul I swear
I will not dine until I see the same.
(*Richard the Third. Act 3. Scene 4. Gloucester speaking.*)

Gallop apace, you fiery-footed steeds,
Towards Phœbus' lodging: such a waggoner
As Phæthon would whip you to the West
And bring in cloudy night immediately.
(*Romeo and Juliet. Act 3. Scene 2. Juliet speaking.*)

I shall remember:
When Cæsar says 'Do this!' it is performed.
(*Julius Cæsar. Act 1. Scene 2. Antony speaking.*)

If you can look into the seeds of time
And say which grain will grow and which will not,
Speak then to me, who neither beg nor fear
Your favours nor your hate.
(*Macbeth. Act 1. Scene 3. Banquo speaking.*)

Hence, horrible shadow!
Unreal mockery, hence!
(*Macbeth. Act 3. Scene 4. Macbeth speaking.*)

At once, good night.
Stand not upon the order of your going,
But go at once.
(*Macbeth. Act 3. Scene 4. Lady Macbeth speaking.*)

Double, double toil and trouble;
Fire burn and cauldron bubble.
(*Macbeth. Act 4. Scene 1. The Three Witches speaking.*)

By the pricking of my thumbs,
Something wicked this way comes.
Open locks,
Whoever knocks!
(*Macbeth. Act 4. Scene 1. Second Witch speaking.*)

Out, damnèd spot! Out, I say!
(*Macbeth. Act 5. Scene 1. Lady Macbeth speaking.*)

Throw physic to the dogs; I'll none of it.
(*Macbeth. Act 5. Scene 3. Macbeth speaking.*)

Hang out our banners on the outward walls;
The cry is still 'They come!'
(*Macbeth. Act 5. Scene 5. Macbeth speaking.*)

I 'gin to be a-weary of the sun
And wish the estate o' the world were now undone.
Ring the alarum-bell! Blow, wind! Come, wrack!
At least we'll die with harness on our back.
(*Macbeth. Act 5. Scene 5. Macbeth speaking.*)

Lay on, Macduff!
And damned be him that first cries 'Hold, enough!'
(*Macbeth. Act 5. Scene 8. Scene 7, The Oxford Shakespeare. Macbeth speaking.*)

GHOST   Swear!
HAMLET   Rest, rest, perturbed spirit!
(*Hamlet. Act 1. Scene 5.*)

More matter, with less art.
(*Hamlet. Act 2. Scene 2. The Queen speaking.*)

Look here, upon this picture, and on this;
The counterfeit presentment of two brothers.
(*Hamlet. Act 3. Scene 4. Hamlet speaking.*)

Let it work;
For 'tis the sport to have the enginer
Hoist with his own petar.
(*Hamlet.   Act* 3.   *Scene* 4.   *Hamlet speaking.*)
Enginer: engineer.
Petar: petard: an engine charged with powder, for the purpose of blowing
    up gates.

The point envenomed, too!
Then, venom, to thy work!   (*Stabs the King.*)
(*Hamlet.   Act* 5.   *Scene* 2.   *Hamlet speaking.*)

Cudgel thy brains no more about it. . . .
(*Hamlet.   Act* 5.   *Scene* 1.   *First Clown speaking.*)

Blow, winds, and crack your cheeks! Rage! Blow!
You cataracts and hurricanoes, spout
Till you have drenched our steeples, drowned the cocks!
You sulphurous and thought-executing fires,
Vaunt-couriers to oak-cleaving thunderbolts,
Singe my white head!
(*King Lear.   Act* 3.   *Scene* 2.   *Lear speaking.*)
Vaunt-couriers: forerunners.

Put out the light, and then put out the light:
If I quench *thee*, thou flaming minister,
I can again thy former light restore
Should I repent me; but once put out *thy* light,
Thou cunning'st pattern of excelling nature,
I know not where is that Promethean heat
That can thy light relume.
(*Othello.   Act* 5.   *Scene* 2.   *Othello speaking.*)

Give me my robe, put on my crown; I have
Immortal longings in me.
(*Antony and Cleopatra.   Act* 5.   *Scene* 2.   *Cleopatra speaking.*)

Section XXXV

IN TOWN AND COUNTRY

You sunburned sicklemen, of August weary,
Come hither from the furrow and be merry.
Make holiday; your rye-straw hats put on,
And these fresh nymphs encounter every one
In country footing.
(**The Tempest.**   *Act* 4.   *Scene* 1.   *Iris speaking.*)

They say this town is full of cozenage;
As, nimble jugglers that deceive the eye,
Dark-working sorcerers that change the mind,
Soul-killing witches that deform the body,
Disguisèd cheaters, prating mountebanks,
And many such-like liberties of sin.
(*The Comedy of Errors. Act* 1. *Scene* 2. *Antipholus of Syracuse speaking.*)

And in the wood, a league without the town,
Where I did meet thee once with Helena
To do observance to a morn of May,
There will I stay for thee.
(*A Midsummer-Night's Dream. Act* 1. *Scene* 1. *Lysander speaking.*)

For call you that keeping for a gentleman of my birth, that differs not from
the stalling of an ox? His horses are bred better; for besides that they
are fair with their feeding, they are taught their manage, and to that
end riders dearly hired.
(*As You Like It. Act* 1. *Scene* 1. *Orlando speaking.*)

Shall I keep your hogs and eat husks with them?
(*As You Like It. Act* 1. *Scene* 1. *Orlando speaking.*)

ROSALIND   Oh, how full of briers is this working-day world!
CELIA   They are but burs, cousin, thrown upon thee in holiday
             foolery: if you walk not in the trodden paths, our very
             petticoats will catch them.
ROSALIND   I could shake them off my coat: these burs are in my heart.
(*As You Like It. Act* 1. *Scene* 3.)

But, poor old man, thou prunest a rotten tree,
That cannot so much as a blossom yield
In lieu of all thy pains and husbandry.
(*As You Like It. Act* 2. *Scene* 3. *Orlando speaking.*)

I remember the kissing of her batlet, and the cow's dugs that her pretty
chopt hands had milked. And I remember the wooing of a peascod,
instead of her; from whom I took two cods and, giving her them
again, said with weeping tears, 'Wear these for my sake.'
(*As You Like It. Act* 2. *Scene* 4. *Touchstone speaking.*)
Batlet: a little bat used by laundresses.

But I am shepherd to another man
And do not shear the fleeces that I graze.
(*As You Like It. Act* 2. *Scene* 4. *Corin speaking.*)

. . . those that are good manners at the court are as ridiculous in the country as the behaviour of the country is most mockable at the court.
(*As You Like It. Act 3. Scene 2. Corin speaking.*)

And will you, being a man of your breeding, be married under a bush like a beggar?
(*As You Like It. Act 3. Scene 3. Jaques speaking.*)

So holy and so perfect is my love,
And I in such a poverty of grace,
That I shall think it a most plenteous crop
To glean the broken ears after the man
That the main harvest reaps: loose now and then
A scattered smile, and that I'll live upon.
(*As You Like It. Act 3. Scene 5. Silvius speaking.*)

It was a lover and his lass,
With a hey, and a ho, and a hey nonino,
That o'er the green corn-field did pass
In the Spring time, the only pretty ring time.
(*As You Like It. Act 5. Scene 3. Two Pages, singing.*)

He's a coward and a coystrill that will not drink to my niece, till his brains turn o' the toe like a parish-top.
(*Twelfth Night. Act 1. Scene 3. Sir Toby speaking.*)
Coystrill: a mean, paltry fellow.
Parish-top: alluding to the large top kept in every village for the peasants to whip in frosty weather. The idea was that they should thus keep themselves both warm and out of mischief.

The country cocks do crow, the clocks do toll,
And the third hour of drowsy morning name.
(*Henry the Fifth. Act 4. Chorus speaking.*)

And to conclude: the shepherd's homely curds,
His cold thin drink out of his leather bottle,
His wonted sleep under a fresh tree's shade,
All which secure and sweetly he enjoys,
Is far beyond a prince's delicates.
(*Henry the Sixth. Part Three. Act 2. Scene 5. The King speaking.*)

To climb steep hills
Requires slow pace at first.
(*Henry the Eighth. Act 1. Scene 1. Norfolk speaking.*)

Why should you want? Behold, the earth hath roots;
Within this mile break forth a hundred springs;
The oaks bear mast, the briers scarlet hips;
The bounteous housewife, nature, on each bush
Lays her full mess before you. Want! Why want?
(*Timon of Athens. Act 4. Scene 3. Timon speaking.*)

It is the bright day that brings forth the adder;
And that craves wary walking.
(*Julius Cæsar. Act 2. Scene 1. Brutus speaking.*)

Section XXXVI

POVERTY AND WEALTH

Then know that I have little wealth to lose.
A man I am, crossed with adversity:
My riches are these poor habiliments,
Of which, if you should here disfurnish me,
You take the sum and substance that I have.
(*The Two Gentlemen of Verona. Act 4. Scene 1. Valentine speaking.*)

Albeit I will confess thy father's wealth
Was the first motive that I wooed thee, Anne,
Yet, wooing thee, I found thee of more value
Than stamps in gold or sums in sealèd bags;
And 'tis the very riches of thyself
That now I aim at.
(*The Merry Wives of Windsor. Act 3. Scene 4. Fenton speaking.*)

If thou art rich, thou'rt poor;
For, like an ass whose back with ingots bows,
Thou bear'st thy heavy riches but a journey
And death unloads thee.
(*Measure For Measure. Act 3. Scene 1. The Duke speaking.*)

Fair gentle sweet,
Your wit makes wise things foolish. When we greet,
With eyes best seeming, heaven's fiery eye,
By light we lose light. Your capacity
Is of that nature that to your huge store
Wise things seem foolish and rich things but poor.
(*Love's Labour's Lost. Act 5. Scene 2. Berowne speaking.*)

Give me your hand, Bassanio.   Fare you well.
Grieve not that I am fallen to this for you;
For herein Fortune shows herself more kind
Than is her custom: it is still her use
To let the wretched man outlive his wealth,
To view with hollow eye and wrinkled brow
An age of poverty; from which lingering penance
Of such a misery doth she cut me off.
(*The Merchant of Venice.   Act 4.   Scene 1.   Antonio speaking.*)

Then, good my liege, mistake me not so much
To think my poverty is treacherous.
(*As You Like It.   Act 1.   Scene 3.   Rosalind speaking.*)

Well, come, my Kate; we will unto your father's
Even in these honest mean habiliments.
Our purses shall be proud, our garments poor;
For 'tis the mind that makes the body rich.
(*The Taming of the Shrew.   Act 4.   Scene 3.   Petruchio speaking.*)

I am not worthy of the wealth I owe,
Nor dare I say 'tis mine, and yet it is;
But, like a timorous thief, most fain would steal
What law does vouch mine own.
(*All's Well That Ends Well.   Act 2.   Scene 5.   Helena speaking.*)
Owe: own.

Oh, world, how apt the poor are to be proud!
(*Twelfth Night.   Act 3.   Scene 1.   Olivia speaking.*)

I am as poor as Job, my lord, but not so patient: your lordship may minister
    the potion of imprisonment to me in respect of poverty; but how I
    should be your patient to follow your prescriptions, the wise may
    make some dram of a scruple, or indeed a scruple itself.
(*Henry the Fourth.   Part Two.   Act 1.   Scene 2.   Falstaff speaking.*)

By Jove, I am not covetous for gold,
Nor care I who doth feed upon my cost;
It yearns me not if men my garments wear;
Such outward things dwell not in my desires:
But if it be a sin to covet honour,
I am the most offending soul alive.
(*Henry the Fifth.   Act 4.   Scene 3.   Henry speaking.*)

What piles of wealth hath he accumulated
To his own portion!   And what expense by the hour
Seems to flow from him!   How i' the name of thrift
Does he rake this together?
(*Henry the Eighth.   Act 3.   Scene 2.   Henry speaking.*)

The last is, for my men; they are the poorest,
But poverty could never draw 'em from me;
That they may have their wages duly paid 'em,
And something over to remember me by.
(*Henry the Eighth. Act 4. Scene 2. Queen Katharine speaking.*)

Oh, she is rich in beauty; only poor
That, when she dies, with beauty dies her store!
(*Romeo and Juliet. Act 1. Scene 1. Romeo speaking.*)

ROMEO   The world is not thy friend, nor the world's law.
               The world affords no law to make thee rich.
               Then be not poor, but break it; and take this.
APOTHECARY   My poverty, but not my will, consents.
ROMEO   I pay thy poverty and not thy will.
(*Romeo and Juliet. Act 5. Scene 1.*)

                    Nay, do not think I flatter;
For what advancement may I hope from thee,
That no revenue hast but thy good spirits
To feed and clothe thee?   Why should the poor be flattered?
No, let the candied tongue lick absurd pomp,
And crook the pregnant hinges of the knee
Where thrift may follow fawning.
(*Hamlet. Act 3. Scene 2. Hamlet speaking.*)

Fairest Cordelia, that art most rich being poor,
Most choice forsaken, and most loved despised,
Thee and thy virtues here I seize upon.
(*King Lear. Act 1. Scene 1. The King of France speaking.*)

How poor are they that have not patience!
What wound did ever heal but by degrees?
Thou know'st we work by wit and not by witchcraft,
And wit depends on dilatory time.
(*Othello. Act 2. Scene 3. Iago speaking.*)

Good name in man and woman, dear my lord,
Is the immediate jewel of their souls.
Who steals my purse steals trash: 'tis something, nothing;
'Twas mine, 'tis his, and has been slave to thousands.
But he that filches from me my good name
Robs me of that which not enriches him
And makes me poor indeed.
(*Othello. Act 3. Scene 3. Iago speaking.*)

Poor and content is rich, and rich enough;
But riches fineless is as poor as Winter
To him that ever fears he shall be poor.
(*Othello.   Act* 3.   *Scene* 3.   *Iago speaking.*)
Fineless: without end.

It is my birthday:
I had thought to have held it poor; but since my lord
Is Antony again, I will be Cleopatra.
(*Antony and Cleopatra.   Act* 3.   *Scene* 13.   *Cleopatra speaking.   Scene* 11,
  The Oxford Shakespeare.)

I am alone the villain of the earth,
And feel I am so most.   Oh, Antony,
Thou mine of bounty!   How would'st thou have paid
My better services, when my turpitude
Thou dost so crown with gold!
(*Antony and Cleopatra.   Act* 4.   *Scene* 6.   *Enobarbus speaking.*)

THIRD FISHERMAN   Master, I marvel how the fishes live in the sea.
FIRST FISHERMAN   Why, as men do a-land: the great ones eat up the
                  little ones.   I can compare our rich misers to
                  nothing so fitly as to a whale: a'plays and tumbles,
                  driving the poor fry before him, and at last devours
                  them all at a mouthful.   Such whales have I heard
                  on o' the land, who never leave gaping till they've
                  swallowed the whole parish, church, steeple, bells,
                  and all.
(*Pericles.   Act* 2.   *Scene* 1.)

Haply I think on thee . . . and then my state,
Like to the lark at break of day arising
From sullen earth, sings hymns at heaven's gate;
For thy sweet love, remembered, such wealth brings
That then I scorn to change my state with kings.
(*Sonnet 29.*)

SECTION XXXVII

MONEY

Seven hundred pounds and possibilities is good gifts.
(*The Merry Wives of Windsor.   Act* 1.   *Scene* 1.   *Evans speaking.*)

. . . of seven groats in mill-sixpences, and two Edward shovel-boards.
(*The Merry Wives of Windsor.   Act* 1.   *Scene* 1.   *Slender speaking.*)
The sixpence was the first coin to have a milled edge.   A shovel-board
  was a shilling used in the game of that name.

FALSTAFF   I will not lend thee a penny.
PISTOL   Why, then the world's mine oyster,
            Which I with sword will open.
            I will retort the sum in equipage.
(*The Merry Wives of Windsor. Act 2. Scene 2.*)

FORD   For, they say, if money go before, all ways do lie open.
FALSTAFF   Money is a good soldier, sir, and will on.
(*The Merry Wives of Windsor. Act 2. Scene 2.*)

Oh! . . . sixpence, that I had a' Wednesday last,
To pay the saddler for my mistress' crupper;
The saddler had it, sir; I kept it not.
(*The Comedy of Errors. Act 1. Scene 2. Dromio of Ephesus speaking.*)

To Adriana, villain, hie thee straight;
Give her this key, and tell her, in the desk
That's covered o'er with Turkish tapestry,
There is a purse of ducats. Let her send it.
Tell her I am arrested in the street,
And that shall bail me.
(*The Comedy of Errors. Act 4. Scene 1. Antipholus of Ephesus speaking.*)

ARMADO   How hast thou purchased this experience?
MOTH   By my penny of observation.
(*Love's Labour's Lost. Act 3. Scene 1.*)

An I had but one penny in the world, thou shouldst have it to buy
    gingerbread. Hold, there is the very remuneration I had of thy
    master, thou halfpenny purse of wit, thou pigeon-egg of discretion.
(*Love's Labour's Lost. Act 5. Scene 1. Costard speaking.*)

BASSANIO   This is Signior Antonio.
SHYLOCK (*aside*) How like a fawning publican he looks!
                I hate him, for he is a Christian;
                But more, for that in low simplicity
                He lends out money gratis and brings down
                The rate of usance here with us in Venice.
(*The Merchant of Venice. Act 1. Scene 3.*)

Shall I bend low, and in a bondman's key,
With bated breath and whispering humbleness,
Say this:
'Fair sir, you spat on me on Wednesday last;
You spurned me such a day; another time
You called me dog; and for these courtesies
I'll lend you thus much moneys'?
(*The Merchant of Venice. Act 1. Scene 3. Shylock speaking.*)

BASSANIO   For thy three thousand ducats here is six.
SHYLOCK   If every ducat in six thousand ducats
           Were in six parts and every part a ducat,
           I would not draw them; I would have my bond.
(*The Merchant of Venice. Act 4. Scene 1.*)

I have five hundred crowns,
The thrifty hire I saved under your father;
Which I did store to be my foster-nurse,
When service should in my old limbs lie lame
And unregarded age in corners thrown.
Take that . . .
(*As You Like It. Act 2. Scene 3. Adam speaking.*)

And that he that wants money, means and content is without three good friends.
(*As You Like It. Act 3. Scene 2. Corin speaking.*)

. . . they were all like one another as half-pence are.
(*As You Like It. Act 3. Scene 2. Rosalind speaking.*)

Why, nothing comes amiss, so money comes withal.
(*The Taming of the Shrew. Act 1. Scene 2. Grumio speaking.*)

SIR TOBY   Why, he has three thousand ducats a year.
MARIA   Ay, but he'll have but a year in all these ducats: he's a very fool
           and a prodigal.
(*Twelfth Night. Act 1. Scene 3.*)

ANTONIO   I must entreat of you some of that money.
VIOLA   What money, sir?
           For the fair kindness you have showed me here,
           And part being prompted by your present trouble,
           Out of my lean and low ability
           I'll lend you something.
(*Twelfth Night. Act 3. Scene 4.*)

He seems to be of great authority.   Close with him, give him gold; and
   though authority be a stubborn bear, yet he is oft led by the nose with
   gold.
(*The Winter's Tale. Act 4. Scene 4. Clown speaking. Scene 3, The Oxford
   Shakespeare.*)

And that's the wavering commons; for their love
Lies in their purses, and whoso empties them
By so much fills their hearts with deadly hate.
(*Richard the Second. Act 2. Scene 2. Bagot speaking.*)

To approve my youth further, I will not: the truth is, I am only old in
    judgment and understanding; and he that will caper with me for a
    thousand marks, let him lend me the money and have at him!
(*Henry the Fourth. Part Two. Act 1. Scene 2. Falstaff speaking.*)

FALSTAFF   Boy!
PAGE   Sir!
FALSTAFF   What money is in my purse?
PAGE   Seven groats and twopence.
FALSTAFF   I can get no remedy against this consumption of the purse:
            borrowing only lingers and lingers it out, but the disease
            is incurable.
(*Henry the Fourth. Part Two. Act 1. Scene 2.*)
Groat: a coin to the value of fourpence.

Quoit him down, Bardolph, like a shove-groat shilling. Nay, an a' do
    enothing but speak nothing, a' shall *be* nothing here.
(*Henry the Fourth. Part Two. Act 2. Scene 4. Falstaff speaking.*)
Quoit: to throw.
Shove-groat shilling: a shilling used in the game of shove-groat.

They will steal anything and call it purchase. Bardolph stole a lute-case,
    bore it twelve leagues and sold it for three half-pence.
(*Henry the Fifth. Act 3. Scene 2. Boy speaking.*)

Gold were as good as twenty orators,
And will, no doubt, tempt him to anything.
(*Richard the Third. Act 4. Scene 2. A Page speaking.*)

OLD LADY   You would not be a queen?
ANNE BULLEN No, not for all the riches under heaven.
OLD LADY   'Tis strange: a three-pence bowed would hire me,
             Old as I am, to queen it.
(*Henry the Eighth. Act 2. Scene 3.*)
Bowed: bent.

She will not stay the siege of loving terms,
Nor bide the encounter of assailing eyes,
Nor ope her lap to saint-seducing gold.
(*Romeo and Juliet. Act 1. Scene 1. Romeo speaking.*)

There is thy gold; worse poison to men's souls,
Doing more murder in this loathsome world,
Than these poor compounds that thou mayst not sell:
I sell *thee* poison; thou hast sold me none.
(*Romeo and Juliet. Act 5. Scene 1. Romeo speaking.*)

Make all the money thou canst: if sanctimony and a frail vow betwixt an erring barbarian and a super-subtle Venetian be not too hard for my wits and all the tribe of hell, thou shalt enjoy her. Therefore make money.
(*Othello. Act 1. Scene 3. Iago speaking.*)

Why tribute? Why should we pay tribute? If Cæsar can hide the sun from us with a blanket, or put the moon in his pocket, we will pay him tribute for light; else, sir, no more tribute, pray you now.
(*Cymbeline. Act 3. Scene 1. Cloten speaking.*)

GUIDERIUS   Money, youth?
ARVIRAGUS   All gold and silver rather turn to dirt!
              As 'tis no better reckoned, but of those
              Who worship dirty gods.
(*Cymbeline. Act 3. Scene 6.*)

SECTION XXXVIII

THE DEITY

I, I, I, myself sometimes, leaving the fear of God on the left hand and hiding mine honour in my necessity, am fain to shuffle, to hedge and to lurch.
(*The Merry Wives of Windsor. Act 2. Scene 2. Falstaff speaking.*)

Why, all the souls that were were forfeit once;
And He that might the vantage best have took
Found out the remedy. How would you be
If He, which is the top of judgment, should
But judge you as you are? Oh, think on that,
And mercy then will breathe within your lips
Like man new made.
(*Measure For Measure. Act 2. Scene 2. Isabella speaking.*)

God help the noble Claudio if he have caught the 'Benedick'! It will cost him a thousand pound ere a' be cured.
(*Much Ado About Nothing. Act 1. Scene 1. Beatrice speaking.*)

LEONATO   Well, niece, I hope to see you one day fitted with a husband.
BEATRICE   Not till God make men of some other metal than earth.
            Would it not grieve a woman to be overmastered with a
            piece of valiant dust, to make an account of her life to
            a clod of wayward marl?
(*Much Ado About Nothing. Act 2. Scene 1.*)

Write down that they hope they serve God; and write God first, for God
defend but God should go before such villains!
(*Much Ado About Nothing.* Act 4. Scene 2. *Dogberry speaking.*)

But mercy is above this sceptred sway;
It is enthronèd in the *hearts* of kings.
It is an attribute to God himself.
And earthly power doth then show likest God's
When mercy seasons justice.
(*The Merchant of Venice.* Act 4. Scene 1. *Portia speaking.*)

NERISSA   Gave it a judge's clerk! No, God's my judge,
             The clerk will ne'er wear hair on's face that had it.
GRATIANO   He will, an if he live to be a man.
NERISSA   Ay, if a *woman* live to be a man.
(*The Merchant of Venice.* Act 5. Scene 1.)

. . . and He that doth the ravens feed,
Yea, providently caters for the sparrow,
Be comfort to my age!
(*As You Like It.* Act 2. Scene 3. *Adam speaking.*)

Do I stand there? I never had a brother;
Nor can there be that deity in my nature
Of here and everywhere. I had a sister
Whom the blind waves and surges have devoured.
(*Twelfth Night.* Act 5. Scene 1. *Sebastian speaking.*)

KING JOHN   From whom hast thou this great commission, France,
             To draw my answer from thy articles?
KING PHILIP From that supernal Judge, that stirs good thoughts
             In any breast of strong authority
             To look into the blots and stains of right.
(*King John.* Act 2. Scene 1.)

Then God forgive the sin of all those souls
That to their everlasting residence,
Before the dew of evening fall, shall fleet
In dreadful trial of our kingdom's king!
(*King John.* Act 2. Scene 1. *King John speaking.*)

God for his Richard hath in heavenly pay
A glorious angel: then, if angels fight,
Weak men must fall, for heaven still guards the right.
(*Richard the Second.* Act 3. Scene 2. *Richard speaking.*)

Well, God give *thee* the spirit of persuasion and *him* the ears of profiting,
that what thou speakest may move and what he hears may be believed;
that the true prince may, for recreation sake, prove a false thief.
(*Henry the Fourth. Part One. Act 1. Scene 2. Falstaff speaking.*)

PRINCE HENRY   Why, thou owest God a death.
FALSTAFF   'Tis not due yet. I would be loath to pay Him before
His day. What need I be so forward with Him
that calls not on me?
(*Henry the Fourth. Part One. Act 5. Scene 1.*)

CHIEF JUSTICE   Well, God send the prince a better companion!
FALSTAFF   God send the companion a better prince! I cannot rid
my hands of him.
(*Henry the Fourth. Part Two. Act 1. Scene 2.*)

Oh, God, that one might read the book of fate,
And see the revolution of the times
Make mountains level, and the continent,
Weary of solid firmness, melt itself
Into the sea!
(*Henry the Fourth. Part Two. Act 3. Scene 1. The King speaking.*)

God's arm strike with us! 'Tis a fearful odds.
(*Henry the Fifth. Act 4. Scene 3. Salisbury speaking.*)

But what a point, my lord, your falcon made,
And what a pitch she flew above the rest!
To see how God in all His creatures works!
Yea, man and birds are fain of climbing high.
(*Henry the Sixth. Part Two. Act 2. Scene 1. The King speaking.*)

. . . for my mind misgives
Some consequence, yet hanging in the stars,
Shall bitterly begin his fearful date
With this night's revels, and expire the term
Of a despised life closèd in my breast
By some vile forfeit of untimely death.
But He that hath the steerage of my course
Direct my sail! On, lusty gentlemen.
(*Romeo and Juliet. Act 1. Scene 4. Romeo speaking.*)

One cried 'God bless us!' and 'Amen' the other,
As they had seen me with these hangman's hands.
Listening their fear, I could not say 'Amen,'
When they did say 'God bless us!'
(*Macbeth. Act 2. Scene 2. Macbeth speaking.*)

Look to the lady.
And when we have our naked frailties hid,
That suffer in exposure, let us meet
And question this most bloody piece of work
To know it further.   Fears and scruples shake us.
In the great hand of God I stand; and thence,
Against the undivulged pretence I fight
Of treasonous malice.
(*Macbeth.   Act 2.   Scene 3.   Banquo speaking.*)

Oh, that this too too solid flesh would melt,
Thaw and resolve itself into a dew!
Or that the Everlasting had not fixed
His canon 'gainst self-slaughter!   Oh, God!   God!
How weary, stale, flat and unprofitable
Seem to me all the uses of this world!
(*Hamlet.   Act 1.   Scene 2.   Hamlet speaking.*)

Oh, God!   That men should put an enemy in their mouths to steal away
    their brains!   That we should, with joy, pleasance, revel and applause,
    transform ourselves into beasts!
(*Othello.   Act 2.   Scene 3.   Cassio speaking.*)

Section **XXXIX**

CHILDHOOD

At first the infant,
Mewling and puking in the nurse's arms.
And then the whining school-boy, with his satchel
And shining morning face, creeping like snail
Unwillingly to school.
(*As You Like It.   Act 2.   Scene 7.   Jaques speaking.*)

ARCHIDAMUS   You have an unspeakable comfort of your young Prince
                        Mamillius: it is a gentleman of the greatest promise
                        that ever came into my note.
CAMILLO   I very well agree with you in the hopes of him.   It is a
                        gallant child; one that indeed physics the subject,
                        makes old hearts fresh.   They that went on crutches
                        ere he was born, desire yet their life to see him a man.
(*The Winter's Tale.   Act 1.   Scene 1.*)

HERMIONE   Come, I'll question you
Of my lord's tricks and yours when you were boys:
You were pretty lordings then?
POLIXENES   We were, fair queen,
Two lads that thought there was no more behind
But such a day to-morrow as to-day;
And to be boy eternal.
(*The Winter's Tale. Act 1. Scene 2.*)

FIRST LADY   Come, my gracious lord,
Shall I be your playfellow?
MAMILLIUS   No, I'll none of you.
FIRST LADY   Why, my sweet lord?
MAMILLIUS   You'll kiss me hard, and speak to me as if I were a baby still.
(*The Winter's Tale. Act 2. Scene 1.*)

MAMILLIUS   I learned it out of women's faces. Pray now,
What colour are your eyebrows?
FIRST LADY   Blue, my lord.
MAMILLIUS   Nay, that's a mock. I have seen a lady's nose
That has been blue, but not her eyebrows.
(*The Winter's Tale. Act 2. Scene 1.*)

Look here upon thy brother Geffrey's face:
These eyes, these brows, were moulded out of his;
This little abstract doth contain that large
Which died in Geffrey, and the hand of time
Shall draw this brief into as huge a volume.
That Geffrey was thy elder brother born,
And this his son. England was Geffrey's right,
And this is Geffrey's. In the name of God
How comes it then that thou art called a king,
When living blood doth in these temples beat
Which own the crown that thou o'ermasterest?
(*King John. Act 2. Scene 1. King Philip of France, addressing King John
    of England and referring to Arthur, King John's young nephew.*)

QUEEN ELINOR (*to Arthur*) Come to thy grandam, child.
CONSTANCE   Do, child. Go to it grandam, child.
Give grandam kingdom, and it grandam will
Give it a plum, a cherry, and a fig:
There's a good grandam!
ARTHUR   Good my mother, peace!
I would that I were low laid in my grave.
I am not worth this coil that's made for me.
(*King John. Act 2. Scene 1.*)
Coil: fuss.

ARTHUR   Must you with hot irons burn out both mine eyes?
HUBERT   Young boy, I must.
ARTHUR   And will you?
HUBERT   And I will.
ARTHUR   Have you the heart? When *your* head did but ache,
          I knit my handkercher about your brows . . .
          The best I had, a princess wrought it me . . .
          And I did never ask it you again;
          And with my hand at midnight held your head,
          And, like the watchful minutes to the hour,
          Still and anon cheered up the heavy time,
          Saying 'What lack you?' and 'Where lies your grief?'
(*King John. Act 4. Scene 1.*)

DUCHESS OF YORK   I long with all my heart to see the prince:
                   I hope he is much grown since last I saw him.
QUEEN ELIZABETH   But I hear, no; they say my son of York
                   Hath almost overta'en him in his growth.
YORK   Ay, mother; but I would not have it so.
DUCHESS OF YORK   Why, my young cousin, it is good to grow.
YORK   Grandam, one night, as we did sit at supper,
                   My uncle Rivers talked how I did grow
                   More than my brother: 'Ay,' quoth my uncle
                       Gloucester,
                   'Small herbs have grace, great weeds do grow apace.'
                   And since, methinks, I would not grow so fast;
                   Because sweet flowers are slow and weeds make haste.
(*Richard the Third. Act 2. Scene 4.*)

'Lo, thus,' quoth Dighton, 'lay those tender babes.'
'Thus, thus,' quoth Forrest, 'girdling one another
Within their innocent alabaster arms.
Their lips were four red roses on a stalk,
Which, in their Summer beauty, kissed each other.
A book of prayers on their pillow lay.'
(*Richard the Third. Act 4. Scene 3. Tyrrel, referring to the murder of the
     Princes in the Tower.*)

CRANMER (*kneeling*) And to your royal Grace and the good queen,
                      My noble partners and myself thus pray:
                      All comfort, joy, in this most gracious lady,
                      Heaven ever laid up to make parents happy,
                      May hourly fall upon ye!
THE KING   Thank you, good lord Archbishop.
                      What is her name?
CRANMER   Elizabeth.
(*Henry the Eighth. Act 5. Scene 5.*)

A' shall not tread on me:
I'll run away till I am bigger, but then I'll fight.
(*Coriolanus.   Act 5.   Scene 3.   Son to Coriolanus speaking.*)

LADY MACDUFF	Sirrah, your father's dead.
	And what will you do now. How will you live?
SON	As birds do, Mother.
LADY MACDUFF	What! With worms and flies?
SON	With what I get, I mean; and so do they.
LADY MACDUFF	Poor bird! Thou'dst never fear the net nor lime,
	The pit-fall nor the gin.
SON	Why should I, Mother? Poor birds they are not set for.
	My father is not dead, for all your saying.
LADY MACDUFF	Yes, he is dead: how wilt thou do for a father?
SON	Nay, how will *you* do for a husband?

(*Macbeth.   Act 4.   Scene 2.*)

MURDERER	Where is your husband?
LADY MACDUFF	I hope in no place so unsanctified
	Where such as thou mayst find him.
MURDERER	He's a traitor.
SON	Thou liest, thou shag-haired villain!
MURDERER	What! You egg!
	Young fry of treachery! (*Stabbing him.*)
SON	He has killed me, Mother!
	Run away, I pray you!

(*Macbeth.   Act 4.   Scene 2.   Temple Shakespeare has: shag-ear'd.*)

HAMLET	How comes it? Do they grow rusty? (*Referring to the players.*)
ROSENCRANTZ	Nay, their endeavour keeps in the wonted pace. But there is, sir, an eyrie of children, little eyases, that cry out on the top of question and are most tyrannically clapped for't.

(*Hamlet.   Act 2.   Scene 2.*)
Eyases: young hawks just taken from the nest.

SECTION XL

SARCASM

Oh, jest unseen, inscrutable, invisible,
As a nose on a man's face or a weathercock on a steeple!
(*The Two Gentlemen of Verona.   Act 2.   Scene 1.   Speed speaking.*)

JULIA   A thousand oaths, an ocean of his tears,
             And instances of infinite of love
             Warrant me welcome to my Proteus.
LUCETTA   All these are servants to deceitful men.
(*The Two Gentlemen of Verona.   Act 2.   Scene 7.*)

Oh, worthy fool!   One that hath been a courtier,
And says, if ladies be but young and fair
They have the gift to know it.
(*As You Like It.   Act 2.   Scene 7.   Jaques speaking.*)

Most friendship is feigning, most loving mere folly.
(*As You Like It.   Act 2.   Scene 7.   Amiens singing.*)

ORLANDO   Can you remember any of the principal evils that he laid to
             the charge of women?
ROSALIND   There were none principal.   They were all like one another
             as half-pence are;   every one fault seeming monstrous
             till his fellow fault came to match it.
(*As You Like It.   Act 3.   Scene 2.*)

ROSALIND   But why did he swear he would come this morning, and
             comes not?
CELIA   Nay, certainly, there is no truth in him.
ROSALIND   Do you think so?
CELIA   Yes.   I think he is not a pick-purse nor a horse-stealer;   but
             for his verity in love, I do think him as concave as a
             covered goblet or a worm-eaten nut.
ROSALIND   Not true in love?
CELIA   Yes, when he is in;   but I think he is not in.
ROSALIND   You have heard him swear downright he was.
CELIA   'Was' is not 'is.'   Besides, the oath of a lover is no stronger
             than the word of a tapster: they are both the confirmers
             of false reckonings.
(*As You Like It.   Act 3.   Scene 4.*)

Oh, that's a brave man!   He writes brave verses, speaks brave words,
     swears brave oaths and breaks them bravely, quite traverse, athwart the
     heart of his lover;   as a puisny tilter that spurs his horse but on one
     side, breaks his staff like a noble goose.   But all's brave that youth
     mounts and folly guides.
(*As You Like It.   Act 3.   Scene 4.   Celia speaking.*)
Puisny: unskilful.

Farewell, Monsieur Traveller.   Look you lisp and wear strange suits;
     disable all the benefits of your own country;   be out of love with your
     nativity and almost chide God for making you the countenance you
     are;   or I will scarce think you have swam in a gondola.
(*As You Like It.   Act 4.   Scene 1.   Rosalind speaking.*)

ORLANDO	Pardon me, dear Rosalind.
ROSALIND	Nay, an you be so tardy, come no more in my sight: I had as lief be wooed of a snail.
ORLANDO	Of a snail!
ROSALIND	Ay, of a snail: for though he comes slowly, he carries his house on his head. A better jointure, I think, than you make a woman.

(*As You Like It.   Act* 4.   *Scene* 1.)

Your 'if' is the only peace-maker; much virtue in 'if.'
(*As You Like It.   Act* 5.   *Scene* 4.   *Touchstone speaking.*)

I am too childish-foolish for this world.
(*Richard the Third.   Act* 1.   *Scene* 3.   *Gloucester, afterwards Richard the Third, speaking.*)

ÆNEAS	Fair leave and large security. How may A stranger to those most imperial looks Know them from eyes of other mortals?
AGAMEMNON	How!
ÆNEAS	Ay. I ask that I might waken reverence, And bid the cheek be ready with a blush Modest as morning when she coldly eyes The youthful Phœbus. Which is that god in office, guiding men? Which is the high and mighty Agamemnon?

(*Troilus and Cressida.   Act* 1.   *Scene* 3.)

| ROMEO | Courage, man; the hurt cannot be much. |
| MERCUTIO | No, 'tis not so deep as a well, nor so wide as a church door; but 'tis enough, 'twill serve. |

(*Romeo and Juliet.   Act* 3.   *Scene* 1.)

SECTION XLI

PUNS

PROTEUS	But what said she? (*Speed nods.*) Did she nod?
SPEED	Ay.
PROTEUS	Nod, ay? Why, that's noddy.

(*The Two Gentlemen of Verona.   Act* 1.   *Scene* 1.)
Noddy: a simpleton.   Also a game of cards.

PANTHINO   Away, ass! You'll lose the tide if you tarry any longer.
LAUNCE   It is no matter if the tied were lost; for it is the unkindest tied
            that ever any man tied.
PANTHINO   What's the unkindest tide?
LAUNCE   Why, he that's tied here: Crab, my dog.
(*The Two Gentlemen of Verona. Act 2. Scene 3.*)

FALSTAFF   Now, the report goes she has all the rule of her husband's
            purse. He hath a legion of angels.
PISTOL   As many devils entertain, and 'To her, boy,'! say I.
(*The Merry Wives of Windsor. Act 1. Scene 3.*)
Angel: an old English coin, worth ten shillings, bearing the figure of the
    archangel Michael.

ANTIPHOLUS OF SYRACUSE   Where is the thousand marks thou hadst of me?
DROMIO OF EPHESUS   I have some marks of yours upon my pate;
                         Some of my mistress' marks upon my shoulders;
                         But not a thousand marks between you both.
                         If I should pay your worship those again,
                         Perchance you will not bear them patiently.
(*The Comedy of Errors. Act 1. Scene 2.*)

BASSANIO   Why dost thou whet thy knife so earnestly?
SHYLOCK (*sharpening his knife on the sole of his shoe*)
            To cut the forfeiture from that bankrupt there.
GRATIANO   Not on thy sole, but on thy soul, harsh Jew,
            Thou mak'st thy knife keen; but no metal can,
            No, not the hangman's axe, bear half the keenness
            Of thy sharp envy. Can no prayers pierce thee?
(*The Merchant of Venice. Act 4. Scene 1.*)

For my part, I had rather bear with you than bear you: yet I should bear
    no cross if I did bear you; for I think you have no money in your purse.
(*As You Like It. Act 2. Scene 4. Touchstone speaking.*)
Cross: misfortune. The ancient penny was stamped with a cross, so that
    it might easily be broken into four pieces.

                        And why, sir, must they so?
The 'why' is plain as way to parish church.
(*As You Like It. Act 2. Scene 7. Jaques speaking.*)
'*Why*' and '*way*' would be pronounced similarly in Shakespeare's day.

CELIA   He was furnished like a hunter.
ROSALIND   Oh, ominous! He comes to kill my heart,
(*As You Like It. Act 3. Scene 2.*)
Heart: hart.

MALVOLIO   M: but then there is no consonancy in the sequel; that
                 suffers under probation. A should follow, but O does.
FABIAN   And O shall end, I hope.
SIR TOBY   Ay, or I'll cudgel him and make him cry 'Oh!'
MALVOLIO   And then I comes behind.
FABIAN   Ay, an you had any eye behind you, you might see more
                 detraction at your heels than fortunes before you.
(*Twelfth Night. Act 2. Scene 5.*)

And yet I lie, for they pray continually to their saint, the commonwealth;
    or rather, not pray *to* her, but prey *on* her, for they ride up and down
    on her and make her their boots.
(*Henry the Fourth. Part One. Act 2. Scene 1. Gadshill speaking.*)

CHIEF JUSTICE Your means are very slender, and your waste is great.
FALSTAFF   I would it were otherwise: I would my means were greater
                   and my waist slenderer.
(*Henry the Fourth. Part Two. Act 1. Scene 2.*)

GLOUCESTER   Thou art reverent
                 Touching thy spiritual function, not thy life.
WINCHESTER   Rome shall remedy this.
WARWICK   Roam thither then.
(*Henry the Sixth. Part One. Act 3. Scene 1.*)

For Suffolk's duke, may he be suffocate
That dims the honour of this war-like isle!
(*Henry the Sixth. Part Two. Act 1. Scene 1. York speaking.*)

MERCUTIO   Nay, gentle Romeo, we must have you dance.
ROMEO   Not I, believe me.   You have dancing shoes
                 With nimble soles; I have a soul of lead
                 So stakes me to the ground I cannot move.
(*Romeo and Juliet. Act 1. Scene 4.*)

When the sun sets, the air doth drizzle dew;
But for the sunset of my brother's son
It rains downright.
How now! A conduit, girl? What! Still in tears?
Evermore showering?
(*Romeo and Juliet. Act 3. Scene 5. Capulet speaking.*)

PETER   I will carry no crotchets. I'll re you, I'll fa you. Do
                     you note me?
FIRST MUSICIAN   An you re us and fa us, *you* note *us.*
(*Romeo and Juliet. Act 4. Scene 5.*)

FLAVIUS   Thou art a cobbler, art thou?
SECOND COMMONER   Truly, sir, all that I live by is with the awl: I meddle
                       with no tradesman's matters, nor women's
                       matters, but with awl. I am indeed, sir, a
                       surgeon to old shoes; when they are in great
                       danger, I re-cover them.
(*Julius Cæsar. Act* 1. *Scene* 1.)

HAMLET (*to Polonius*) My lord, you played once i' the university, you say?
POLONIUS   That did I, my lord; and was accounted a good actor.
HAMLET   What did you enact?
POLONIUS   I did enact Julius Cæsar: I was killed i' the Capitol;
                       Brutus killed me.
HAMLET   It was a brute part of him to kill so capital a calf there.
(*Hamlet. Act* 3. *Scene* 2.)

SECTION XLII

COMFORT AND REBUKE

My lord Sebastian,
The truth you speak doth lack some gentleness,
And time to speak it in: you rub the sore
When you should bring the plaster.
(*The Tempest. Act* 2. *Scene* 1. *Gonzalo speaking.*)

But, mistress, know yourself: down on your knees
And thank heaven, fasting, for a good man's love.
For I must tell you friendly in your ear,
Sell when you can; you are not for all markets.
(*As You Like It. Act* 3. *Scene* 5. *Rosalind, reproving Phebe.*)

Peace, lady! Pause, or be more temperate.
It ill beseems this presence to cry aim
To these ill-tunèd repetitions.
(*King John. Act* 2. *Scene* 1. *King Philip speaking.*)

Comfort's in heaven; and we are on the earth
Where nothing lives but crosses, cares, and grief.
(*Richard the Second. Act* 2. *Scene* 2. *York speaking.*)

Of comfort no man speak:
Let's talk of graves, of worms, and epitaphs.
(*Richard the Second. Act* 3. *Scene* 2. *Richard speaking.*)

The posts come tiring on,
And not a man of them brings other news
Than they have learnt of me: from Rumour's tongues
They bring smooth comforts false, worse than true wrongs.
(*Henry the Fourth. Part Two. Induction. Rumour speaking.*)

PRINCE HENRY   I never thought to hear you speak again.
THE KING   Thy wish was father, Harry, to that thought:
                          I stay too long by thee, I weary thee.
                          Dost thou so hunger for my empty chair
                          That thou wilt needs invest thee with mine honours
                          Before thy hour be ripe?
(*Henry the Fourth. Part Two. Act 4. Scene 5.*)

FALSTAFF   My king! My Jove! I speak to thee, my heart.
PRINCE HENRY (*newly-crowned Henry the Fifth*)
                          I know thee not, old man. Fall to thy prayers.
                          How ill white hairs become a fool and jester!
(*Henry the Fourth. Part Two. Act 5. Scene 5.*)

Upon his royal face there is no note
How dread an army hath enrounded him;
Nor doth he dedicate one jot of colour
Unto the weary and all-watchèd night:
But freshly looks and overbears attaint
With cheerful semblance and sweet majesty;
That every wretch, pining and pale before,
Beholding him, plucks comfort from his looks.
A largesse universal, like the sun,
His liberal eye doth give to everyone,
Thawing cold fear.
(*Henry the Fifth. Act 4. Chorus.*)

SUFFOLK   Comfort, my sovereign! Gracious Henry, comfort!
THE KING   What, doth my lord of Suffolk comfort me?
                          Came he right now to sing a raven's note,
                          Whose dismal tune bereft my vital powers;
                          And thinks he that the chirping of a wren,
                          By crying comfort from a hollow breast,
                          Can chase away the first-conceivèd sound?
(*Henry the Sixth. Part Two. Act 3. Scene 2.*)

Oh, my good lord, that comfort comes too late;
'Tis like a pardon after execution:
That gentle physic, given in time, had cured me;
But now I am past all comforts here but prayers.
(*Henry the Eighth. Act 4. Scene 2. Queen Katharine speaking.*)

Would I could answer
This comfort with the like! But I have words
That would be howled out in the desert air,
Where hearing should not latch them.
(*Macbeth. Act 4. Scene 3. Ross speaking.*)
Latch: to lay hold of.

MALCOLM   Be comforted.
           Let's make us medicine of our great revenge,
           To cure this deadly grief.
MACDUFF   *He* has no children. All my pretty ones?
           Did you say all? Oh, hell-kite! All?
           What, all my pretty chickens and their dam
           At one fell swoop?
(*Macbeth. Act 4. Scene 3.*)

POLONIUS   Your noble son is mad:
           Mad call I it; for, to define true madness,
           What is't but to be nothing else but mad?
           But let that go.
THE QUEEN More matter, with less art.
(*Hamlet. Act 2. Scene 2.*)

                      Come, let's away to prison;
We two alone will sing like birds i' the cage:
When thou dost ask me blessing, I'll kneel down
And ask of thee forgiveness. So we'll live,
And pray, and sing, and tell old tales, and laugh
At gilded butterflies, and hear poor rogues
Talk of court news.
(*King Lear. Act 5. Scene 3. Lear speaking.*)

If e'er my will did trespass 'gainst his love
Either in discourse of thought or actual deed,
Or that mine eyes, mine ears, or any sense,
Delighted them in any other form;
Or that I do not yet, and ever did,
And ever will, though he do shake me off
To beggarly divorcement, love him dearly,
Comfort forswear me!
(*Othello. Act 4. Scene 2. Desdemona speaking.*)

           Oh, most false love!
Where be the sacred vials thou should'st fill
With sorrowful water? Now, I see, I see
In Fulvia's death how mine received shall be.
(*Antony and Cleopatra. Act 1. Scene 3. Cleopatra speaking.*)

Farewell, my dearest sister; fare thee well:
The elements be kind to thee and make
Thy spirits all of comfort! Fare thee well!
(*Antony and Cleopatra. Act 3. Scene 2. Octavius Cæsar speaking.*)

               Cheer your heart;
Be you not troubled with the time, which drives
O'er your content these strong necessities,
But let determined things to destiny
Hold unbewailed their way.
(*Antony and Cleopatra. Act 3. Scene 6. Octavius Cæsar speaking.*)

Most noble sir, arise; the queen approaches.
Her head's declined, and death will seize her but
Your comfort makes the rescue.
(*Antony and Cleopatra. Act 3. Scene 11. Eros speaking. Scene 9, The Oxford Shakespeare.*)

Egypt, thou knew'st too well
My heart was to thy rudder tied by the strings,
And thou should'st tow me after; o'er my spirit
Thy full supremacy thou knew'st, and that
Thy beck might from the bidding of the gods
Command me.
(*Antony and Cleopatra. Act 3. Scene 11. Antony, to Cleopatra. Scene 9, The Oxford Shakespeare.*)

To let a fellow that will take rewards
And say 'God quit you!' be familiar with
My playfellow, your hand; this kingly seal
And plighter of high hearts!
(*Antony and Cleopatra. Act 3. Scene 13. Antony, rebuking Cleopatra. Scene 11, The Oxford Shakespeare.*)

CHARMIAN   Be comforted, dear madam.
CLEOPATRA   No, I will not.
      All strange and terrible events are welcome,
      But comforts we despise. Our size of sorrow,
      Proportioned to our cause, must be as great
      As that which makes it.
(*Antony and Cleopatra. Act 4. Scene 15. Scene 13, The Oxford Shakespeare.*)

               Thou art all the comfort
The gods will diet me with.
(*Cymbeline. Act 3. Scene 4. Imogen speaking.*)

Beseech your majesty,
Forbear sharp speeches to her; she's a lady
So tender of rebukes that words are strokes,
And strokes death to her.
(*Cymbeline. Act 3. Scene· 5. The Queen speaking.*)

Be cheerful, wipe thine eyes.
Some falls are means the happier to arise.
(*Cymbeline. Act 4. Scene 2. Lucius speaking.*)

As a decrepit father takes delight
To see his active child do deeds of youth,
So I, made lame by fortune's dearest spite,
Take all my comfort of thy worth and truth.
(*Sonnet 37.*)

Section XLIII

PHILOSOPHY

I pray thee, peace! I will be flesh and blood;
For there was never yet philosopher
That could endure the toothache patiently,
However they have writ the style of gods
And made a push at chance and sufferance.
(*Much Ado About Nothing. Act 5. Scene 1. Leonato speaking.*)

I hold the world but as the world, Gratiano:
A stage, where every man must play a part,
And mine a sad one.
(*The Merchant of Venice. Act 1. Scene 1. Antonio speaking.*)

ROSALIND   Oh, how full of briers is this working-day world!
CELIA   They are but burs, cousin, thrown upon thee in holiday
           foolery: if we walk not in the trodden paths, our very
           petticoats will catch them.
(*As You Like It. Act 1. Scene 3.*)

Now, my co-mates and brothers in exile,
Hath not old custom made this life more sweet
Than that of painted pomp? Are not these woods
More free from peril than the envious court?
Here feel we but the penalty of Adam,
The seasons' difference; as the icy fang
And churlish chiding of the Winter's wind,

Which, when it bites and blows upon my body
Even till I shrink with cold, I smile and say
'This is no flattery: these are counsellors
That feelingly persuade me what I am.'
Sweet are the uses of adversity
Which, like the toad, ugly and venomous,
Wears yet a precious jewel in his head;
And this our life exempt from public haunt
Finds tongues in trees, books in the running brooks,
Sermons in stones and good in every thing.
I would not change it.
(*As You Like It.   Act 2.   Scene 1.   The Banished Duke speaking.*)

TOUCHSTONE   Hast any philosophy in thee, shepherd?
CORIN   No more but that I know the more one sickens the worse
                at ease he is; and that he that wants money, means and
                content is without three good friends; that the
                property of rain is to wet and fire to burn; that good
                pasture makes fat sheep, and that a great cause of the
                night is lack of the sun; that he that hath learned no
                wit by nature nor art may complain of good breeding
                or comes of very dull kindred.
TOUCHSTONE   Such a one is a natural philosopher.
(*As You Like It.   Act 3.   Scene 2.*)

Oft expectation fails, and most oft there
Where most it promises; and oft it hits
Where hope is coldest and despair most fits.
(*All's Well That Ends Well.   Act 2.   Scene 1.   Helena speaking.*)

They say miracles are past; and we have our philosophical persons, to make
        modern and familiar, things supernatural and causeless. Hence is it
        that we make trifles of terrors; ensconcing ourselves into seeming
        knowledge, when we should submit ourselves to an unknown fear.
(*All's Well That Ends Well.   Act 2.   Scene 3.   Lafeu speaking.*)

Methinks I am a prophet new inspired
And thus expiring do foretell of him:
His rash fierce blaze of riot cannot last,
For violent fires soon burn out themselves;
Small showers last long, but sudden storms are short;
He tires betimes that spurs too fast betimes;
With eager feeding, food doth choke the feeder.
(*Richard the Second.   Act 2.   Scene 1.   John of Gaunt speaking.*)

Each substance of a grief hath twenty shadows,
Which shows like grief itself but is not so;
For sorrow's eye, glazèd with blinding tears,
Divides one thing entire to many objects. . . .
(*Richard the Second. Act 2. Scene 2. Bushy speaking.*)

Why, courage, then! What cannot be avoided
'Twere childish weakness to lament or fear.
(*Henry the Sixth. Part Three. Act 5. Scene 4. Queen Margaret speaking.*)

They that stand high have many blasts to shake them;
And if they fall, they dash themselves to pieces.
(*Richard the Third. Act 1. Scene 3. Queen Margaret speaking.*)

So much the more
Must pity drop upon her. Verily,
I swear, 'tis better to be lowly born
And range with humble livers in content,
Than to be perked up in a glistering grief
And wear a golden sorrow.
(*Henry the Eighth. Act 2. Scene 3. Anne Bullen speaking.*)

One touch of nature makes the whole world kin;
That all with one consent praise new-born gawds,
Though they are made and moulded of things past,
And give to dust that is a little gilt
More laud than gilt o'er-dusted.
The present eye praises the present object.
(*Troilus and Cressida. Act 3. Scene 3. Ulysses speaking.*)

Two such opposèd kings encamp them still
In man as well as herbs: grace and rude will.
And where the worser is predominant,
Full soon the canker, death, eats up that plant.
(*Romeo and Juliet. Act 2. Scene 3. Friar Laurence speaking.*)

There is no time so miserable but a man may be true.
(*Timon of Athens. Act 4. Scene 3. First Bandit speaking.*)

It is the bright day that brings forth the adder;
And that craves wary walking.
(*Julius Cæsar. Act 2. Scene 1. Brutus speaking.*)

There is a tide in the affairs of men
Which, taken at the flood, leads on to fortune;
Omitted, all the voyage of their life
Is bound in shallows and in miseries.
(*Julius Cæsar. Act 4. Scene 3. Brutus speaking.*)

Of your philosophy you make no use,
If you give place to accidental evils.
(*Julius Cæsar. Act 4. Scene 3. Cassius speaking.*)

Things at the worst will cease, or else climb upward
To what they were before.
(*Macbeth. Act 4. Scene 2. Ross speaking.*)

Out, out, brief candle!
Life's but a walking shadow, a poor player
That struts and frets his hour upon the stage
And then is heard no more. It is a tale
Told by an idiot, full of sound and fury,
Signifying nothing.
(*Macbeth. Act 5. Scene 5. Macbeth speaking.*)

HORATIO   Oh, day and night, but this is wondrous strange!
HAMLET   And therefore as a stranger give it welcome.
          There are more things in heaven and earth, Horatio,
          Than are dreamt of in your philosophy.
(*Hamlet. Act 1. Scene 5.*)

It is not very strange; for my uncle is king of Denmark, and those that
    would make mows at him while my father lived, give twenty, forty,
    fifty, a hundred ducats a-piece for his picture in little. 'Sblood, there
    is something in this more than natural, if philosophy could find it out.
(*Hamlet. Act 2. Scenc 2. Hamlet speaking.*)
Mows: faces, grimaces.

To what base uses we may return, Horatio! Why may not imagination
    trace the noble dust of Alexander, till he find it stopping a bung-hole?
                . . . .
Imperious Cæsar, dead and turned to clay,
Might stop a hole to keep the wind away;
Oh, that that earth, which kept the world in awe,
Should patch a wall to expel the Winter's flaw!
(*Hamlet. Act 5. Scene 1. Hamlet speaking.*)
Flaw: a sudden gust of wind.

Rashly,
And praised be rashness for it, let us know,
Our indiscretion sometimes serves us well
When our deep plots do pall; and that should learn us
There's a divinity that shapes our ends,
Rough-hew them how we will.
(*Hamlet. Act 5. Scene 2. Hamlet speaking.*)

To mourn a mischief that is past and gone
Is the next way to draw new mischief on.
What cannot be preserved when fortune takes,
Patience her injury a mockery makes.
The robbed that smiles steals something from the thief;
He robs himself that spends a bootless grief.
(*Othello. Act* 1. *Scene* 3. *The Duke of Venice speaking.*)

We, ignorant of ourselves,
Beg often our own harms, which the wise powers
Deny us for our good; so find we profit
By losing of our prayers.
(*Antony and Cleopatra. Act* 2. *Scene* 1. *Menecrates speaking.*)

SECTION XLIV

PHYSICAL BEAUTY

What! Have I 'scaped love-letters in the holiday time of my beauty, and
am I now a subject for them?
(*The Merry Wives of Windsor. Act* 2. *Scene* 1. *Mistress Page speaking.*)

Since that my beauty cannot please his eye,
I'll weep what's left away; and weeping, die.
(*The Comedy of Errors. Act* 2. *Scene* 1. *Adriana speaking.*)

Let every eye negotiate for itself,
And trust no agent; for beauty is a witch
Against whose charms faith melteth into blood.
(*Much Ado About Nothing. Act* 2. *Scene* 1. *Claudio speaking.*)

For thee I'll lock up all the gates of love,
And on my eyelids shall conjecture hang
To turn all beauty into thoughts of harm;
And never shall it more be gracious.
(*Much Ado About Nothing. Act* 4. *Scene* 1. *Claudio speaking.*)

Good Lord Boyet, my beauty, though but mean,
Needs not the painted flourish of your praise.
Beauty is bought by judgment of the eye,
Not uttered by base sale of chapmen's tongues.
(*Love's Labour's Lost. Act* 2. *Scene* 1. *Princess of France speaking.*)

Lend me the flourish of all gentle tongues . . .
Fie, painted rhetoric! Oh, she needs it not:
To things of sale a seller's praise belongs;
She passes praise, then praise too short doth blot.
A withered hermit, five-score Winters worn,
Might shake off fifty, looking in her eye:
Beauty doth varnish age, as if new-born,
And gives the crutch the cradle's infancy.
(*Love's Labour's Lost. Act 4. Scene 3. Berowne speaking.*)

For when would you, my liege, or you, or you,
In leaden contemplation have found out
Such fiery numbers as the prompting eyes
Of beauty's tutors have enriched you with?
(*Love's Labour's Lost. Act 4. Scene 3. Berowne speaking.*)

Oh, happy fair!
Your eyes are lode-stars; and your tongue's sweet air
More tuneable than lark to shepherd's ear
When wheat is green, when hawthorn buds appear.
(*A Midsummer-Night's Dream. Act 1. Scene 1. Helena speaking.*)

Look on beauty,
And you shall see 'tis purchased by the weight;
Which therein works a miracle in nature,
Making them lightest that wear most of it.
(*The Merchant of Venice. Act 3. Scene 2. Bassanio speaking.*)

Beauty provoketh thieves sooner than gold.
(*As You Like It. Act 1. Scene 3. Rosalind speaking.*)

Tranio, I saw her coral lips to move
And with her breath she did perfume the air:
Sacred and sweet was all I saw in her.
(*The Taming of the Shrew. Act 1. Scene 1. Lucentio speaking.*)

Kate, like the hazel-twig,
Is straight and slender; and as brown in hue
As hazel-nuts and sweeter than the kernels.
(*The Taming of the Shrew. Act 2. Scene 1. Petruchio speaking.*)

Kindness in women, not their beauteous looks,
Shall win my love.
(*The Taming of the Shrew. Act 4. Scene 2. Hortensio speaking.*)

Most radiant, exquisite and unmatchable beauty . . .
I pray you tell me if this be the lady of the house, for
I never saw her.
(*Twelfth Night. Act 1. Scene 5. Viola speaking.*)

OLIVIA Look you, sir, such a one I was this present. Is't not well done?
      (Unveiling.)
VIOLA Excellently done, if God did all.
OLIVIA 'Tis in grain, sir; 'twill endure wind and weather.
VIOLA 'Tis beauty truly blent, whose red and white
      Nature's own sweet and cunning hand laid on.
(Twelfth Night. Act 1. Scene 5.)

I see you what you are: you are too proud.
But, if you were the devil, you are fair.
My lord and master loves you. Oh, such love
Could be but recompensed, though you were crowned
The nonpareil of beauty!
(Twelfth Night. Act 1. Scene 5. Viola speaking.)

LEONTES His princess, say you, with him?
GENTLEMAN Ay, the most peerless piece of earth, I think,
      That e'er the sun shone bright on.
(The Winter's Tale. Act 5. Scene 1.)

The beauty that is borne here in the face
The bearer knows not, but commends itself
To others' eyes.
(Troilus and Cressida. Act 3. Scene 3. Achilles speaking.)

BENVOLIO Then she hath sworn that she will still live chaste?
ROMEO She hath, and in that sparing makes huge waste;
      For beauty, starved with her severity,
      Cuts beauty off from all posterity.
(Romeo and Juliet. Act 1. Scene 1.)

BENVOLIO Be ruled by me. Forget to think of her.
ROMEO Oh, teach me how I should forget to think!
BENVOLIO By giving liberty unto thine eyes:
      Examine other beauties.
(Romeo and Juliet. Act 1. Scene 1.)

BENVOLIO Go thither, and with unattainted eye
      Compare her face with some that I shall show;
      And I will make thee think thy swan a crow.
ROMEO When the devout religion of mine eye
      Maintains such falsehood, then turn tears to fires;
      And these, who, often drowned, could never die,
      Transparent heretics, be burnt for liars!
      One fairer than my love! The all-seeing sun
      Ne'er saw her match since first the world begun.

BENVOLIO Tut! You saw her fair, none else being by:
        Herself poised with herself, in either eye.
(*Romeo and Juliet. Act 1. Scene 2.*)

What say you? Can you love the gentleman?
This night you shall behold him at our feast.
Read o'er the volume of young Paris' face,
And find delight writ there with beauty's pen.
(*Romeo and Juliet. Act 1. Scene 3. Lady Capulet speaking.*)

Oh, she doth teach the torches to burn bright!
It seems she hangs upon the cheek of night
Like a rich jewel in an Ethiop's ear:
Beauty too rich for use, for earth too dear!
(*Romeo and Juliet. Act 1. Scene 5. Romeo speaking.*)

                    Oh, my love! My wife!
Death, that hath sucked the honey of thy breath,
Hath had no power yet upon thy beauty.
Thou art not conquered; beauty's ensign yet
Is crimson in thy lips and in thy cheeks,
And death's pale flag is not advancèd there.
(*Romeo and Juliet. Act 5. Scene 3. Romeo speaking.*)

                    For her own person,
It beggared all description. She did lie
In her pavilion . . . cloth-of-gold of tissue. . . .
O'er-picturing that Venus, where we see
The fancy outwork nature.
(*Antony and Cleopatra. Act 2. Scene 2. Enobarbus speaking.*)

From fairest creatures we desire increase,
That thereby beauty's rose might never die;
But as the riper should by time decease,
His tender heir might bear his memory.
(*Sonnet 1.*)

How much more praise deserved thy beauty's use,
If thou couldst answer, 'This fair child of mine
Shall sum my count, and make my old excuse,'
Proving his beauty by succession thine!
(*Sonnet 2.*)

Unthrifty loveliness, why dost thou spend
Upon thyself thy beauty's legacy?
(*Sonnet 4.*)

Then, were not Summer's distillation left,
A liquid prisoner pent in walls of glass,
Beauty's effect with beauty were bereft ;
Nor it, nor no remembrance what it was.
But flowers distilled, though they with Winter meet,
Lease but their show; their substance still lives sweet.
(*Sonnet* 5.)

Then let not Winter's ragged hand deface
In thee thy Summer, ere thou be distilled:
Make sweet some vial; treasure thou some place
With beauty's treasure, ere it be self-killed.
(*Sonnet* 6.)

But beauty's waste hath in the world an end;
And kept unused, the user so destroys it.
No love toward others in that bosom sits
That on himself such murderous shame commits.
(*Sonnet* 9.)

If I could write the beauty of your eyes
And in fresh numbers number all your graces,
The age to come would say, 'This poet lies;
Such heavenly touches ne'er touched earthly faces.'
(*Sonnet* 17.)

Oh, how much more doth beauty beauteous seem
By that sweet ornament which truth doth give !
The rose looks fair, but fairer we it deem
For that sweet odour which doth in it live.
(*Sonnet* 54.)

Since brass, nor stone, nor earth, nor boundless sea,
But sad mortality o'ersways their power,
How with this rage shall beauty hold a plea,
Whose action is no stronger than a flower?
(*Sonnet* 65.)

When in the chronicle of wasted time
I see description of the fairest wights;
And beauty making beautiful old rhyme,
In praise of ladies dead and lovely knights;
Then, in the blazon of sweet beauty's best,
Of hand, of foot, of lip, of eye, of brow,
I see their antique pen would have expressed
Even such a beauty as you master now.
(*Sonnet* 106.)

SECTION XLV

HUMILITY AND PRIDE

Let me be ignorant, and in nothing good,
But graciously to know I am no better.
(*Measure For Measure. Act 2. Scene 4. Isabella speaking.*)

But the full sum of me
Is sum of nothing, which, to term in gross,
Is an unlessoned girl, unschooled, unpractised;
Happy in this, she is not yet so old
But she may learn; happier than this,
She is not bred so dull but she *can* learn;
Happiest of all is that her gentle spirit
Commits itself to yours to be directed,
As from her lord, her governor, her king.
(*The Merchant of Venice. Act 3. Scene 2. Portia speaking.*)

He calls us back: my pride fell with my fortunes;
I'll ask him what he would. Did you call, sir?
(*As You Like It. Act 1. Scene 2. Rosalind speaking.*)

Why, who cries out on pride,
That can therein tax any private party?
Doth it not flow as hugely as the sea,
Till that the weary very means do ebb?
(*As You Like It. Act 2. Scene 7. Jaques speaking.*)

'Twere all one
That I should love a bright particular star
And think to wed it, he is so above me.
(*All's Well That Ends Well. Act 1. Scene 1. Helena speaking.*)

Then call them to our presence; face to face,
And frowning brow to brow, ourselves will hear
The accuser and the accusèd freely speak.
High-stomached are they both and full of ire;
In rage deaf as the sea, hasty as fire.
(*Richard the Second. Act 1. Scene 1. Richard speaking.*)

Have I not reason to look pale and dead?
All souls that will be safe, fly from my side;
For time hath set a blot upon my pride.
(*Richard the Second. Act 3. Scene 2. Richard speaking.*)

And then I stole all courtesy from heaven,
And dressed myself in such humility
That I did pluck allegiance from men's hearts,
Loud shouts and salutations from their mouths,
Even in the presence of the crownèd king.
(*Henry the Fourth. Part One. Act* 3. *Scene* 2. *The King speaking.*)

Once more unto the breach, dear friends, once more;
Or close the wall up with our English dead.
In peace there's nothing so becomes a man
As modest stillness and humility;
But when the blast of war blows in our ears,
Then imitate the action of the tiger. . . .
(*Henry the Fifth. Act* 3. *Scene* 1. *The King speaking.*)

I cannot tell
What heaven hath given him; let some graver eye
Pierce into that.   But I can see his pride
Peep through each part of him: whence has he that?
If not from hell, the devil is a niggard
Or has given all before; and he begins
A new hell in himself.
(*Henry the Eighth. Act* 1. *Scene* 1. *Abergavenny speaking.*)

His overthrow heaped happiness upon him;
For then, and not till then, he felt himself,
And found the blessedness of being little.
(*Henry the Eighth. Act* 4. *Scene* 2. *Griffith speaking.*)

Section XLVI

APPAREL AND JEWELRY

SPEED	Because Love is blind. Oh, that you had mine eyes; or your own eyes had the lights they were wont to have when you chid at Sir Proteus for going ungartered!
VALENTINE	What should I see then?
SPEED	Your own present folly and her passing deformity: for he, being in love, could not see to garter his hose; and you, being in love, cannot see to put on your hose.
VALENTINE	Belike, boy, then *you* are in love; for last morning you could not see to wipe my shoes.
SPEED	True, sir. I was in love with my bed.

(*The Two Gentlemen of Verona. Act* 2. *Scene* 1.)

LUCETTA	What fashion, madam, shall I make your breeches?
JULIA	That fits as well as 'Tell me, good my lord,
	What compass will you wear your farthingale?'
	Why, even what fashion thou best lik'st, Lucetta.
LUCETTA	You must needs have them with a cod-piece, madam.
JULIA	Out, out, Lucetta! That will be ill-favoured.
LUCETTA	A round hose, madam, now's not worth a pin,
	Unless you have a cod-piece to stick pins on.

(*The Two Gentlemen of Verona. Act 2. Scene 7.*)
Cod-piece: a padded front-fastening to the breeches.
Round hose: long stockings, probably turned back in a roll at the top.

Win her with gifts, if she respect not words:
Dumb jewels often in their silent kind
More than quick words do move a woman's mind.
(*The Two Gentlemen of Verona. Act 3. Scene 1. Valentine speaking.*)

MISTRESS FORD	My maid's aunt, the fat woman of Brainford, has a gown above.
MISTRESS PAGE	On my word, it will serve him; she's as big as he is. And there's her thrummed hat and her muffler too. Run up, Sir John.

(*The Merry Wives of Windsor. Act 4. Scene 2.*)
Thrummed hat: a hat made of coarse woollen cloth.
Brainford: Brentford.

I see, the jewel best enamelled
Will lose his beauty; and though gold bides still
That others touch, yet often touching will
Wear gold.
(*The Comedy of Errors. Act 2. Scene 1. Adriana speaking.*)

My wife is shrewish when I keep not hours;
Say that I lingered with you at your shop
To see the making of her carkanet.
(*The Comedy of Errors. Act 3. Scene 1. Antipholus of Ephesus speaking.*)
Carkanet: a necklace.

All this I see; and I see that the fashion wears out more apparel than the man. But art not thou thyself giddy with the fashion too, that thou hast shifted out of thy tale into telling me of the fashion?
(*Much Ado About Nothing. Act 3. Scene 3. Conrade speaking.*)

MARGARET	Troth, I think your other rabato were better.
HERO	No, pray thee, good Meg, I'll wear this.

(*Much Ado About Nothing. Act 3. Scene 4.*)
Rabato: a collar or ruff.

MARGARET   I saw the Duchess of Milan's gown that they praise so.
HERO   Oh, that exceeds, they say.
MARGARET   By my troth's but a night-gown in respect of yours: cloth
            o' gold, and cuts, and laced with silver, set with pearls,
            down sleeves, side sleeves, and skirts round, underborne
            with a bluish tinsel. But for a fine, quaint, graceful and
            excellent fashion, yours is worth ten on't.

(*Much Ado About Nothing. Act 3. Scene 4.*)

Sweet hearts, we shall be rich ere we depart,
If fairings come thus plentifully in.
A lady walled about with diamonds!
Look you what I have from the loving king.

(*Love's Labour's Lost. Act 5. Scene 2. The Princess speaking.*)

Fairings: presents.

MARIA   This, and these pearls to me sent Longaville.
           The letter is too long by half a mile.
PRINCESS   I think no less. Dost thou not wish in heart
           The chain were longer and the letter short?

(*Love's Labour's Lost. Act 5. Scene 2.*)

He is a proper man's picture, but, alas, who can converse with a dumb-
    show? How oddly he's suited! I think he bought his doublet in
    Italy, his round hose in France, his bonnet in Germany, and his
    behaviour everywhere.

(*The Merchant of Venice. Act 1. Scene 2. Portia speaking.*)

TUBAL   One of them showed me a ring that he had of your daughter
           for a monkey.
SHYLOCK   Out upon her! Thou torturest me, Tubal. It was my
           turquoise; I had it of Leah when I was a bachelor. I
           would not have given it for a wilderness of monkeys!

(*The Merchant of Venice. Act 3. Scene 1.*)

Myself and what is mine to you and yours
Is now converted: but now I was the lord
Of this fair mansion, master of my servants,
Queen o'er myself; and even now, but now,
This house, these servants, and this same myself
Are yours, my lord. I give them with this ring;
Which when you part from, lose, or give away,
Let it presage the ruin of your love,
And be my vantage to exclaim on you.

(*The Merchant of Venice. Act 3. Scene 2. Portia speaking.*)

PORTIA	A quarrel, ho, already! What's the matter?
GRATIANO	About a hoop of gold, a paltry ring
	That she did give me, whose poesy was
	For all the world like cutlers' poetry
	Upon a knife: 'Love me and leave me not.'

(The Merchant of Venice. Act 5. Scene 1.)

(Giving Orlando a chain from her neck.) Gentleman,
Wear this for me; one out of suits with fortune
That could give more, but that her hand lacks means.
(As You Like It. Act 1. Scene 2. Rosalind speaking.)

I could find in my heart to disgrace my man's apparel and to cry like a
woman; but I must comfort the weaker vessel, as doublet and hose
ought to show itself courageous to petticoat.
(As You Like It. Act 2. Scene 4. Rosalind speaking.)

Motley's the only wear.
(As You Like It. Act 2. Scene 7. Jaques speaking.)
Motley: parti-coloured costume worn by professional fools.

You are full of pretty answers. Have you not been acquainted with
goldsmiths' wives, and conned them out of rings?
(As You Like It. Act 3. Scene 2. Jaques speaking.)

ORLANDO	Where dwell you, pretty youth?
ROSALIND	With this shepherdess, my sister: here in the skirts of the
	forest, like fringe upon a petticoat.

(As You Like It. Act 3. Scene 2.)

Then your hose should be ungartered, your bonnet unbanded, your sleeve
unbuttoned, your shoe untied, and everything about you demonstrating
a careless desolation. But you are no such man: you are rather point-
device in your accoutrements; as loving yourself than seeming the
lover of any other.
(As You Like It. Act 3. Scene 2. Rosalind speaking.)
Point-device: trim, faultless.

We will have rings, and things, and fine array;
And, kiss me, Kate, we will be married o' Sunday.
(The Taming of the Shrew. Act 2. Scene 1. Petruchio speaking.)

Why, Petruchio is coming, in a new hat and an old jerkin, a pair of old breeches thrice turned, a pair of boots that have been candle-cases, one buckled, another laced; an old rusty sword ta'en out of the town armoury, with a broken hilt, and chapelesss; with two broken points. . . .

(*The Taming of the Shrew. Act 3. Scene 2. Biondello speaking.*)

Chapeless: the chape was the metal at the end of the scabbard.

Points: laces with tags, used to fasten parts of the costume.

BAPTISTA   Who comes with him?

BIONDELLO   Oh, sir, his lackey, for all the world caparisoned like the horse; with a linen stock on one leg and a kersey boot-hose on the other, gartered with a red and blue list; an old hat, and the 'humour of forty fancies' pricked in't for a feather. A monster, a very monster in apparel, and not like a Christian footboy or a gentleman's lackey.

(*The Taming of the Shrew. Act 3. Scene 2.*)

Stock: stocking.

Boot-hose: stockings suited to wear with boots.

The 'humour of forty fancies': probably the title of a collection of ballads.

Pricked: pinned.

With silken coats and caps and golden rings,
With ruffs and cuffs and fardingales and things;
With scarfs and fans and double change of bravery,
With amber bracelets, beads and all this knavery.

(*The Taming of the Shrew. Act 4. Scene 3. Petruchio speaking.*)

HABERDASHER   Here is the cap your worship did bespeak.

PETRUCHIO   Why, this was moulded on a porringer;
A velvet dish. Fie, fie! 'Tis lewd and filthy.
Why, 'tis a cockle or a walnut-shell,
A knack, a toy, a trick, a baby's cap.
Away with it! Come, let me have a bigger.

KATHARINA   I'll have no bigger: this doth fit the time;
And gentlewomen wear such caps as these.

(*The Taming of the Shrew. Act 4. Scene 3.*)

Thy gown? Why, ay; come, tailor, let us see't.
Oh, mercy, God! What masquing stuff is here?
What's this? A sleeve? 'Tis like a demi-cannon.
What, up and down, carved like an apple-tart?
Here's snip and nip and cut and slish and slash,
Like to a censer in a barber's shop.

(*The Taming of the Shrew. Act 4. Scene 3. Petruchio speaking.*)

Demi-cannon: a sort of ordnance.

Censer: a fire pan, used for burning perfumes.

What am I, sir! Nay, what are you, sir? Oh, immortal gods! Oh, fine villain! A silken doublet! A velvet hose! A scarlet cloak! And a copatain hat! Oh, I am undone!
(*The Taming of the Shrew. Act 5. Scene 1. Vincentio speaking.*)
A copatain hat: a hat with a very high crown.

| MARIA | Ay, but you must confine yourself within the modest limits of order. |
| SIR TOBY | Confine! I'll confine myself no finer than I am: these clothes are good enough to drink in; and so be these boots too. An they be not, let them hang themselves in their own straps. |

(*Twelfth Night. Act 1. Scene 3.*)

| SIR TOBY | Is it a world to hide virtues in? I did think, by the excellent constitution of thy leg, it was formed under the star of a galliard. |
| SIR ANDREW | Ay, 'tis strong; and it does indifferent well in a flame-coloured stock. |

(*Twelfth Night. Act 1. Scene 3.*)
Galliard: a lively French dance.

| FESTE | Not so, neither; but I am resolved on two points. |
| MARIA | That if one break, the other will hold; or if both break, your gaskins fall. |

(*Twelfth Night. Act 1. Scene 5.*)
Gaskins: loose breeches.

None of my lord's ring! Why, he sent her none.
I am the man! If it be so, as 'tis,
Poor lady, she were better love a dream.
Disguise, I see thou art a wickedness
Wherein the pregnant enemy does much.
(*Twelfth Night. Act 2. Scene 2. Viola speaking.*)

| MALVOLIO | Calling my officers about me, in my branched velvet gown; having come from a day-bed, where I left Olivia sleeping. . . . |
| SIR TOBY | Fire and brimstone! |

(*Twelfth Night. Act 2. Scene 5.*)
Branched: adorned with needlework, representing flowers and twigs.
Day-bed: a couch or sofa.

'Remember who commended thy yellow stockings, and wished to see thee
ever cross-gartered.'
(*Twelfth Night. Act 2. Scene 5. Malvolio, reading from a letter.*)
Yellow stockings: these were very popular in Shakespeare's day. It is
interesting to note that they still survive in the yellow stockings worn
by the Blue Coat boys.
Cross-gartered: it was fashionable to wear garters crossed, over the stockings.
The pattern of the cross-gartering was left to the fancy of the individual.

You have said, sir. To see this age! A sentence is but a cheveril glove
to a good wit: how quickly the wrong side may be turned outward!
(*Twelfth Night. Act 3. Scene 1. Feste speaking.*)
Cheveril: kid leather. The word is used by Shakespeare as a symbol of
flexibility.

Here; wear this jewel for me. 'Tis my picture.
Refuse it not. *It* hath no tongue to vex you.
(*Twelfth Night. Act 3. Scene 4. Olivia speaking.*)

He hath ribbons of all the colours i' the rainbow; points, more than all the
lawyers in Bohemia can learnedly handle though they come to him
by the gross. Inkles, caddisses, cambrics, lawns; why, he sings 'em
over as they were gods or goddesses. You would think a smock were
a she-angel, he so chants to the sleeve-hand and the work about the
square on't.
(*The Winter's Tale. Act 4. Scene 4. A servant speaking. Scene 3. The
Oxford Shakespeare.*)
Points: tagged laces. *Inkles:* a sort of tape.
Caddisses: worsted ribbon. *Sleeve-hand:* wristband.

Lawn as white as driven snow,
Cypress black as e'er was crow,
Gloves as sweet as damask roses,
Masks for faces and for noses,
Bugle bracelet, necklace amber,
Perfume for a lady's chamber,
Golden quoifs and stomachers
For my lads to give their dears,
Pins and poking-sticks of steel,
What maids lack from head to heel:
Come buy of me, come! Come buy, come buy!
(*The Winter's Tale. Act 4. Scene 4. Autolycus singing. Scene 3. The
Oxford Shakespeare.*)
Cypress: crape. *Bugle:* a bead of black glass.
Quoifs: hoods. *Poking-sticks:* small metal rods which were heated and
used for setting the pleats of ruffs.

Come, you promised me a tawdry-lace and a pair of sweet gloves.
(*The Winter's Tale. Act* 4. *Scene* 4. *Mopsa speaking. Scene* 3. *The Oxford Shakespeare.*)
Tawdry-lace: a rustic necklace. 'Tawdry' is a corruption from 'Saint Audrey' (Saint Etheldreda) on whose day, October 17th, a fair was held in the Isle of Ely. At this fair, all sorts of toys and trinkets were sold.

A jewel in a ten-times-barred-up chest
Is a bold spirit in a loyal breast.
(*Richard the Second. Act* 1. *Scene* 1. *Mowbray speaking.*)

Come, shelter, shelter! I have removed Falstaff's horse, and he frets like a gummed velvet.
(*Henry the Fourth. Part One. Act* 2. *Scene* 2. *Poins speaking.*)
Gummed velvet: velvet, stiffened with gum to strengthen it.

MISTRESS QUICKLY You owe me money, Sir John, and now you pick a quarrel to beguile me of it: I bought you a dozen of shirts to your back.
FALSTAFF   Dowlas, filthy dowlas.
(*Henry the Fourth. Part One. Act* 3. *Scene* 3.)
Dowlas: a coarse linen.

What said Master Dombledon about the satin for my short cloak and my slops?
(*Henry the Fourth. Part Two. Act* 1. *Scene* 2. *Falstaff speaking.*)
Slops: large, baggy trousers.

Look, how thy ring encompasseth thy finger
Even so thy breast encloseth my poor heart;
Wear both of them, for both of them are thine.
(*Richard the Third. Act* 1. *Scene* 2. *Gloucester speaking.*)

. . . renouncing clean
The faith they have in tennis and tall stockings,
Short blistered breeches, and those types of travel.
(*Henry the Eighth. Act* 1. *Scene* 3. *Lovell speaking.*)
Blistered: puffed and slashed.

He counsels a divorce; a loss of her
That like a jewel has hung twenty years
About his neck, yet never lost her lustre.
(*Henry the Eighth. Act* 2. *Scene* 2. *Norfolk speaking.*)

There was a haberdasher's wife of small wit near him, that railed upon me
   till her pinked porringer fell off her head.
(*Henry the Eighth. Act 5. Scene 4. The Porter's Man speaking.*)
Pinked: pierced with holes.
Porringer: a small round (bowl-shaped) cap.

You i' the camlet, get up o' the rail.
(*Henry the Eighth. Act 5. Scene 4. A Porter speaking.*)
Camlet: a light warm material, made from camel's hair.

A plague of opinion! A man may wear it on both sides, like a leather
   jerkin.
(*Troilus and Cressida. Act 3. Scene 3. Thersites speaking.*)

Where is thy leather apron and thy rule?
What dost thou with thy best apparel on?
(*Julius Cæsar. Act 1. Scene 1. Marullus speaking.*)

My lord, as I was sewing in my closet,
Lord Hamlet, with his doublet all unbraced,
No hat upon his head, his stockings fouled,
Ungartered and down-gyvèd to his ankle,
Pale as his shirt, his knees knocking each other,
And with a look so piteous in purport
As if he had been loosèd out of hell
To speak of horrors, he comes before me.
(*Hamlet. Act 2. Scene 1. Ophelia speaking.*)

Marry, I would not do such a thing for a joint-ring, nor for measures of
   lawn, nor for gowns, petticoats, nor caps, nor any petty exhibition.
   But for the whole world! Why, who would not make her husband
   a cuckold to make him a monarch? I would venture purgatory for't.
(*Othello. Act 4. Scene 3. Emilia speaking.*)
Joint-ring: a lover's token; a ring consisting of two halves, jointed.

IMOGEN	Then waved his handkerchief?
PISANIO	And kissed it, madam.
IMOGEN	Senseless linen, happier therein than I!
	And that was all?
PISANIO	No, madam. For so long
	As he could make me with this eye or ear
	Distinguish him from others, he did keep
	The deck, with glove, or hat, or handkerchief,
	Still waving; as the fits and stirs of's mind
	Could best express how slow his soul sailed on,
	How swift his ship.

(*Cymbeline. Act 1. Scene 3.*)

Oh, no, no, no! 'Tis true.   Here, take this too.

(*Gives Iachimo the ring.*)

It is a basilisk unto mine eye;
Kills me to look on't.   Let there be no honour
Where there is beauty; truth where semblance; love
Where there's another man; the vows of women
Of no more bondage be to where they are made
Than *they* are to their virtues, which is nothing.
Oh, above measure false!
(*Cymbeline.   Act 2.   Scene 4.   Posthumus speaking.*)

Till whatsoever star that guides my moving
Points on me graciously with fair aspect,
And puts apparel on my tattered loving
To show me worthy of thy sweet respect.
(*Sonnet 26.*)

For then my thoughts . . . from far where I abide . . .
Intend a zealous pilgrimage to thee;
And keep my drooping eyelids open wide,
Looking on darkness which the blind do see:
Save that my soul's imaginary sight
Presents thy shadow to my sightless view,
Which, like a jewel hung in ghastly night,
Makes black night beauteous and her old face new.
(*Sonnet 27.*)

Oh, fearful meditation!   Where, alack,
Shall Time's best jewel from Time's chest lie hid?
(*Sonnet 65.*)

As on the finger of a thrònèd queen
The basest jewel will be well esteemed,
So are those errors that in thee are seen
To truth translated and for true things deemed.
(*Sonnet 96.*)

SECTION XLVII

PROMISES

Pardon, master:
I will be correspondent to command,
And do my spiriting gently.
(*The Tempest.   Act 1.   Scene 2.   Ariel speaking.*)

Shortly shall all my labours end, and thou
Shalt have the air at freedom.
(*The Tempest.   Act 4.   Scene 1.   Prospero speaking.*)

                              Oh, good Gonzalo,
My true preserver and a loyal sir
To him thou follow'st!   I will pay thy graces
Home both in word and deed.
(*The Tempest.   Act 5.   Scene 1.   Prospero speaking.*)

Did not the heavenly rhetoric of thine eye,
'Gainst whom the world cannot hold argument,
Persuade my heart to this false perjury?
Vows for thee broke deserve not punishment.
A woman I forswore; but I will prove,
Thou being a goddess, I forswore not thee:
My vow was earthly, thou a heavenly love;
Thy grace being gained cures all disgrace in me:
Vows are but breath, and breath a vapour is:
Then thou, fair sun, which on my earth dost shine,
Exhalest this vapour-vow; in thee it is:
If broken then, it is no fault of mine:
If by me broke, what fool is not so wise
To lose an oath to win a paradise?
(*Love's Labour's Lost.   Act 4.   Scene 3.   Longaville, reading.*)

Then fools you were these women to forswear;
Or, keeping what is sworn, you will prove fools.
For wisdom's sake, a word that all men love,
Or for love's sake, a word that loves all men,
Or for men's sake, the authors of these women,
Or women's sake, by whom we men are men,
Let us once lose our oaths to find ourselves
Or else we lose ourselves to keep our oaths.
It is religion to be thus forsworn. . . .
(*Love's Labour's Lost.   Act 4.   Scene 3.   Berowne speaking.*)

I owe you much, and, like a wilful youth,
That which I owe is lost; but if you please
To shoot another arrow that self way
Which you did shoot the first, I do not doubt
As I will watch the aim, or to find both,
Or bring your latter hazard back again
And thankfully rest debtor for the first.
(*The Merchant of Venice.   Act 1.   Scene 1.   Bassanio speaking.*)

                    But when this ring
Parts from this finger, then parts life from hence.
Oh, then be bold to say Bassanio's dead.
(*The Merchant of Venice. Act 3. Scene 2. Bassanio speaking.*)

ROSALIND   Why, how now, Orlando! Where have you been all this
            while? You a lover? An you serve me such another
            trick, never come in my sight more.
ORLANDO   My fair Rosalind, I come within an hour of my promise.
ROSALIND   Break an hour's promise in love! He that will divide a
            minute into a thousand parts, and break but a part of the
            thousandth part of a minute in the affairs of love, it may
            be said of him that Cupid hath clapped him o' the
            shoulder, but I'll warrant him heart-whole.
(*As You Like It. Act 4. Scene 1.*)

Fear not, sweet wench; they shall not touch thee, Kate:
I'll buckler thee against a million.
(*The Taming of the Shrew. Act 3. Scene 2. Petruchio speaking.*)
Buckler: to shield.

HORTENSIO   Signior Lucentio
            Here is my hand, and here I firmly vow
            Never to woo her more, but do forswear her
            As one unworthy all the former favours
            That I have fondly flattered her withal.
TRANIO   And here I take the like unfeignèd oath:
            Never to marry with her though she would entreat.
(*The Taming of the Shrew. Act 4. Scene 2.*)

                    Was not this love indeed?
We men may say more, swear more, but indeed
Our shows are more than will; for still we prove
Much in our vows, but little in our love.
(*Twelfth Night. Act 2. Scene 4. Viola speaking.*)

And all those sayings will I over-swear;
And all those swearings keep as true in soul
As doth that orbèd continent, the fire
That severs day from night.
(*Twelfth Night. Act 5. Scene 1. Viola speaking.*)

CAMILLO   This is desperate, sir.
FLORIZEL   So call it.   But it does fulfil my vow;
             I needs must think it honesty.   Camillo,
             Not for Bohemia, nor the pomp that may
             Be thereat gleaned; for all the sun sees, or
             The close earth wombs, or the profound seas hide
             In unknown fathoms, will I break my oath
             To this my fair beloved.
(*The Winter's Tale.   Act 4.   Scene 4.   Scene 3, The Oxford Shakespeare.*)

MISTRESS QUICKLY (*to Falstaff*)
             And didst thou not, when she was gone downstairs, desire me
                 to be no more so familiarity with such poor people;
                 saying that ere long they should call me madam?   And
                 didst thou not kiss me and bid me fetch thee thirty
                 shillings?   I put thee now to thy book-oath.   Deny it if
                 thou canst.
FALSTAFF (*to the Chief Justice*)
             My lord, this is a poor mad soul; and she says up and down
                 the town that her eldest son is like you.   She hath been
                 in good case; and the truth is, poverty hath distracted her.
(*Henry the Fourth.   Part Two.   Act 2.   Scene 1.*)

If I be false, or swerve a hair from truth,
When time is old and hath forgot itself,
When water-drops have worn the stones of Troy
And blind oblivion swallowed cities up,
And mighty states characterless are grated
To dusty nothing, yet let memory,
From false to false, among false maids in love
Upbraid my falsehood!
(*Troilus and Cressida.   Act 3.   Scene 2.   Cressida speaking.*)

It is the purpose that makes strong the vow;
But vows to every purpose must not hold.
(*Troilus and Cressida.   Act 5.   Scene 3.   Cassandra speaking.*)

ROMEO   Lady, by yonder blessèd moon I swear,
             That tips with silver all these fruit-tree tops. . .
JULIET   Oh, swear not by the moon, th'inconstant moon
             That monthly changes in her circled orb,
             Lest that thy love prove likewise variable.
ROMEO   What shall I swear by?
JULIET   Do not swear at all;
             Or, if thou wilt, swear by thy gracious self
             Which is the god of my idolatry,
             And I'll believe thee.
(*Romeo and Juliet.   Act 2.   Scene 2.*)

HAMLET   Upon my sword.
MARCELLUS   We have sworn, my lord, already.
HAMLET   Indeed, upon my sword, indeed!
GHOST (*beneath*) Swear.
HAMLET   Ah, ha, boy! Say'st thou so? Art thou there, true-penny?
              Come on. You hear this fellow in the cellarage.
              Consent to swear.
HORATIO   Propose the oath, my lord.
HAMLET   Never to speak of this that you have seen.
              Swear, by my sword.
GHOST (*beneath*) Swear.
(*Hamlet. Act* 1. *Scene* 5.)
True-penny: honest fellow.

Why should I think you can be mine and true,
Though you in swearing shake the thronèd gods,
Who have been false to Fulvia? Riotous madness,
To be entangled with those mouth-made vows
Which break themselves in swearing!
(*Antony and Cleopatra. Act* 1. *Scene* 3. *Cleopatra speaking.*)

SECTION XLVIII

PRAYERS, ENTREATIES AND THREATS

Wish me partaker in thy happiness,
When thou dost meet good hap; and in thy danger,
If ever danger do environ thee,
Commend thy grievance to my holy prayers,
For I will be thy beadsman, Valentine.
(*The Two Gentlemen of Verona. Act* 1. *Scene* 1. *Proteus speaking.*)
Beadsman: someone hired to pray for another.

SILVIA   And when it's writ, for my sake read it over,
              And if it please you, so; if not, why, so.
VALENTINE   If it please me, madam, what then?
SILVIA   Why, if it please you, take it for your labour:
              And so, good morrow, servant.   (*Exit.*)
SPEED   Oh, jest unseen, inscrutable, invisible,
              As a nose on a man's face, or a weathercock on a steeple!
              My master sues to her; and she hath taught her suitor,
              He being her pupil, to become her tutor.
(*The Two Gentlemen of Verona. Act* 2. *Scene* 1.)

ANGELO   Were he my kinsman, brother, or my son,
                It should be thus with him: he must die to-morrow.
ISABELLA   To-morrow! Oh, that's sudden. Spare him, spare him!
                He's not prepared for death. Even for our kitchens
                We kill the fowl of season: shall we serve heaven
                With less respect than we do minister
                To our gross selves? Good, good my lord, bethink you;
                Who is it that hath died for this offence!
                There's many have committed it.
(*Measure For Measure. Act 2. Scene 2.*)

An I may hide my face, let me play Thisbe too. I'll speak in a monstrous
    little voice.
(*A Midsummer-Night's Dream. Act 1. Scene 2. Bottom speaking.*)

If I can catch him once upon the hip,
I will feed fat the ancient grudge I bear him.
He hates our sacred nation; and he rails,
Even there where merchants most do congregate,
On me, my bargains, and my well-won thrift,
Which he calls interest. Cursèd be my tribe,
If I forgive him!
(*The Merchant of Venice. Act 1. Scene 3. Shylock speaking.*)

                    Mark you this, Bassanio:
The devil can cite Scripture for his purpose.
An evil soul, producing holy witness,
Is like a villain with a smiling cheek;
A goodly apple rotten at the heart.
Oh, what a goodly outside falsehood hath!
(*The Merchant of Venice. Act 1. Scene 3. Antonio speaking.*)

Mislike me not for my complexion;
The shadowed livery of the burnished sun,
To whom I am a neighbour and near bred.
(*The Merchant of Venice. Act 2. Scene 1. Morocco speaking.*)

If a Jew wrong a Christian, what is his humility? Revenge. If a Christian
    wrong a Jew, what should his sufferance be by Christian example?
    Why, revenge. The villany you teach me I will execute; and it shall
    go hard but I will better the instruction.
(*The Merchant of Venice. Act 3. Scene 1. Shylock speaking.*)

SHYLOCK   I pray you, give me leave to go from hence;
                I am not well. Send the deed after me
                And I will sign it.

DUKE   Get thee gone, but do it.
GRATIANO   In christening shalt thou have two godfathers:
              Had I been judge, thou shouldst have had ten more,
              To bring thee to the gallows, not the font.
(*The Merchant of Venice. Act 4. Scene 1.*)

TOUCHSTONE   . . . or, to wit, I kill thee, make thee away, translate thy
              life into death, thy liberty into bondage; I will deal
              in poison with thee, or in bastinado, or in steel; I will
              bandy with thee in faction; I will o'er-run thee with
              policy; I will kill thee a hundred and fifty ways.
              Therefore, tremble and depart.
AUDREY   Do, good William.
WILLIAM   God rest you merry, sir!
(*As You Like It. Act 5. Scene 1.*)

Oh, God of battles, steel my soldiers' hearts!
Possess them not with fear; take from them now
The sense of reckoning, if the opposed numbers
Pluck their hearts from them.
(*Henry the Fifth. Act 4. Scene 1. The King speaking.*)

FLUELLEN If I owe you anything, I will pay you in cudgels: you shall be
          a woodmonger, and buy nothing of me but cudgels. God
          be wi' you, and keep you, and heal your pate.   (*Exit.*)
PISTOL   All hell shall stir for this!
(*Henry the Fifth. Act 5. Scene 1.*)

                    Oh, Lord, that lends me life,
Lend me a heart replete with thankfulness!
(*Henry the Sixth. Part Two. Act 1. Scene 1. The King speaking.*)

Could I come near your beauty with my nails,
I'd set my ten commandments in your face.
(*Henry the Sixth. Part Two. Act 1. Scene 3. Duchess of Gloucester
    speaking.*)

Let me have men about me that are fat;
Sleek-headed men, and such as sleep o' nights.
Yond Cassius has a lean and hungry look:
He thinks too much. Such men are dangerous.
(*Julius Cæsar. Act 1. Scene 2. Cæsar speaking.*)

Oh, pardon me, thou bleeding piece of earth,
That I am meek and gentle with these butchers!
(*Julius Cæsar. Act 3. Scene 1. Antony speaking.*)

Friends, Romans, countrymen, lend me your ears;
I come to bury Cæsar, not to praise him.
The evil that men do lives after them,
The good is oft interrèd with their bones;
So let it be with Cæsar.
(*Julius Cæsar. Act 3. Scene 2. Antony speaking.*)

If you have tears, prepare to shed them now.
(*Julius Cæsar. Act 3. Scene 2' Antony speaking.*)

                    Thou sure and firm-set earth,
Hear not my steps, which way they walk, for fear
Thy very stones prate of my whereabout,
And take the present horror from the time
Which now suits with it.
(*Macbeth. Act 2. Scene 1. Macbeth speaking.*)

                    But, good my brother,
Do not, as some ungracious pastors do,
Show me the steep and thorny way to heaven;
Whilst, like a puffed and reckless libertine,
Himself the primrose path of dalliance treads
And recks not his own rede.
(*Hamlet. Act 1. Scene 3. Ophelia speaking.*)

                    My fate cries out
And makes each petty artery in this body
As hardy as the Nemean lion's nerve.
Still am I called. Unhand me, gentlemen;
By heaven I'll make a ghost of him that lets me.
I say, away! Go on; I'll follow thee.
(*Hamlet. Act 1. Scene 4. Hamlet speaking.*)

                    Soft you now!
The fair Ophelia! Nymph, in thy orisons
Be all my sins remembered.
(*Hamlet. Act 3. Scene 1. Hamlet speaking.*)

Speak the speech, I pray you, as I pronounced it to you, trippingly on the
    tongue; but if you mouth it, as many of your players do, I had as lief
    the town-crier spoke my lines. Nor do not saw the air too much with
    your hand, thus. . . . Oh, it offends me to the soul to hear a
    robustious periwig-pated fellow tear a passion to tatters, to very rags,
    to split the ears of the groundlings, who, for the most part, are capable

of nothing but inexplicable dumb-shows and noise. I would have
such a fellow whipped for o'er-doing Termagant: it out-herods Herod.
Pray you, avoid it.

(*Hamlet   Act* 3. *Scene* 2. *Hamlet speaking.*)

Termagant: a supposed Mohammedan female deity, represented in our old
plays as a most violent character.

Soft!   Now to my mother.
Oh, heart, lose not thy nature; let not ever
The soul of Nero enter this firm bosom;
Let me be cruel, not unnatural;
I will speak daggers to her, but use none.

(*Hamlet.   Act* 3. *Scene* 2. *Hamlet speaking.*)

Mother, for love of grace,
Lay not that flattering unction to your soul,
That not your trespass but my madness speaks:
It will but skin and film the ulcerous place,
Whiles rank corruption, mining all within,
Infects unseen.

(*Hamlet.   Act* 3. *Scene* 4. *Hamlet speaking.*)

You that look pale and tremble at this chance,
That are but mutes or audience to this act,
Had I but time . . . as this fell sergeant, Death,
Is strict in his arrest. . . .   Oh, I could tell you . . .
But let it be.   Horatio, I am dead.
Thou livest; report me and my cause aright
To the unsatisfied.

. . . .

If thou didst ever hold me in thy heart,
Absent thee from felicity a while;
And in this harsh world draw thy breath in pain,
To tell my story.

(*Hamlet.   Act* 5. *Scene* 2. *Hamlet speaking.*)

You see me here, you gods, a poor old man,
As full of grief as age; wretched in both.
If it be you that stirs these daughters' hearts
Against their father, fool me not so much
To bear it tamely.   Touch me with noble anger
And let not woman's weapons, water-drops,
Stain my man's cheeks!

(*King Lear.   Act* 2. *Scene* 4. *Lear speaking.*)

Oh, let the heavens
Give him defence against the elements,
For I have lost him on a dangerous sea.
(*Othello. Act 2. Scene 1. Cassio speaking.*)

I pray you, in your letters,
When you shall these unlucky deeds relate,
Speak of me as I am; nothing extenuate,
Nor set down aught in malice: then must you speak
Of one that loved not wisely but too well. . . .
(*Othello. Act 5. Scene 2. Othello speaking.*)

Section XLIX

HONOUR AND HONESTY

MISTRESS FORD   Oh, woman, if it were not for one trifling respect, I could come to such honour!

MISTRESS PAGE   Hang the trifle, woman; take the honour. What is it? Dispense with trifles. What is it?

MISTRESS FORD   If I would but go to hell for an eternal moment or so, I could be knighted.

MISTRESS PAGE   What? Thou liest. Sir Alice Ford! These knights will hack; and so thou shouldst not alter the article of thy gentry.

MISTRESS FORD   We burn daylight: here, read, read; perceive how I might be knighted.
(*The Merry Wives of Windsor. Act 2. Scene 1.*)
Hack: to grow common, plentiful.

DOGBERRY   Goodman Verges, sir, speaks a little off the matter: an old man, sir, and his wits are not so blunt as, God help, I would desire they were; but, in faith, honest as the skin between his brows.

VERGES   Yes, I thank God I am as honest as any man living that is an old man and no honester than I.

DOGBERRY   Comparisons are odorous: palabras, neighbour Verges.
(*Much Ado About Nothing. Act 3. Scene 5.*)
Palabras: pocas palabras, Spanish for 'few words'; otherwise 'shut up.'

What should I say, sweet lady?
I was enforced to send it after him.
I was beset with shame and courtesy;
My honour would not let ingratitude
So much besmear it.
(*The Merchant of Venice. Act 5. Scene 1. Bassanio speaking.*)

A poor virgin, sir, an ill-favoured thing, sir, but mine own; a poor humour
  of mine, sir, to take that that no man else will: rich honesty dwells
  like a miser, sir, in a poor house; as your pearl in your foul oyster.
(*As You Like It. Act 5. Scene 4. Touchstone, referring to Audrey.*)

Our purses shall be proud, our garments poor,
For 'tis the mind that makes the body rich;
And as the sun breaks through the darkest clouds,
So honour peereth in the meanest habit.
(*The Taming of the Shrew. Act 4. Scene 3. Petruchio speaking.*)

To the wars, my boy; to the wars!
He wears his honour in a box, unseen,
That hugs his kicky-wicky here at home,
Spending his manly marrow in her arms
Which should sustain the bound and high curvet
Of Mar's fiery steed.
(*All's Well That Ends Well. Act 2. Scene 3. Parolles speaking.*)

Well, Diana, take heed of this French earl: the honour of a maid is her
  name; and no legacy is so rich as honesty.
(*All's Well That Ends Well. Act 3. Scene 5. Mariana speaking.*)

Ha, ha! What a fool Honesty is! And Trust, his sworn brother, a very
  simple gentleman!
(*The Winter's Tale. Act 4. Scene 4. Act 4, Scene 3, The Oxford Shakespeare.
  Autolycus speaking.*)

A foot of honour better than I was;
But many a foot of land the worse!
Well, now can I make any Joan a lady.
'Good den, Sir Richard!' . . . 'God-a-mercy, fellow!' . . .
And if his name be George, I'll call him Peter;
For new-made honour doth forget men's names:
'Tis too respective and too sociable
For your conversion.
(*King John. Act 1. Scene 1. The Bastard speaking.*)

Mine honour is my life; both grow in one.
Take honour from me, and my life is done.
Then, dear my liege, mine honour let me try;
In that I live and for that will I die.
(*Richard the Second. Act 1. Scene 1. Mowbray speaking.*)

Live in thy shame, but die not shame with thee!
These words hereafter thy tormentors be!
Convey me to my bed, then to my grave:
Love they to live that love and honour have.
(*Richard the Second. Act 2. Scene 1. John of Gaunt speaking.*)

There's neither honesty, manhood, nor good fellowship in thee, nor thou
camest not of the blood royal, if thou darest not stand for ten shillings.
(*Henry the Fourth. Part One. Act 1. Scene 2. Falstaff speaking.*)

HOTSPUR	Send danger from the East unto the West,
	So honour cross it from the North to South,
	And let them grapple. Oh, the blood more stirs
	To rouse a lion than to start a hare!
NORTHUMBERLAND	Imagination of some great exploit
	Drives him beyond the bounds of patience.
HOTSPUR	By heaven, methinks it were an easy leap
	To pluck bright honour from the pale-faced moon,
	Or dive into the bottom of the deep,
	Where fathom-line could never touch the ground,
	And pluck up drownèd honour by the locks;
	So he that doth redeem her thence might wear
	Without corrival all her dignities.

(*Henry the Fourth. Part One. Act 1. Scene 3.*)

Well, 'tis no matter; honour pricks me on. Yea, but how if honour prick
me off when I come on? How then? Can honour set to a leg? No.
Or an arm? No. Or take away the grief of a wound? No.
Honour hath no skill in surgery, then? No. What is honour? A
word. What is that word honour? Air. A trim reckoning! Who
hath it? He that died o' Wednesday. Doth he feel it? No. Doth
he hear it? No. It is insensible, then? Yea, to the dead. But will
it not live with the living? No. Why? Detraction will not suffer
it. Therefore I'll none of it. Honour is a mere scutcheon; and so
ends my catechism.
(*Henry the Fourth. Part One. Act 5. Scene 1. Falstaff speaking.*)
N.B.: The Everyman Edition is worded slightly differently. The reference
here used is that of *The Oxford Shakespeare.*

What's he that wishes so?
My cousin Westmoreland? No, my fair cousin:
If we are marked to die, we are enow
To do our country loss; and if to live,
The fewer men the greater share of honour.
God's will! I pray thee, wish not one man more.
By Jove, I am not covetous for gold,
Nor care I who doth feed upon my cost;
It yearns me not if men my garments wear;
Such outward things dwell not in my desires.
But if it be a sin to covet honour,
I am the most offending soul alive.
(*Henry the Fifth. Act 4. Scene 3. The King speaking.*)

An honest tale speeds best being plainly told.
(*Richard the Third. Act 4. Scene 4. Elizabeth speaking.*)

Perseverance, dear my lord,
Keeps honour bright: to have done, is to hang
Quite out of fashion, like a rusty mail
In monumental mockery. Take the instant way;
For honour travels in a strait so narrow,
Where one but goes abreast.
(*Troilus and Cressida. Act 3. Scene 3. Ulysses speaking.*)

Mine honour keeps the weather of my fate:
Life every man holds dear; but the dear man
Holds honour far more precious-dear than life.
(*Troilus and Cressida. Act 5. Scene 3. Hector speaking.*)

His nature is too noble for the world:
He would not flatter Neptune for his trident,
Or Jove for's power to thunder. His heart's his mouth:
What his breast forges, that his tongue must vent;
And, being angry, does forget that ever
He heard the name of death.
(*Coriolanus. Act 3. Scene 1. Menenius speaking.*)

Here's that which is too weak to be a sinner: honest water, which ne'er left
    man i' the mire.
(*Timon of Athens. Act 1. Scene 2. Apemantus speaking.*)

Every man has his fault, and honesty is his. I ha' told him on't, but I
    could ne'er get him from't.
(*Timon of Athens. Act 3. Scene 1. Lucullus speaking.*)

What is it that you would impart to me?
If it be aught toward the general good,
Set honour in one eye and death i' the other
And I will look on both indifferently;
For let the gods so speed me as I love
The name of honour more than I fear death.
(*Julius Cæsar. Act 1. Scene 2. Brutus speaking.*)

The noble Brutus
Hath told you Cæsar was ambitious:
If it were so, it was a grievous fault,
And grievously hath Cæsar answered it.
Here, under leave of Brutus and the rest . . .
For Brutus is an honourable man;
So are they all, all honourable men . . .
Come I to speak in Cæsar's funeral.
(*Julius Cæsar. Act 3. Scene 2. Antony speaking.*)

There is no terror, Cassius, in your threats;
For I am armed so strong in honesty,
That they pass by me as the idle wind
Which I respect not.
(*Julius Cæsar.   Act 4.   Scene 3.   Brutus speaking.*)

Ay, sir; to be honest, as this world goes, is to be one man picked out of
   ten thousand.
(*Hamlet.   Act 2.   Scene 2.   Hamlet speaking.*)

HAMLET   Ha, ha! Are you honest?
OPHELIA   My lord?
HAMLET   Are you fair?
OPHELIA   What means your lordship?
HAMLET   That if you be honest and fair, your honesty should admit no
            discourse to your beauty.
OPHELIA   Could beauty, my lord, have better commerce than with
            honesty?
HAMLET   Ay, truly; for the power of beauty will sooner transform
            honesty from what it is to a bawd, than the force of honesty
            can translate beauty into his likeness: this was sometime a
            paradox, but now the time gives it proof.
(*Hamlet.   Act 3.   Scene 1.*)

                  Rightly to be great
Is not to stir without great argument,
But greatly to find quarrel in a straw
When honour's at the stake.
(*Hamlet.   Act 4.   Scene 4.   Hamlet speaking.*)

Good name in man and woman, dear my lord,
Is the immediate jewel of their souls:
Who steals my purse steals trash; 'tis something, nothing;
'Twas mine, 'tis his, and has been slave to thousands;
But he that filches from me my good name
Robs me of that which not enriches him
And makes me poor indeed.
(*Othello.   Act 3.   Scene 3.   Iago speaking.*)

OTHELLO   If thou dost slander her and torture me,
            Never pray more; abandon all remorse;
            On horror's head, horrors accumulate;
            Do deeds to make heaven weep, all earth amazed;
            For nothing canst thou to damnation add
            Greater than that.

IAGO   Oh, grace! Oh, heaven defend me!
          Are you a man? Have you a soul, or sense?
          God be wi' you; take mine office. Oh, wretched fool,
          That livest to make thine honesty a vice!
          Oh, monstrous world! Take note, take note, oh world,
          To be direct and honest is not safe.
          I thank you for this profit, and from hence
          I'll love no friend sith love breeds such offence.
OTHELLO   Nay, stay; thou shouldst be honest.
IAGO   I should be wise; for honesty's a fool,
          And loses what it works for.
(*Othello*. *Act* 3. *Scene* 3.)

He sits 'mongst men like a descended god:
He hath a kind of honour sets him off,
More than a mortal seeming.
(*Cymbeline*. *Act* 1. *Scene* 6. *Iachimo speaking*.)

SECTION L

MISCELLANEOUS

Alas, the storm is come again! My best way is to creep under his gaberdine;
     there is no other shelter hereabout. Misery acquaints a man with
     strange bed-fellows. I will here shroud till the dregs of the storm
     be past.
(*The Tempest*. *Act* 2. *Scene* 2. *Trinculo speaking*.)

                         Sit down and rest.
Even here I will put off my hope, and keep it
No longer for my flatterer.
(*The Tempest*. *Act* 3. *Scene* 3. *Alonso speaking*.)

                    I cannot too much muse
Such shapes, such gesture, and such sound, expressing . . .
Although they want the use of tongue . . . a kind
Of excellent dumb discourse.
(*The Tempest*. *Act* 3. *Scene* 3. *Alonso speaking*.)

JULIA   Your reason?
LUCETTA   I have no other but a woman's reason:
           I think him so, because I think him so.
(*The Two Gentlemen of Verona*. *Act* 1. *Scene* 2.)

Marry, this is the short and the long of it; you have brought her into such
a canaries as 'tis wonderful.
(*The Merry Wives of Windsor. Act 2. Scene 2. Mistress Quickly speaking.*)
Canaries: here used to denote a state of excitement. The Canary was a
lively dance.

FORD   Where had you this pretty weathercock?
MISTRESS PAGE   I cannot tell what the dickens his name is my husband
                had him of. (*To Robin*) What do you call your
                knight's name, sirrah?
(*The Merry Wives of Windsor. Act 3. Scene 2.*)

Think of that; a man of my kidney! Think of that, that am as subject
to heat as butter; a man of continual dissolution and thaw.
(*The Merry Wives of Windsor. Act 3. Scene 5. Falstaff speaking.*)

. . . so curses all Eve's daughters, of what complexion soever.
(*The Merry Wives of Windsor. Act 4. Scene 2. Mistress Page speaking.*)

Prithee, no more prattling; go. I'll hold. This is the third time; I hope
good luck lies in odd numbers. Away! Go! They say there is
divinity in odd numbers, either in nativity, chance, or death. Away!
(*The Merry Wives of Windsor. Act 5. Scene 1. Falstaff speaking.*)

He hath indeed better bettered expectation than you must expect of me to
tell you how.
(*Much Ado About Nothing. Act 1. Scene 1. A Messenger speaking.*)

MESSENGER   He hath done good service, lady, in these wars.
BEATRICE   You had musty victual, and he hath holp to eat it. He is a
             very valiant trencher-man; he hath an excellent stomach.
(*Much Ado About Nothing. Act 1. Scene 1.*)

BEATRICE   He wears his faith but as the fashion of his hat: it ever changes
             with the next block.
MESSENGER   I see, lady, the gentleman is not in your books.
BEATRICE   No; an he were, I would burn my study.
(*Much Ado About Nothing. Act 1. Scene 1.*)

He shows me where the bachelors sit, and there live we as merry as the
day is long.
(*Much Ado About Nothing. Act 2. Scene 1. Beatrice speaking.*)

LEONATO   Cousin, you apprehend passing shrewdly.
BEATRICE   I have a good eye, uncle; I can see a church by daylight.
(*Much Ado About Nothing. Act 2. Scene 1.*)

No, I was not born under a rhyming planet, nor I cannot woo in festival terms.
(*Much Ado About Nothing. Act 5. Scene 2. Benedick speaking.*)

THE KING   A letter from the magnificent Armado.
BEROWNE   How low soever the matter, I hope in God for high words.
LONGAVILLE   A high hope for a low heaven. God grant us patience!
(*Love's Labour's Lost. Act 1. Scene 1.*)

. . . 'with a child of our grandmother Eve, a female; or, for thy more sweet understanding, a woman.'
(*Love's Labour's Lost. Act 1. Scene 1. The King, reading a letter.*)

QUINCE   An you should do it too terribly, you would fright the duchess and the ladies, that they would shriek; and that were enough to hang us all.
ALL   That would hang us, every mother's son.
(*A Midsummer-Night's Dream. Act 1. Scene 2.*)

I'll put a girdle round about the earth
In forty minutes.
(*A Midsummer-Night's Dream. Act 2. Scene 1. Puck speaking.*)

Bless thee, Bottom! Bless thee! Thou art translated.
(*A Midsummer-Night's Dream. Act 3. Scene 1. Quince speaking.*)

OBERON   About the wood go swifter than the wind,
          And Helena of Athens look thou find.
          All fancy-sick she is and pale of cheer
          With sighs of love, that costs the fresh blood dear.
          By some illusion see thou bring her here.
          I'll charm his eyes against she do appear.
PUCK   I go, I go; look how I go:
          Swifter than arrow from the Tartar's bow.
(*A Midsummer-Night's Dream. Act 3. Scene 2.*)

If we offend, it is with our good will.
That you should think, we come not to offend,
But with good will. To show our simple skill,
That is the true beginning of our end.
          .   .   .   .
Gentles, perchance you wonder at this show;
But wonder on, till truth make all things plain.
(*A Midsummer-Night's Dream. Act 5. Scene 1. Quince, speaking as Prologue.*)

Well, if Fortune be a woman, she's a good wench for this gear. Father,
    come; I'll take my leave of the Jew in the twinkling of an eye.
(*The Merchant of Venice. Act 2. Scene 2. Launcelot speaking.*)

PORTIA   Thus hath the candle singed the moth.
        Oh, these deliberate fools! When they do choose,
        They have the wisdom by their wit to lose.
NERISSA   The ancient saying is no heresy;
        Hanging and wiving goes by destiny.
(*The Merchant of Venice. Act 2. Scene 9.*)

A second Daniel! A Daniel, Jew!
Now, infidel, I have thee on the hip.
(*The Merchant of Venice. Act 4. Scene 1. Gratiano speaking.*)

Hereafter, in a better world than this,
I shall desire more love and knowledge of you.
(*As You Like It. Act 1. Scene 2. Le Beau speaking.*)

Chewing the food of sweet and bitter fancy.
(*As You Like It. Act 4. Scene 3. Oliver speaking.*)

GRUMIO   First, know, my horse is tired; my master and mistress fallen out.
CURTIS   How?
GRUMIO   Out of their saddles into the dirt; and thereby hangs a tale.
(*The Taming of the Shrew. Act 4. Scene 1.*)

My cake is dough: but I'll in among the rest;
Out of hope of all but my share of the feast.
(*The Taming of the Shrew. Act 5. Scene 1. Gremio speaking.*)

           He lost a wife
Whose beauty did astonish the survey
Of richest eyes, whose words all ears took captive,
Whose dear perfection hearts that scorned to serve
Humbly called mistress.
(*All's Well That Ends Well. Act 5. Scene 3. Lafeu speaking.*)

I am sure care's an enemy to life.
(*Twelfth Night. Act 1. Scene 3. Sir Toby speaking.*)

If this were played upon a stage now, I could condemn it as an improbable
    fiction.
(*Twelfth Night. Act 3. Scene 4. Fabian speaking.*)

. . . yet they say we are
Almost as like as eggs.
(*The Winter's Tale. Act 1. Scene 2. Leontes speaking.*)

My father named me Autolycus; who being, as I am, littered under
Mercury, was likewise a snapper-up of unconsidered trifles.
(*The Winter's Tale. Act 4. Scene 3. . . . Act 4, Scene 2 in The Oxford
Shakespeare. . . . Autolycus speaking.*)

Saint George, that swinged the dragon, and e'er since
Sits on his horse-back at mine hostess' door.
(*King John. Act 2. Scene 1. The Bastard speaking.*)

Ay, marry, now my soul hath elbow-room;
It would not out at windows nor at doors.
There is so hot a Summer in my bosom
That all my bowels crumble up to dust.
I am a scribbled form, drawn with a pen
Upon a parchment; and against this fire
Do I shrink up.
(*King John. Act 5. Scene 7. The King speaking.*)

Evermore thanks, the exchequer of the poor;
Which, till my infant fortune comes to years,
Stands for my bounty.
(*Richard the Second. Act 2. Scene 3. Bolingbroke speaking.*)

PRINCE HENRY   I see a good amendment of life in thee; from praying
to purse-taking.
FALSTAFF   Why, Hal, 'tis my vocation, Hal; 'tis no sin for a man
to labour in his vocation.
(*Henry the Fourth. Part One. Act 1. Scene 2.*)

POINS   Good morrow, sweet Hal. What says Monsieur
Remorse? What says Sir John Sack and Sugar?
Jack, how agrees the devil and thee about thy soul,
that thou soldest him on Good Friday last for a cup
of Madeira and a cold capon's leg?
PRINCE HENRY   Sir John stands to his word; the devil shall have his
bargain. For he was never yet a breaker of proverbs:
he will give the devil his due.
(*Henry the Fourth. Part One. Act 1. Scene 2.*)

Came there a certain lord, neat, and trimly dressed,
Fresh as a bridegroom.
(*Henry the Fourth. Part One. Act 1. Scene 3. Hotspur speaking.*)

I know a trick worth two of that, i' faith.
(*Henry the Fourth. Part One. Act 2. Scene 1. First Carrier speaking.*)

'Zounds, an I were now by this rascal, I could brain him with his lady's fan.
(*Henry the Fourth. Part One. Act 2. Scene 3. Hotspur speaking.*)

Give you a reason on compulsion! If reasons were as plentiful as black-
berries, I would give no man a reason upon compulsion, I.
(*Henry the Fourth. Part One. Act 2. Scene 4. Falstaff speaking.*)

A plague of sighing and grief! It blows a man up like a bladder.
(*Henry the Fourth. Part One. Act 2. Scene 4. Falstaff speaking.*)

PRINCE HENRY   I never did see such pitiful rascals.
FALSTAFF   Tut, tut! Good enough to toss. Food for powder,
                         food for powder; they'll fill a pit as well as better.
                         Tush, man; mortal men, mortal men.
(*Henry the Fourth. Part One. Act 4. Scene 2.*)

He hath eaten me out of house and home.
(*Henry the Fourth. Part Two. Act 2. Scene 1. Mistress Quickly speaking.*)

. . . for, by my troth, I do now remember the poor creature: small beer.
(*Henry the Fourth. Part Two. Act 2. Scene 2. Prince Henry speaking.*)

SHALLOW   Ha, cousin Silence, that thou hadst seen that that this knight
                  and I have seen! Ha, Sir John, said I well?
FALSTAFF   We have heard the chimes at midnight, Master Shallow.
(*Henry the Fourth. Part Two. Act 3. Scene 2.*)

PRINCE HENRY   I never thought to hear you speak again.
THE KING   Thy wish was father, Harry, to that thought:
                         I stay too long by thee; I weary thee.
(*Henry the Fourth. Part Two. Act 4. Scene 5.*)

Oh, for a Muse of fire, that would ascend
The brightest heaven of invention;
A kingdom for a stage, princes to act,
And monarchs to behold the swelling scene.
(*Henry the Fifth. Prologue to Act 1. Chorus speaking.*)

. . . yea, at that very moment,
Consideration like an angel came
And whipped the offending Adam out of him;
Leaving his body as a paradise,
To envelope and contain celestial spirits.
(*Henry the Fifth. Act 1. Scene 1. The Archbishop of Canterbury speaking.*)

It must be as it may; though patience be a tired mare, yet she will plod.
(*Henry the Fifth. Act 2. Scene 1. Nym speaking.*)

This day is called the feast of Crispian.
He that outlives this day and comes safe home
Will stand a tip-toe when this day is named,
And rouse him at the name of Crispian.
(*Henry the Fifth. Act 4. Scene 3. The King speaking.*)

A sweeter and a lovelier gentleman,
Framed in the prodigality of nature,
Young, valiant, wise, and, no doubt, right royal,
The spacious world cannot again afford.
(*Richard the Third. Act 1. Scene 2. Gloucester speaking.*)

Thy head is as full of quarrels as an egg is full of meat; and yet thy head
    hath been beaten as addle as an egg for quarrelling.
(*Romeo and Juliet. Act 3. Scene 1. Mercutio speaking.*)

Nay, an I tell you that, I'll ne'er look you i' the face again, but those that
    understood him smiled at one another and shook their heads; but for
    mine own part, it was Greek to me.
(*Julius Cæsar. Act 1. Scene 2. Casca speaking.*)

He reads much;
He is a great observer, and he looks
Quite through the deeds of men. He loves no plays,
As thou dost, Antony; he hears no music;
Seldom he smiles, and smiles in such a sort
As if he mocked himself, and scorned his spirit
That could be moved to smile at anything.
(*Julius Cæsar. Act 1. Scene 2. Cæsar speaking.*)

And, gentle friends,
Let's kill him boldly, but not wrathfully;
Let's carve him as a dish fit for the gods,
Not hew him as a carcass fit for hounds.
(*Julius Cæsar. Act 2. Scene 1. Brutus speaking.*)

CASCA   Speak, hands, for me! (*They stab Cæsar.*)
CÆSAR   Et tu, Brute? Then fall, Cæsar! (*Dies.*)
(*Julius Cæsar. Act 3. Scene 1.*)

But yesterday the word of Cæsar might
Have stood against the world: now lies he there,
And none so poor to do him reverence.
(*Julius Cæsar. Act 3. Scene 2. Antony speaking.*)

This was the most unkindest cut of all;
For when the noble Cæsar saw him stab,
Ingratitude, more strong than traitors' arms,
Quite vanquished him.   Then burst his mighty heart;
And, in his mantle muffling up his face,
Even at the base of Pompey's statue,
Which all the while ran blood, great Cæsar fell.
Oh, what a fall was there, my countrymen!
Then I, and you, and all of us fell down,
Whilst bloody treason flourished over us.
(*Julius Cæsar.   Act* 3.   *Scene* 2.   *Antony speaking.*)

Oh, never
Shall sun that morrow see!
Your face, my thane, is as a book where men
May read strange matters.   To beguile the time,
Look like the time; bear welcome in your eye,
Your hand, your tongue: look like the innocent flower,
But be the serpent under't.
(*Macbeth.   Act* 1.   *Scene* 5.   *Lady Macbeth speaking.*)

Yet do I fear thy nature;
It is too full o' the milk of human kindness
To catch the nearest way.
(*Macbeth.   Act* 1.   *Scene* 5.   *Lady Macbeth speaking.*)

If it were done when 'tis done, then 'twere well
It were done quickly.
(*Macbeth.   Act* 1.   *Scene* 7.   *Macbeth speaking.*)

There's husbandry in heaven:
Their candles are all out.
(*Macbeth.   Act* 2.   *Scene* 1.   *Banquo speaking.*)
Husbandry: economy.

To Ireland, I.   Our separated fortune
Shall keep us both the safer: where we are
There's daggers in men's smiles.
(*Macbeth.   Act* 2.   *Scene* 3.   *Donalbain speaking.*)

Then comes my fit again: I had else been perfect,
Whole as the marble, founded as the rock,
As broad and general as the casing air:
But now I am cabined, cribbed, confined, bound in
To saucy doubts and fears.
(*Macbeth.   Act* 3.   *Scene* 4.   *Macbeth, speaking aside.*)

U

Then live, Macduff: what need I fear of thee?
But yet I'll make assurance doubly sure,
And take a bond of fate: thou shalt not live;
That I may tell pale-hearted fear it lies,
And sleep in spite of thunder.
(*Macbeth. Act 4. Scene 1. Macbeth speaking.*)
The Oxford Shakespeare has 'double sure' in place of 'doubly sure.'

Here's the smell of the blood still: all the perfumes of Arabia will not
  sweeten this little hand. Oh, oh, oh!
(*Macbeth. Act 5. Scene 1. Lady Macbeth speaking.*)

But look, the morn, in russet mantle clad,
Walks o'er the dew of yon high eastward hill.
(*Hamlet. Act 1. Scene 1. Horatio speaking.*)

A little more than kin, and less than kind.
(*Hamlet. Act 1. Scene 2. Hamlet, speaking aside.*)

Ay, springes to catch woodcocks. I do know,
When the blood burns, how prodigal the soul
Lends the tongue vows.
(*Hamlet. Act 1. Scene 3. Polonius speaking.*)

Something is rotten in the state of Denmark.
(*Hamlet. Act 1. Scene 4. Marcellus speaking.*)

GHOST   But know, thou noble youth,
            The serpent that did sting thy father's life
            Now wears his crown.
HAMLET   Oh, my prophetic soul!
            My uncle!
(*Hamlet. Act 1. Scene 5.*)

The time is out of joint. Oh, cursèd spite,
That ever I was born to set it right!
(*Hamlet. Act 1. Scene 5. Hamlet speaking.*)

Though this be madness, yet there is method in't.
(*Hamlet. Act 2. Scene 2. Polonius, speaking aside.*)

Beggar that I am, I am even poor in thanks; but I thank you.
(*Hamlet. Act 2. Scene 2. Hamlet speaking.*)

I'll have grounds

More relative than this.   The play's the thing
Wherein I'll catch the conscience of the king.
(*Hamlet.   Act* 2.   *Scene* 2.   *Hamlet speaking.*)

This is the very coinage of your brain:
This bodiless creation, ecstasy
Is very cunning in.
(*Hamlet.   Act* 3.   *Scene* 4.   *The Queen speaking.*)

One woe doth tread upon another's heel,
So fast they follow: your sister's drowned, Laertes.
(*Hamlet.   Act* 4.   *Scene* 7.   *The Queen speaking.*)

Alas, poor Yorick! I knew him, Horatio: a fellow of infinite jest, of most
excellent fancy.
(*Hamlet.   Act* 5.   *Scene* 1.   *Hamlet speaking.*)

Sweets to the sweet: farewell!
(*Hamlet.   Act* 5.   *Scene* 1.   *The Queen speaking, as she scatters flowers on
Ophelia's grave.*)

Sir, I will walk here in the hall: if it please his majesty, it is the breathing
time of day with me.
(*Hamlet.   Act* 5.   *Scene* 2.   *Hamlet speaking.*)

I am a man

More sinned against than sinning.
(*King Lear.   Act* 3.   *Scene* 2.   *Lear speaking.*)

Reputation, reputation, reputation! Oh, I have lost my reputation!
I have lost the immortal part of myself, and what remains is bestial.
(*Othello.   Act* 2.   *Scene* 3.   *Cassio speaking.*)

Nay, that's certain. But yet the pity of it. Iago! Oh, Iago, the pity
of it, Iago!
(*Othello.   Act* 4.   *Scene* 1.   *Othello speaking.*)

CLEOPATRA   By Isis, I will give thee bloody teeth
             If thou with Cæsar paragon again
             My man of men.
CHARMIAN   By your most gracious pardon,
             I sing but after you.
CLEOPATRA   My salad days,
             When I was green in judgment, cold in blood
             To say as I said then!
(*Antony and Cleopatra.   Act* 1.   *Scene* 5.)

                    For her own person,
It beggared all description.
(*Antony and Cleopatra.   Act* 2.   *Scene* 2.   *Enobarbus speaking.*)

Age cannot wither her, nor custom stale
Her infinite variety.
(*Antony and Cleopatra.   Act* 2.   *Scene* 2.   *Enobarbus speaking.*)

                    THE END

INDEX OF FAMILIAR QUOTATIONS